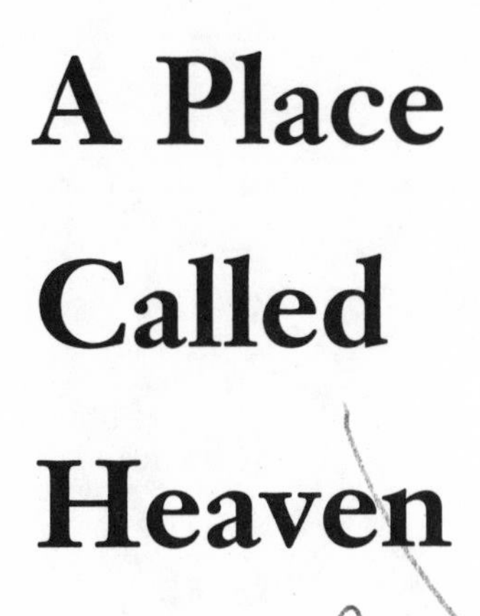

A Place Called Heaven

ALSO BY CECIL FOSTER

Fiction
No Man in the House
Sleep On, Beloved

Non-Fiction
Caribana: The Greatest Celebration
Distorted Mirror: Canada's Racist Face

A Place Called Heaven

The Meaning of Being Black in Canada

Cecil Foster

HarperCollins*PublishersLtd*

Affectionately dedicated to
Stephen and Earl

Names in this book have been changed to protect the identities of the people involved, except when the individual is or has been a public figure or has been the subject of media attention

A PLACE CALLED HEAVEN:
THE MEANING OF BEING BLACK IN CANADA
 For information address HarperCollins Publishers Ltd, Suite 2900, Hazelton Lanes, 55 Avenue Road, Toronto, Canada M5R 3L2.

http://www.harpercollins.com/canada

First edition

Canadian Cataloguing in Publication Data

Foster, Cecil, 1954-
A place called heaven : the meaning of being Black in Canada

ISBN 0-00-638028-X

1. Blacks - Canada. 2. Black Canadians.* 3. Racism - Canada. 4. Canada - Race relations. I. Title.

FC106.B6F67 1996 305.896'071 C96-930742-X
F1035.N3F67 1996

---

96 97 98 99 ❖HC 10 9 8 7 6 5 4 3 2 1

Printed and bound in the United States

CONTENTS

ACKNOWLEDGEMENTS

There are many people I would like to thank for assisting me with this book. Needless to say, at the top of the list are all of my friends and associates—I hope they have not now become former friends and associates—who will recognize themselves in these pages. Every one of you has contributed and is contributing to making Canada a better place for all of us. In addition, I would like to thank everyone who granted me interviews or took time out to return a phone call or, as was the case with Celia Donnelly, librarian at *The Globe and Mail*, never hesitated to check a fact or two. If there are any errors in this book, of course, they are mine.

I would also like to thank the staff at HarperCollins Publishers Canada Ltd., and in particular Iris Tupholme for her encouragement and timely advice not to rush the work because, unfortunately, human nature being what it is, there will always be a need for a book like this; Maya Mavjee for helping to shape and formulate the book, for always challenging and probing, for always believing in the book and my ability to pull it off; and Don Loney whose editing and suggestions were timely and insightful. You are a great team!

I remain indebted to Ed Carson, president and chief executive officer of HarperCollins Canada Ltd. One afternoon six years ago, Ed generously spent about an hour talking on the phone to a stranger about writing. That stranger was me. Ed was then in charge of publishing at Random House of Canada. Before he left that position, he had laid the groundwork for the publication of my first two novels. Later, I would write a pamphlet on racism in Canada for HarperCollins, and now this book.

Special thanks also to the Canada Arts Council, the Ontario Arts Council and Multiculturalism Canada, without whose financial assistance this book would not have been possible.

Finally, special thanks to my agent Bev Slopen; my friend Ayanna Black for the encouragement and a drink or two; to my brother Errol and family; to my buddy Orville Folkes. And, of course, a very special thanks to my family, especially my three sons.

Toronto
July 1996

INTRODUCTION

A PLACE IN THE SUN?

The evening of February 24, 1996, was unusually warm, with a beguiling touch of an early spring in the air. For the first time in a long while, I felt happy with the events in my life. The winter that appeared to be slipping away had been harsh in many respects, not the least financially, as I despaired about the likelihood of finding another job in a Canadian newsroom. I had found myself walking the streets of Toronto with empty pockets.

On this evening, it appeared the sky was once again the limit for me. Two hours earlier, I had completed my first talk show, *Cecil Foster Urbantalk* on CFRB AM 1010, the Toronto radio station that arguably has the largest listenership in Canada. To say I was elated at having my own talk show is to state the very obvious. Here was a chance for me to do something that I liked, to feel part of the news-gathering and dissemination business again. Over the years, I had been a guest and commentator on several radio and television stations in Canada, the United States and the Caribbean. But this was the first time I hosted my own show. Wasn't Canada a wonderful place, where a young Black from a little island like Barbados, dreaming of a future beyond the horizon, could arrive with a few dollars in his pockets and in less than two decades carve out a rewarding career as a journalist, radio and television commentator, newspaper and magazine reporter and columnist, author of fiction and now ... radio talk-show host? For what more could I possibly ask?

On an evening like this, with a hint of spring and a sense of renewal in the air, I was once again in love with Canada. Immigrating to this country in 1979 was one of the best decisions—if not *the* best—I had ever made. Obviously, this place can be heavenly when it wants to be, a place to raise my kids and offer them all those opportunities that I could only have dreamt about for myself. But alas, as we all know, as is so typical of Canada, one pleasant evening does not mean the end to a harsh winter. The unusual warmth can be just a delusion, a passing respite at most, something to lull us into dropping our guard. Appropriately, this winter of 1995–96 would prove to be one of the harshest, lasting well past the time when the cold wind and snow should have relented and melted away, when we should have started to enjoy the bliss that is a Canadian summer.

As I drove along, I kept thinking how the talk show could be another career turning-point for me, another point of arrival. It could be the end of a three-year drought that started when I was chased from my last full-time job as a senior editor at *The Financial Post* for, ironically, writing a story that would turn out to be bang-on. However, vindication would be cold comfort as I received rejection after rejection from the major newspapers around Toronto, and as I saw former colleagues easily jump from job to job in an incestuous network of one friend helping another with no regard for real talent, track record or what the government of the day calls the "merit principle."

I had tried to get by on 11 hours of weekly teaching at the Humber College School of Journalism, a few hours in the journalism department at Ryerson Polytechnic University and some uncertain freelance work. Even those teaching hours were disappearing. A new provincial government had come to power and was slashing budgets so deeply that Humber College had put me on notice that I should not count on retaining my teaching post. Part-time work in the newsrooms of CBC National Radio and Television, employment that had supplemented the teaching, had dried up—once again because of government spending cuts.

I knew that a lot was riding on how well I performed on-air. The previous week, *The Toronto Star* had announced to the world that I had become the "Black Voice" on CFRB, a radio station that, according to the same newspaper, had been criticized for being white, male, anti-immigrant and rabidly right wing. Several prominent members of the black community were involved in an open dispute with the radio station;

the race relations committee of the city of Toronto had condemned the station; several people had complained to the federal regulator and had asked that the station's licence be pulled or modified. My voice on the radio station was to be a signal of change, from within, that minorities and liberals were not to be shut out of talk radio in Canada. It was to be a new beginning of sorts for both sides, and I felt proud that I might be useful in helping to break down barriers of misunderstanding and mistrust.

And it was a personal achievement. As far as I knew, there was no other black talk-show host on any mainstream radio station in the country. From the telephone calls I received at home and at the station, I soon realized that many in the black community were demanding of me that I succeed—for myself, yes, but also to show that black people can reflect, comment and pontificate on just about any subject, just like anybody else. Once again, I was reminded of what so many pioneers of the black community know so well, what I call in this book the "double burden" of being black. And just to prove that, ultimately, we rate success by how it plays among the closest members of our family—the people who really matter—back home in Barbados, I knew some very dear and precious people were also wondering how I was making out. Tony Best, the North American correspondent for the *Nation* newspaper in Barbados, from his base in New York had alerted the entire island that a son of the soil had made it onto the air waves of a major Canadian station. "Foster Making Waves in Canada" ran the headline, expressing the dream of every immigrant, to send news back home that he or she has at least seen the Promised Land, if not entered it.

So on this pleasant evening, as I zipped down the Don Valley Parkway, the main north-south artery in Toronto, I was happy with the way the show went, even though it had been a trial run. If I proved I could handle the job, then I would have an expanded show. Management was promising some interesting possibilities if I turned out to be the personality they had been looking for. I felt I had done better than expected on my first show. A few seconds of dead air here and there, a bit of a case of nerves, yes, but nothing that time and familiarity with the format and technique of radio couldn't correct.

Our first topic invited a lively discussion about Canadian citizenship and whether immigrants should be required to take an oath to the Queen and her heirs. The show could have lasted much longer than the allotted time. The calls just kept pouring in—a sign, I hoped, that although the host of the show was black, racism wasn't the only thing he could talk about, and that the city was ready for the kind of show I had in mind.

Now, it was time to celebrate. Many from the black artistic community in the Toronto area were having a party at a restaurant on the Toronto lakeshore to celebrate the completion of a successful run for a black dance troupe at the nearby Harbourfront theatre. I wanted to join in the celebration and to unwind from my personal high. That high was about to abruptly end.

I saw flashing lights in my rear-view mirror. The police. *Shit,* I thought, *what's up now?* At the first break in the traffic, which had been pushing me along as part of the flow, I pulled over to the side of the roadway and waited for the policeman to pull up behind me. He approached from the passenger side. I rolled down the window and waited.

"Is this *your* car?" he asked. *So that is why he stopped me,* I thought. *He is on the lookout for a stolen car.*

"Yes," I said.

"Well, *where* could you be going in such a hurry that I clocked you at 120 in a 90-kilometre zone?" he demanded. The tone was obviously condescending and demeaning. I looked at him. He was young.

"I don't think I was going *that* fast," I said. Right away, I was careful not to engage him in any discussion that would make him angrier. After all, he and I were the only two people on the scene. No other witnesses. History told me I was badly outnumbered. Only a fool of a black man would not be extremely careful in this situation.

"Your driver's licence!" he snapped.

Slowly, I opened the front of my overcoat and jacket to let the officer see that I was reaching for my wallet, and not for a weapon. I very deliberately took out my wallet, removed the licence in its plastic folder and handed it to him. He took a quick look at the picture and then at me, matching my face with the picture on the licence.

"Ownership and insurance," he demanded. By now he was leaning into the car, his elbows propped on the window, noisily flicking the end of the licence with his fingers, as if showing his impatience, intolerance and superiority.

"They are in the glove compartment," I said, and once again *slowly* reached over and released the latch. I found the ownership certificate and handed it to the policeman. I continued rummaging through envelopes, the car manual and other assorted things in the glove compartment for the insurance.

"Oh, it's a *leased* car," he said reading the document, the inflection in his voice most notable. "Well, since it's *leased,* you don't have to show me the insurance."

Taking my licence and the car ownership with him, he went back to the cruiser, must have run some checks, and about five minutes later returned. "I have written out the ticket for what I clocked you at," he said. "The yellow piece of paper is your ticket and summons; the white tells you what to do if you want to go to court." He threw the ticket and my licence and ownership onto the passenger seat of the car. Brusquely, he turned and walked back to his cruiser.

Through my rear-view mirror, I watched this representative of Metro's finest get into the car, turn off the flashing lights and merge with the traffic zooming by. I still wondered why he was so angry and why he would use that tone for an alleged traffic violation. And I remembered all the stories and anecdotes by Blacks about how they were stopped by the police for driving fancy cars—not that my fairly new Chrysler Intrepid was all that fancy—and how not so long ago police used to hand out DWBBs—Driving While Being Black violations—just for the fun of it. And I reflected on how in the past week I had tried to explain, as a guest on a talk show on CFRB, why so many black people everywhere are distrustful of the police, why they do not like the way some bad apples in the force treat Blacks and how, as I had said, we all have to start breaking down barriers, build bridges of understanding and trust, stop shouting at one another and open a dialogue in the hope of producing a better society.

And while sitting in my car, I remembered something else about February 24, 1996. That was the day the black community buried the black man in Toronto most recently killed by a police bullet—in this case three bullets and all apparently fired from close range. Tommy Barnett, a 22-year-old, was gunned down when police said they were driving by in their cruiser and stopped to deal with a man brandishing a Samurai sword in the middle of the road early one morning. Once again, the black community had questioned the killing and was calling for an independent investigation. Barnett's family had delayed the burial for 46 days so an independent pathologist could come into the city and examine the body. Ironically, the family included an elder sister who, as a respected community activist, had campaigned relentlessly for Blacks to gain a better appreciation of police work. Now, she found that justification for the shooting was lacking, and wondered how she could continue to work to raise the level of respect between the police and black youth. At the funeral earlier that day, the eulogy for Tommy Barnett remarked upon the appalling state of relations between police and the black community. Several notable black activists had denounced the police as racist and suggested that the investigation of the shooting was a mere formality. Even then, newspaper reports had indicated that the police officer would be exonerated, even though the investigators promptly announced that the report was premature. Many Blacks doubted it was. Several months later, the formal exoneration came, just as the newspapers had predicted.

I wondered if Officer 1439 in Platoon D of the City Unit was reacting to what he might have heard about the funeral and eulogy when he was dealing with me. And because he might have been angry with the black community, I wondered, could this be why he was so rude and handed me a ticket for $141.25 in the first instance? It was bad enough that I had to pay this penalty for an offence I disputed, but I also knew I would continue to pay for several years because, even if I fought the charge, this policeman had the full weight of the system backing him. Whether he was right or wrong, I would have to pay on several fronts. My insurance company would undoubtedly jack up my premiums over the next while because of this violation, which meant that I could look forward to paying much more for many years. So much for the argument that racism is costless or that we tend to be too sensitive! There is always a real cost, which reminded me of the other anecdotes making the rounds in the black community, all of which illustrated the high cost in actual out-of-pocket expenses, missed opportunities and spoiled dreams for those of us who are the victims of racism.

I recalled the story of a female friend who worked in Jamaica dealing with business customers for a local branch of the Royal Bank of Canada. When she arrived in Toronto two decades ago and joined the Royal

Bank, she was deemed not qualified for business banking. Finally, after working her way through regular banking, from cashier up, she was selected for training as a business banker, only to discover that what she was learning was what she had studied and had done in Jamaica almost 20 years earlier. In the meanwhile, she had missed out on two decades of self-actualization she would have gained from working in her chosen field, to say nothing of the two decades of the extra salary she would have received if she had gone directly into business banking. The price for being black—and the victims of what has been documented in government reports as the virulent strain of anti-Black racism in Canada—is as high for many of us.

Later, at the party, I told anyone who would listen about my experience with PC 1439. Just about everyone shook his or her head knowingly and sympathetically. They knew what I was talking about. Yes, we agreed, there is the approach of lodging a formal complaint against the officer. But how do you make a case against the *tone* of an officer? It would have been so much easier to argue and produce evidence if racism were still blatant and open, but that is not so in Canada. After all, driving is a privilege and the police officer has a right to ask questions, even if his words and tone are coded, just the way suspected criminals are described as "having a Jamaican or Caribbean accent"—coded words for black or West Indian. But how can you argue against tone? In any case, the complaint would amount to a case of the word of a black man against a white policeman, and everyone knew the likely outcome.

One high-profile case was brought against Metro police by a Jamaican woman who claimed she was strip-searched on a sidewalk by three Toronto police officers. The case essentially became the trial of the visitor, who, beyond that indignity, had to suffer the suggestion that she was a drug dealer. Somehow, the gist of her complaint got lost in the process. Needless to say, the police were exonerated and the visitor chided for getting what she deserved.

Everyone I spoke to at the party agreed that a formal complaint would be a waste of time, except for the satisfaction of making a point. And just about everyone also agreed that I should fight the ticket in court. "What do you have to lose?" asked Sandra Whiting, a folklorist, storyteller and the president of the Black Business and Professional Association of

Canada. "They aren't likely to increase the fine, so why not fight it and hope the bastard doesn't show up?"

Similarly, black lawyers and a former chair of the Metro Toronto Police Services Board suggested that I should lay a complaint, not because they expected me to win, but because it might help someone later on. One lawyer told me, when I raised the issue on a panel when we were discussing black experiences in Canada, that my complaint would be a mark against the cop and that maybe sometime down the road an accumulation of complaints would embarrass the Police Board into taking action against this officer, and eventually get him out of the way of harassing other Blacks. And as Susan Eng, the former chair of the Police Board, admonished, "If people like you who have a profile and with it some protection don't complain, what can we expect of those less fortunate and with less protection from recriminations?"

My option was to simply settle the matter out of court and move on with my life. I decided to plea bargain in the hope that I would not lose demerit points and thereby find myself on a slippery slope that could cause me to lose my licence. I arrived on the appointed evening to meet with the Crown prosecutor. The young lawyer showed me into his office, pointed out that our conversations were being taped and we sat down to talk.

"As you know, you can lose four demerit points for this offence," he says. "But that is not up to us. We have nothing to do with demerit points—that's the Ministry of Transportation." He proceeded to read out the charge and then made me his best offer. "I am willing to reduce your speed by two kilometres," he said. "That is the best I can do. It would at least save you a demerit point or two."

"Two kilometres?" I asked. If that is the best he can offer, I might as well take my chances in court, I told him. Also, there was a matter of principle here in that I didn't believe I was going that fast and I was still considering filing a complaint against the cop.

"How fast would you say you were going?" he asked.

"At the most 100 kilometres," I said.

"Nah," he said shaking his head. "Two kilometres—that's the best I can do."

"What are my options, then?" I asked.

"You can go to court, but remember this is your only chance at a plea bargain."

Some bargain, I thought. I would take my chances before the courts. After signing the relevant documents, I left the meeting with a court date, but also wondering how a plea-bargaining system can work—a system that is supposed to ease the clutter of cases before the courts—when the bargain is a reduction of two kilometres. And, I wondered, why was it that all the others who had gone in to see this agent of the provincial government had come out smiling, obviously satisfied with the outcome of the bargaining? Perhaps it mattered that they were all white.

My experience was so predictable. About this time the provincial government released a damning study of the judicial system in Ontario,[1] yet another official study on the bias and racism in the police and in the courts. It found that Blacks are far more likely than Whites to be charged for a given offence; that when they are charged, Blacks are far more likely to have to pay higher bail and are more likely to be refused bail; that they are far less likely to get a plea bargain; that they are much more likely to be convicted in court and are far more likely to get hit with the maximum penalty.

Black friends who are in the police force offered me their understanding and sympathy: yes, even if I was going that fast, the traffic cop probably could have used his discretion and lowered the speed in the hope that I would learn a lesson from the possibility of acquiring demerit points; yes, the Crown prosecutors are usually more accommodating; and yes, what can they say, such is my experience because I am black.

It is because of experiences like this—experiences that are so routine for Blacks at the hands of Whites and that the white community can choose to ignore—that I decided to write this book. It appeared to me that something is very awry in this beautiful country, where the cauldron of race relations is boiling over. Everyone is putting up barricades as if preparing for a long battle, a fight nobody can possibly win. Worse, people are entrenched in their positions, their ears and eyes closed, purposely unwilling to reason and to respect differences. And this is in a country that claims to be multicultural, that supposedly celebrates and encourages diversity and differences!

For this is a time when it seems to be fair game to pick on immigrants and to blame Blacks and other minorities for just about every wrong in the

[1] *A Report of the Commission on Systemic Racism in the Ontario Criminal Justice System.* Toronto: Commission on Systemic Racism in the Ontario Criminal Justice Sysytem, 1995.

country. There is a hardening of feelings, for this is a time of the ascendancy of tough-talking, right-wing parties with their coded words about taking back Canada and making the streets safe, of choosing the right immigrants to reflect the traditional Canadian way of life, of dealing harshly with welfare bums, of discarding employment equity and so-called preference for minorities over white males—all the stereotypes and angry arguments that are the well-known shorthand for the leeches of society, for all those who are not white and deserving of entrenched preferences. For this is a time when, for example, we see the rise in popularity of the Reform Party to become essentially the federal government in waiting, a party with several candidates who openly espouse racist views—some of them so ugly that the candidates had to be dropped during the last federal election—a party in which several members take great glee in calling themselves "rednecks." They wear this label as a badge of honour, defiantly sending out a message that they do not care about the hurt feelings of those for whom this label symbolizes so much pain. The label is a proud claim that bleeding-heart liberals have no place in public life. This is no different from members of a major political party claiming they are proud to be called Nazis or Stasis. They are rednecks and proud of it, promising the chilling prospect of a government of rednecks, as all North America appears to be lurching to the far right of the political spectrum.

And even as I write this introduction in late spring, the same Reform Party is in the throes of controversy over comments made by the party whip, Bob Ringma, in the House of Commons. He claimed that he could see nothing wrong with a shop owner firing, or hiding in the back of a store, a gay or black employee if a bigoted customer objected to the presence of that employee. Ironically, this comment was made while the Canadian Parliament was discussing extending human rights to same-sex couples. At first, Ringma stood his ground and refused to retract his statement. He had no apology to make, he asserted defiantly. It took a public outcry to get him to apologize and to resign his party position. But the damage has been done: bigots have had their position articulated and sanctioned, if the outpouring on some radio talk shows is any indication. Minorities have been offended because of calculated statements by a prominent member of Parliament, a calculation that I believe included taking a chance that if his political balloon did not fly he could always apologize and be no worse off. Maybe, some day, Blacks and other minorities will be less forgiving and less tolerant of those who try to hurt us and then extend an insincere apology. Sometimes apologies, especially when the action is calculated, when the mea culpa is forced, are not acceptable. But that, too, might be the Canadian brand of racism.

This hardening of position also shows up in other areas, such as the treatment of black immigrants, and the demonization of Blacks. So that in the spring of 1996, it was still possible for the government of Canada to deport to the land of their birth people who have lived virtually all their lives in Canada. In one notable case, the government deported a 22-year-old man who had left Jamaica as a child at the age of 17 months, who had never returned to the island, who had learned all his criminality in Canada, including extended stints when he was a ward of the state and in the care of the Canadian Children's Aid Society. But, obviously, the government was bent on sending out a strong signal to all those complaining that black crime is out of control. So it deported this criminal to a country that he does not know, where he has no family and no ties, except for having had his navel string buried some place on that island. Canadians conveniently forget that this criminal is a product of the Canadian system, unless they are making the argument that immigrants are congenitally criminal.

But positions are also hardening in the black community. I see it, most alarmingly, at the two extremes, in the young and the elderly. Both groups are so disillusioned. The elderly are angry and are giving up on Canada because they feel robbed of their youth and have no prospect of getting anything back in return. Many of them immigrated to Canada with their heads full of dreams. They were going to do well and succeed, become an example for all those back home. Now, in the middle of the night, they find themselves scratching their heads and asking what went wrong. For they did not attain their dream, and what is even more significant, they now despair that their kids will be worse off than they.

And yes, black youths know they face a hard lot. I hear many of them defiantly ask why they should try to enter the mainstream, why they should integrate with the dominant cultures that form the mainstream of Canadian society, which are for the most part white. Why should they work as hard and sacrifice as much as their parents only to be denied?

And in visits to schools, I hear disillusioned black youths question why they should continue to listen to any of us telling them to remain in school and study hard. "We know that our parents' generation cannot get us a job, and we look at white students in our class whose parents have connections to get them a job. So we ask, why should we listen to you middle-class Blacks who tell us to stay in school and study hard?" Those words are etched in my memory, words from a female, teenage student who at such an early age is giving up, espousing words and sentiments to which I have no real answers because of the truth they contain. Words that seem to be the ultimate in blasphemy for those of us who are immigrants, who always believed that a solid education would bring liberation and at least middle-class status. And I also think of a young black male who wonders why he should try to enter the mainstream when he looks at his mother and sees how she "lives for the j-o-b, is never at home, is always so tired," but has so few material possessions to show for this effort. Or when the black youths heap scorn on the so-called black role models that they see as sell-outs to the wider society, people whose main job, as the youths see it, is to preach appeasement and get young Blacks to become compliant. So-called role models with a tenuous hold on a middle-level management job, a partially successful profession, but with no real clout to change anything.

As I watch two of my own children enter their teenage years—one of the most perilous periods for black males, when statistically they are more likely to develop problems in high school and risk dropping out, when they start running with their own crowd, when the police might come knocking—I wonder what the future will be like for them. A future that will be part of a new millennium, a time of change. When I was their age, I could start dreaming of getting away to a paradise of sorts. They do not have the luxury of that dream. So how can I encourage them to keep dreaming? If I can help to break down some of the barriers, to get people to start talking for a while, to get the wider Canadian society to recognize that the experience of being black isn't as great as many of them think, to get Blacks to acknowledge that although the situation is tough we cannot afford to despair and must keep hope alive—then I will be doing something for my kids, for all kids, and, I hope, for all of us in Canada.

I hope this book will clear up some of the misconceptions on all sides and at the same time encourage black youths to celebrate who they are, and the long history and legacy of Blacks in Canada, and our unique perspective as a special kind of people.

Understanding the black reality in Canada must start with the recognition that Canada's black population is unique and that it certainly isn't a carbon copy of the African-American population south of the border. It is surprising how many non-black Canadians do not understand or appreciate this difference, a misunderstanding that to a large extent only aggravates the situation. Too often, the rest of Canada tries to treat Canadian Blacks are if they were an offshoot from what they see on television in Los Angeles, New York, Chicago or Detroit. There is an important difference, and perhaps no issue illustrates this better than what happened in Toronto in 1993. Internationally acclaimed impresario Garth Drabinsky thought he had pulled off a world-class coup when he announced that he had obtained the performing rights to the American musical *Showboat*. He hired the brilliant producer Hal Prince and some of Broadway's best talent to update the play, which he planned to use for the inauguration of a world-class theatre in Metro Toronto. To his surprise, members of the Toronto black community rose up against the play. They described it as racist and demeaning to Blacks. Drabinsky argued that the play was well loved in the United States and trotted out a number of African-American luminaries—such as actor James Earl Jones and Harvard University academic Louis Henry Gates Jr.—to support his opinion. If these African-Americans find no fault with this play, why would Toronto Blacks be so offended? He even hired Dr. Gates to prepare educational kits that put the play in a historical perspective.

What Drabinsky overlooked was that Blacks in Toronto and Canada are different from those he was more familiar with, that many Canadian Blacks have a different sensitivity and a well-developed sense of pride because of where they came from before arriving in Canada. James Earl Jones and Dr. Gates could not appease this crowd. The show went ahead and opened to stellar reviews, even in the African-American press. "How could this be?" was a question that many people, including Drabinsky, asked. The answer is simple: Canadian Blacks are not African-Americans. Which leads to another question that I hope this book will help to answer: Why do Blacks who have immigrated to Canada from the

Caribbean not have the same levels of success as Caribbean Blacks who immigrated to the United States? Chances are that if two brothers who grew up in the same home in the Caribbean, with one going to Canada and the other to the United States, the brother who immigrated to Canada would be less successful. Why? The answer undoubtedly is that Caribbean Blacks have always been seen by themselves and by native Blacks as different. In Canada, these same Caribbean Blacks are seen as no different from the native African-Americans and are therefore forced to adopt many of the same outward characteristics of African-Americans. The result is that Caribbean Blacks in Canada are much more frustrated because they do not attain the same heights and realize the same potential as their brothers and sisters in the United States.

A word about my approach to writing this book, an approach that banks on a blend of reporting and commentary: I rely on anecdotes, including my own experiences and observations as a journalist, to tell the story of what it means to be black in Canada today. It is an experience that can be so full of hope and promise but at the same time can also be darkened by what Blacks have come to recognize as benign racism—racism with a smile on its face. By telling anecdotes, I also hope to show that the black community is varied and multifaceted. Indeed, there are thousands of Blacks who have not been stopped by police for speeding or for any other violation. And there are also hundreds of thousands of Blacks—indeed, the vast majority—who are just regular Canadians. They want a job and a place in the sun: they want their kids to grow up and find jobs and stay out of trouble, and to drive a nice car, just like the next guy, just like any other Canadian. And they, too, want to be able to laugh at themselves, for as the Toronto author Austin Clarke says in his collection of short stories, *Nine Men Who Laugh,* sometimes members of a community have to be able to laugh at themselves to survive. Let's hope that as we enter a new millennium, we in the black community will do more than just survive, that we will take our pride of place in all things Canadian.

CHAPTER 1

WHAT THE PRESENT HAS BROUGHT US

The children on the stage are enthusiastically singing, somewhat off-key, but to the delight of the audience, hymns in honour of their hero, Marcus Garvey. The occasion is a school graduation, and the older brothers and sisters of the singers on stage can, after several years of practice, sing flawlessly what is called the "African Anthem" or the "National Negro Hymn":

Lift ev'ry voice and sing,
Till earth and heaven ring,
Ring with the harmonies of liberty.

The youngsters lead the way, their voices ringing every stanza of this paean to African glory and pride. A song every graduating class has sung for 25 years.

It is a good thing the teenagers take the lead, as many elders in the audience do not know the words to this anthem, to this song that we sing right after the Canadian national anthem. This inspirational call sends out the signal that this gathering recognizes—indeed, even asserts defiantly—it is not a mainstream Canadian community. We, as black people, are indulging in what our brothers and sisters in the United States would call honouring the double consciousness of being African and American. In Canada, that consciousness has many more layers. Our African anthem carries strong symbolism, and it is quite significant that we sing the anthem *after* the Canadian anthem.

There is a good reason why many parents do not know the words of this African anthem. For years, the only anthems most of us knew were those of the young and emerging countries in the Caribbean and Africa. These are countries where nobody felt the need for a world-wide rallying song for all people of the same universal tribe. Usually, there was only one consciousness, a nationalistic fervour tied to the land. The parents at this gathering were nurtured on the necessity for a series of national anthems—one for each new country—each accentuating differences, and not the common struggles, among people of the same race. Each anthem asserted unquestionable national fidelity. It emphasized the common pride and aspirations of all the people living within a given geographical boundary. And it obliterated any ambiguity of belonging and inclusion.

What these parents do know is our history and everyday experiences: all the stories, myths and heroes pulled together from various lands around the world. And we also know one specific consciousness—what it is to be members of a minority group living in Canada. We know now what it means to live with daily psychological and social segregation, to feel that the national anthem of the country in which we live does not quite represent us. This consciousness does not fully inspire us or make us confident about our future. So we must look for additional inspiration. As parents, we have a burning desire to pass on our history and experiences of surviving; of why some of us even consciously choose to live apart from the dominant culture in the land we now call home. We know personally and intimately what this African anthem means as we sing—

[A] song full of the faith
The dark past has taught us;
Sing a song full of the hope
That the present has brought us.

These are words that, for us, the Canadian anthem cannot match for inspiration, history and shared experiences. For us as a people, there is no ambiguity in these words written by an African-American nationalist, James Weldon Johnson.

Immediately after the African anthem is concluded, one of the parents moves to the front of the hall. Dressed in traditional African garb, he invokes the African blessings before allowing us to feast on an array of foods from the Caribbean, Africa and, of course, the usual Canadian fare—the latter for those poor deculturalized souls, our children, who shamefully do not eat ethnic foods.

The invoker raises his glass and, in the African tradition, purposely spills some water. He encourages all of us sitting at tables named Barbados, St. Lucia, Guyana, Trinidad, Jamaica, Ghana, Nkrumah and Mandela to join in the invitation for African spirits to guide and protect us. The invitations come through speeches calling upon such heroes as Sojourner Truth, Frederick Douglass, Malcolm X, Nelson Mandela, Marcus Garvey. We need their strength and vision to see us through these tough times, the speaker says, to survive in this country where we are a people set apart.

Markedly, none of the spirits invited to move among us would qualify as a typical Canadian hero. They are not the icons and saints found in regular school books, in popular literature or in short television documentaries depicting important points and heroes in Canadian nation building. Indeed, none of these role models has lived the Canadian experience for which they are supposed to strengthen us.

We are attending the season's final meeting of the African-Canadian Heritage Association, a group of parents who gather every Saturday in a Toronto school hall to prepare their offspring for life in what many of them consider an alien culture. These parents are actually running a complementary school program, taking the responsibility to fill in the blanks about African people in the official school curriculum. On this day, the parents want to show how far their children have come toward achieving this goal of self-education. They want to demonstrate how well this next generation of community leaders has been schooled for life as black Canadians. This is a seminal part of the responsibility of being black in Canada; to rely on no one, not even the school system that collects your taxes or even the federal government, which preaches national unity through diversity.

So these group therapies are crucial for spiritual sustenance. And what better way to mark the end of this part of the journey on a long, hard road to community self-sufficiency and respect than by having a feast, a true African celebration with flags and pictures from as many African and Caribbean countries as possible? What better way to signal the start of summer, when the children will be freed from their weekend sacrifices of taking extra lessons to learn about their culture, free to play road hockey, softball and basketball? To do all the things the Canadian mind turns to in the warm, carefree months.

Still, nobody can fail to detect the irony in this meeting. Most of the people attending are physically, if not psychologically, far removed from Africa, some of them by centuries. Of the 500,000 or so Blacks in Canada, only a small number were born on the African continent. On this day, however, place of birth doesn't matter as much as the shared experience in the African diaspora. Most parents are from the Caribbean, with very few of them ever breathing the air of the much-touted Motherland. Africa and Africanness are simply a state of mind and, in this case, a protective mechanism. Some parents are indeed from continental Africa—those who could proudly boast of being African without a wince of self-doubt. A few are from the United States and Canada.

This mix represents the uniqueness of Canada's black population. It is not the Caribbean where, after centuries of separation from the continent and other forms of acculturation, the black majority are in control of governments and powerful institutions, but a region nonetheless where this majority had to learn to get by with other minorities. It is not a typical community in Africa, where most of the people are of the same colour and have not suffered separation from the culture of their ancestors and the native land. Similarly, it is not Europe, where Blacks primarily from Africa and the Caribbean seem to have no sense of belonging. And it is not Brazil's black population, the largest outside of Africa, a majority with little political power and still shackled by having been born in one of the last countries to officially abolish slavery. This mix is also different from that in the United States, home for what is now an indigenous black population that has been Americanized over the past century, but that still remains a minority in American society and is suspicious of Blacks born elsewhere.

We Blacks in Canada have our own history and experiences that make our expectations and levels of national and cultural consciousness different from those of Blacks in other countries. But the community, perhaps because of its relatively small size, has always had to reach outside of Canada for renewal. This meeting suggests that it still does. We must fuel our expectations and dreams with the raw materials of Blacks from around the world, so that parents, in calling on non-Canadians to inspire our children, are acknowledging a belief that few Blacks ever achieve their full potential in Canada. For where is the abundance of black heroes, the black statesmen and stateswomen, the black politicians, the black astronauts, black police chiefs and black chief executive officers? These parents know well a history that begs the questions: Would a runaway slave like Frederick Douglass, who, on escaping, decided to stay in New York rather than flee to Canada, have gone on to become a successful pioneer in publishing and one of the earliest African-American civil rights leaders? Would the environment in Canada have nurtured Douglass into becoming a role model to Canadians? The evidence from history suggests to us that the people who provided Douglass with a safe house when he escaped to New York from the South also made the right call by advising him not to go to Canada. For there must have been many people as talented as Frederick Douglass who escaped through the Underground Railroad to Canada. Yet, we know nothing of them. We cannot point to them when we are holding up heroes and role models to our children. And some of us think we know why there might be no Canadian Frederick Douglasses for our children—not because there weren't any of the same mettle and intellect, but because this society never nurtured them. And because we fear there is something inherent in the Canadian system that disinherits our young, talented Frederick Douglasses, it is necessary to teach our children differently. This is why we try to get them to look outside of Canada and its school books for inspiration and dreams of how great they can become.

The black Canadian community has evolved into a population that has many of the characteristics and the diversity of the Caribbean Blacks because of the dominance of people from that region. But it is also a community exhibiting the traits—particularly the long suffering—of those who have lived in an environment similar to that proscribed for Blacks in Europe and the United States. This diversity presents its own challenges and obstacles. The question that arises is whether we can create a community, as the organizers of this African feast and celebration suggest we can. Just as important is whether a people can have a community without their own heroes and myths, when they must borrow from other societies, rather than venerate and elevate their own.

Some Blacks even have problems with all of us laying claim to this

Africanness in Canada. "I am writing in response to [a] letter headlined 'I am not an African-Canadian,'" wrote Olyfemi Ogunkoya in the Toronto black newspaper *Share* in the spring of 1995. "Who are African-Canadians? [the writer] asked. I answer: African-Canadians are people who care to know their roots."

In cities across this country and in various publications, I have heard different versions of this debate. It has occurred over bottles of Mount Gay Rum at kitchen tables, over beers in basement dwellings and in makeshift mosques of the Nation of Islam. I have heard the subject discussed passionately at street-corner demonstrations and protests, at summer barbecues and at street festivals. Serious discussion on this same issue springs up during political and social meetings and in classrooms and school cafeterias. And I have encountered similar talks around tables, while sitting on the plush carpeting of expensive condominiums owned by the elite among the black—or is it African?—members of our community. This debate goes on endlessly. Every generation has its own take on the argument; the notion of Africanness rising or falling depending on the climate of acceptance created by the dominant culture for the aspirations of black people, on how anxious older Blacks feel about the future of their children. Usually, the debate is most heated when shaped in terms of whether Blacks, as a very visible minority group, feel so put upon that they must rise up as one, must set aside their personal differences and their claim to their humanity and their civil rights in order to fight for the promise of a better future for their children. Indeed, our blackness is a refuge and shield in the Canadian society. It is the one visible sign that there is a direct lineage to Africa—an identity that can be meaningful to us, if only because others seek to hurt us because of who we are. And it is proof—and a kind of balm—for us that the discrimination and denial heaped on Blacks result from this proud identity, from our being the descendants, despite the centuries of physical disconnection for so many of us, from a common Motherland, Africa. So while others see our Africanness as a curse, we claim and celebrate it as a blessing.

Still, more questions remain. And before going any further, we should deal immediately with one that bedevils even Blacks: Is there really such a thing as a black—or, as some call it, an African—community in Canada? Another way of posing the question is to ask whether there isn't another legacy of Africa that we have to deal with as well. For some would suggest that as descendants of Africans, and because we have been so scattered over the globe before coming together in Canada, we are so culturally different and dispersed that there is no real bond or common denominator among us. Beyond, as some would say, the superficiality of skin colour, are we a community?

If implicit in this discussion is the notion of a *homogeneous* group of people that, within boundaries, thinks and acts alike, the answer is, we are not. Even if we apply the weaker standard of a common language, religion or homeland—as the Sikhs, Jews, Armenians, Germans have—the answer is still, no. But are these the only conditions necessary for a community? I think not.

As I pointed out earlier, Canada's black population is indeed unique and has several distinct segments. What members of these groups have in common is the challenge of realizing that the mainstream does not differentiate among these groups. Ironically, no matter how much these individuals strut their perceived differences, most Canadians see us as forming one homogeneous group. And how we are seen and treated by Canadians at large might, in the end, be the deciding factor. For how we are perceived will govern how we react to the wider community, determine whether we can ever become genuine Canadians, settle what the conditions are under which we will live as individuals and as friends and family. In other words, this answer implies how we are to survive collectively as a community and what our place is, and role in Canada.

There are three main groups of Blacks in Canada: Caribbean immigrants, African immigrants and those who have lived in North America for several generations. But even here I am over-generalizing. For even within the Caribbean community, there are inter-island rivalries. For example, every now and then someone pops up in the media to pose this question: Do Jamaicans bring a bad name on all Blacks, primarily those from the Caribbean, by being in trouble too often with the law? The implication here is that all Blacks, that all Caribbean people, are not alike and, therefore, should not be lumped together as a community.

This parochialism shows up in other questions and stereotypes: Are Barbadians too smug, accommodating, law abiding and less likely to disrupt the system? Are Trinidadians too fun loving because they equate life to a party, and is the Toronto festival, Caribana, always in disarray because its leadership is traditionally Trinidadian? And what about those small-islanders? Do French-speaking Haitians in Quebec see themselves as French nationalists in black skins or Blacks who happen to speak French? Should they be included as allophones—a group made up of mainly immigrants from other than English-speaking or French-speaking countries—or are they members of the elite Francophone community in Quebec because their language is that of the dominant group in that province?

There are also rivalries in what might be called African segments of the black community. For example, do immigrants from Ghana have the same disposition as Nigerians or Somalian refugees? And what about those French-speaking immigrants from Zaire; are they as corrupt as the international media paint them? There are even suspicions among the established black community of several generations. Do native-born Blacks in such cities as Halifax, with their roots planted deeply in the Canadian soil for at least seven generations, have the same outlook on life as those "recently arrived" native Blacks nearby in Sydney, Nova Scotia, people who can boast only a few generations in this country? And what about those century-old black communities in southern Ontario, Winnipeg and Edmonton? And those African-Americans who decided they wanted to live in a kinder and gentler country and opted for Canada—where do they fit in this community? There are no clear answers, even from the black population.

A letter to the editor of the Montreal black newspaper, *Community Contact,* published in August 1995, illustrates these suspicions and the hurt that flows from them.

> In my interactions with Caribbean Blacks, I constantly hear derogatory statements about indigenous Black Canadians (Nova Scotians). For example, Canadian Blacks "don't know how to cook" and are "soft" (have never endured hard times), "do not fight for their rights," and Nova Scotian women are "cheap and easy."
>
> I have found that the majority of people I have met from the [Caribbean] Islands are ignorant about the history of

> Canadian Blacks. Consequently, their statements do not consider the struggle of those first Blacks who had to surmount numerous obstacles and barriers to survive in this country (e.g., societal, structural and institutional racism). In addition, a knowledge of Canadian Blacks would show that Nova Scotian Blacks are descendants of Blacks from Jamaica (Maroons), Barbados and the United States.

The writer, Susan Lucas, signed the letter "a proud but disgruntled Nova Scotian." If she is right—and she is—history therefore argues that we are a community.

However, a community is also defined by how outsiders see it. And this is important, because we must recognize that most black people in Canada have one common trait: *they sold themselves into colonialism.* Many black immigrants to Canada came from societies that were in a colonial relationship with a metropolitan centre. Many immigrant Blacks have subconsciously agreed to live, although perhaps for not too long a time, in a colonial relationship in their adopted country. That was the price for immigrating from a country they know well to one that is alien to them, from a country where they formed the dominant group to one where they are a minority. And for that price of admission came the promise of success.

But the receiving country also had an idea of its colonial role. Much has been made of Canada's never having had the status of a colonial power in the same sense that European countries have had, and in more modern times, the United States. But although it is true that Canada did not have colonies abroad, it did have what might amount to the same thing within its border. The Aboriginal peoples on the reserves and the indigenous black populations, in communities separated from the seats of power, were certainly in a colonial relationship. And with this relationship came the usual colonialists' stereotypes of the dominated groups: that the "others" are lazy, indolent, lawless and untrustworthy. According to this colonial perception, these people were best suited for hard work. So it is no coincidence that for decades the only jobs Blacks in Canada could aspire to were porters on the railway and domestic servants. Indeed, the last wave of black immigration to Canada started with efforts to meet a need for domestic labourers, for a pool of cheap labour. This is why Canada still relies so heavily on thousands of Caribbean and Mexican farm workers to reap its agricultural harvest every year. These harvesters, the backbone of a billion-dollar agricultural business, are largely invisible in Canada. They arrive at an airport and head straight for a farm, where they work until it is time to make the return trip to the airport.

Blacks who live in the cities have a tad more visibility, but they are still relegated into what are essentially job ghettoes. Current research by Statistics Canada, in a report prepared by Karen Kelly called "Visible Minorities—A Diverse Group," shows that black Canadians are employed in disproportionately low-paying menial jobs in manufacturing, the hotel and tourism sectors, medical services—such as nurses and nursing assistants—and as domestic workers. A 1992 study for Multiculturalism and Citizenship Canada of the occupations of Blacks in the Greater Toronto Area—the region that accounts for more than 75 percent of the Canadian black population—found that the largest job classifications for Blacks are in clerical (21 percent), manufacturing (16 percent) and services (13 percent). The same study found that 83 percent of Blacks living in the area have an annual income of $25,000 or less. Of this number, some 23 percent of Blacks have no wages, resulting from the higher rates of unemployment among Blacks and their reliance on government assistance as a sole income. Of those who find work, 16 percent make between $25,000 and $49,999, and a paltry few (less than 1 percent) make $50,000 or more. Few of them make it into management and certainly fewer still, if any at all, actually make it into the rarefied atmosphere of corporate boardrooms.

The stereotyping of the receiving culture indicates a belief that black people from around the world are no different from the already marginalized Blacks living in Canada. So the people with political and economic power and influence simply treat the entire lot—the new immigrants and the existing black citizens—as one group. They see us as having the same set of attributes and the same lack of aspiration, and therefore sharing all the attributes of a community.

The idea of a single community was taken a step further when the report showed that the mainstream Canadian culture sees no difference between the Blacks in Canada and those in the United States. This is the reason that in trying to understand its black population, Canada fails when it tries to adopt solutions and models that might have worked in the United States. The black communities in the two countries—although claiming the same source of Africanness and even some of the same heroes and spiritual leaders—are strikingly different in their attitudes and history, and in the way they see themselves fitting into the wider society. It might, in fact, be more worthwhile for Canada to look for social, political and cultural models from the Caribbean.

Be that as it may, there is still a lasting dichotomy of perception in some circles as to whether we are a community or a collection of individuals who happen to be black. Realistically, this difference is only in the minds of those Blacks looking for some reason—class, money, profession, nationality—to stratify the community socially. Although the average immigrant might see himself or herself in a nationalist gaze—Barbadian, Jamaican, Ghanaian—living in Canada, and although indigenous Blacks might marvel at the pushiness and upstart ways of these newcomers, the wider society sees no real difference between these groups.

We are all *blacked out* into a common community. And if the dominant culture agrees that the black community—a people that sold itself into colonialism—is a community, then a community we become. That is how we are forced to relate to the wider society, as a community, even if members are from different backgrounds and circumstances.

The other problem is how the wider Canadian society defines this community it sees living in its midst. When most Canadians think of a black community, invariably they think of Caribbean immigrants. There is a reason for this: through their numbers, Caribbean Blacks have been able to transplant their culture to Canadian soil. We—and I speak as a Caribbean Black—have also hijacked the political and social agenda by foisting our views on the black community already established in Canada, sometimes to the point of ignoring issues of concern to indigenous Blacks. Sometimes we have even refused to acknowledge their long tradition of fighting for civil rights, of, indeed, making it easier for Caribbean and African Blacks to immigrate to this country. However, as the Caribbean black population ages and as our children come to wrestle with different racial issues in Canada, there will be a need for the meeting of minds and greater co-operation between the indigenous black community and those of us from the

Caribbean. But undoubtedly, because of our numbers, Caribbean Blacks will be setting the agenda for some time in the Canadian black community. If only for this reason, the black community in virtually every major Canadian city has a distinct Caribbean character.

* * *

Other ironies are just as obvious as we meet on this Sunday afternoon in the last days of spring to celebrate our particular brand of Africanness, the Canadian version we are forging as a community. One of the these ironies is acutely accentuated along generational lines. Although the majority of their parents were born elsewhere, for most of the children celebrating their African roots Canada is the only country they know. A few were born abroad and others might have gone on trips to places their parents call *back home*. But for most of the children, home is what is written on their Canadian birth certificates or their citizenship documents. Home is where their navel string is buried, to use a Caribbean saying. For most children in this hall celebrating their Africanness, the burials have been in many hospitals around Toronto, Montreal, Winnipeg, Vancouver—somewhere in Canada.

This generational difference takes another form that is perhaps even more telling. It is a difference that is very important in understanding what political power is available to the black community. It is crucial in understanding how much leverage there is in the community to make this country a better place for the future generations of black Canadians; essential in understanding why this leverage is not felt in the mainstream, why so many Blacks, especially the youth, drop out—some would say are forced out—of the Canadian society. And as they grow up, they often remain outside the mainstream, as if by force of habit, as if this early conditioning that they must be separate and apart has become second nature to them. For if we are to believe the generally accepted wisdom, even among leaders of the community, Blacks will advance in this country only as they band together in groups and derive strength from single-mindedly going after specific goals in such areas as business and politics. This, according to the accepted wisdom, is how other minority groups such as the Jews and Italians, and now the Sikhs, have won acceptance in this country.

Citizenship is usually one of the most potent forms of identification with or commitment to a country. Yet, many Caribbean and African immigrants have not taken the step of applying for Canadian citizenship. The result is that they have very little political clout to demand changes that would improve the quality of life. Yet, there are very few Blacks who do not believe that there is much to be gained through politics. The problem is that too many of us feel that the political system is determined to keep Blacks powerless. So instead of trying to change the system by participating, we choose to sit on the sidelines and watch. This situation is brought home during elections when enumerators from the black community seem unable to get Blacks to sign up to vote. It is almost as if nobody can be bothered to think long term, that political goals can be achieved through diligent work and over time. Only surviving from day to day matters. No commitment to sticking around to benefit from any long-term advances. Maybe it will take a shock such as the election of more right-wing anti-Black governments to frighten these immigrants into taking out Canadian citizenship and voting—perhaps a shock similar to the election of Newt Gingrich in the American Congress, which galvanized Caribbean and African immigrants living in America to start recruitment drives and get involved as citizens and voters.

Why do members of the black community choose to sit on the sidelines rather than actively get involved? One answer is steeped in history. Not taking out citizenship—and making a permanent commitment to Canada—is a carry-over from the days when most of the immigrants felt it was merely a matter of time before they would flee the tough, alien life of living in North America. It is the same problem hundreds of thousands of Caribbean Blacks living in the United States also face. They continue to cling to the now highly improbable dream of escaping to the warmth and familial paradise in the Caribbean and Africa, to clutch resolutely the ingrained idea of eventually returning home. And in holding onto this dream, they are no different from some of their African ancestors centuries earlier, who refused to buy into the idea that the Caribbean could become home. They would not be part of the new society. Some of them set up colonies in places where land was plentiful, or rugged enough to stop outsiders from penetrating, and continued to live defiantly the way they believed their ancestors did in the Motherland. In many North American cities, we now see Caribbean and African immigrants who have had to adjust their goals by realizing that life will never be as they had expected. They had arrived in Canada knowing full well they were selling themselves into colonialism, but hoping this status would be temporary. Now, they realize, they are trapped. Worse, they recognize that this permanence threatens the future of their kids. The youths cannot escape the status into which they were born. So, many immigrants from the Caribbean simply pretend that they still have a choice—a freedom to live in Canada as if they were back home. They behave as if they are not part of the Canadian mosaic, but marooned visitors unable to get back home.

Another possible answer is cultural. Blacks in general have little confidence in the political system, so collectively they ask, Why bother?, especially if the dream is still to go back home. Involvement in politics, as in other manifestations of citizenry, would indicate a buying into the existing order. And since this one excludes Blacks from the centre, why bother getting involved?

Although the cultural argument still holds much weight, particularly with black youth, this invocation of history is losing its appeal. Children of these immigrants do not have the same choices. They have no dreams of going back home to numb the daily pain of surviving in a place where they feel not wanted. These children became Canadians with their first breaths. They didn't have to consciously decide if they wanted this citizenship and nationality. They are born into the system whether they like it or not. The result is that Blacks in Canada have come to acknowledge the presence of segregation, although not the cruel, uncouth forms of forcing groups to live in specific areas—except for the Aboriginal peoples—or the kinds associated with the United States—busing and black ghettoes. It is done by tacitly drawing lines of demarcation, lines that are so well entrenched that Blacks themselves often enforce them, that Blacks themselves often seek refuge and shelter behind them.

On this day, as we meet in separation to celebrate who we are, there is another irony—a realization that this separation isn't all our doing and might be no more than a reflex move to hide our hurt and disappointment. Below the surface, after we scrape away the proud African rhetoric, this gathering, in fact, might be a potent example of how the wider society has excluded us. The graduation ceremony is taking place in the North York Memorial Hall, in the heart of the Canadian city with the largest black, or African, population. This hall is a memorial to all those Canadian—read "white"—soldiers who fought and died to build this country. The celebration is also occurring when the entire country is marking the 50th anniversary of the Allied victory in Europe, a time to reflect on the sacrifices of all those men and women on the battlefield and the home front. But when most people in the wider society think of Canada, they automatically assume White. So when the television and radio networks, the newspapers and other forms of the media discuss the contribution of the Canadian soldier to building and preserving this country, they automatically think and depict Whites. There is no mention of the role played by the sons and daughters of Africa in past wars, no acknowledgement of their sacrifice to build Canada. Indeed, the celebrations to mark the end of the Second World War coincide with a very bitter debate about the presence of Blacks in Canada. It is a debate in which the majority-voice seems to be saying all too loudly that Blacks in Canada are refugees, recently arrived immigrants, a drain on society, criminals and welfare bums who should be sent back to where they came from.

In the heat of this debate, this memorial building would be a place of refuge for many young men and women claiming the legacy of all those who fought and died for Canada. A refuge for those feeling they must fight the suspicions and low expectations of mainstream Canada to survive in this country. Except for the people meeting in this hall, most Canadians have demonstrated through their actions the assumption that none of these soldiers could have been black. Such expectations are part of the reality of being black in Canada.

In the hall, the people gathered for this event have no second thoughts about who they are. They are African, a connection that through the colour of their skin binds them together as a repressed people; a connection that makes them rally together to arm their children to help them survive in a country where it is a distinct disadvantage to have any shade of black skin. An event like this is where they teach their children about the double burden of being black, the meaning of a lifetime of discrimination: of always being qualified only for menial jobs; of feeling judged by different and harsher standards at school, work and on the streets; of having security men chasing away groups of black youths from malls; of feeling spied upon and policed differently; of seeing virtually no reflection of ourselves in the mainstream media and popular culture; of having to deal with the wider expectations that to be black means to be headed for failure or prison; of expecting to be dismissed as a whiner for speaking out against the conditions that create these fears and expectations.

And it is an experience, we tell our children, that makes no difference whether a navel string is buried in Canada, the United States, Britain, Jamaica or Ghana. A black man whom we quote—the Jamaican reggae singer Peter Tosh—is an African, no explanation needed, no apology given. And in Canada, Africans are expected to view the passing parade of all things Canadian from the sidelines rather than joining in. Being black means we will be treated differently.

And so, although the people in the hall would have to search for their navel strings in various places around the world, because they live in Canada, live on the North American continent with a history of discrimination and prejudice, they have to assert their Africanness as a collective weapon and shield. They have to teach their children yet another anthem.

May we forever stand,
True to our God,
True to our native land.

The youngsters lead us in the singing of the African anthem. On this day, their voices rising in unison with other Africans in Atlanta, New York, Miami. In all places where people may not know the words but still sing the same tune.

As the singing dies and we sit to eat, one question begs an answer. Why, in a country like Canada—with its envious international reputation as a gentler and kinder place, with its history as a multicultural haven for people from around the world—is it still necessary for us as black parents to teach our children social segregation in order to prepare them for the future?

CHAPTER 2

COMING TO CANADA

Why it is even necessary to discuss the issues of separation and integration in the first place? Why raise them after a continuous black and African presence in Canada spanning 500 years—a period that cannot be claimed by many of the groups that are now so quick to treat Blacks as outsiders, as interlopers? And shouldn't these questions be answered in a context that takes into account Canada's warm international image as a country that welcomes refugees and minorities? After all, doesn't Canada have a charter of rights and freedoms outlawing discrimination by race, colour, creed and gender?

And isn't this the same country that has been built by immigrants, where it is said that with the exception of Native people, every Canadian is either an immigrant or can trace the start of his or her lineage to an immigrant? Is not Canada a multicultural country where, according to the political views in the ascendency these days, merit and not colour of skin is the only criterion that decides the future and standard of living for every boy or girl, immigrant or native born, black or white?

In Canada, the prevailing view suggests, nobody has doors slammed in their faces because of the colour of their skin, for Canada has the potential to be one big, comfortable home for all people fortunate to live within its boundaries. And as that prevailing view holds, Canada has never practised the blatant racism so obvious in the United States, Europe and even parts of Africa and the Caribbean. Canada is viewed as a kinder and gentler place for minorities, where civil and human rights have been won through quiet persuasion—not in confrontation with water cannons, snarling police dogs, armed guardsmen and security forces who "bust head" at peaceful sit-ins.

No, the prevailing view argues, minority groups have no reason to whine or complain. Not in Canada, not in the place that had been the terminus of freedom for the Underground Railroad for American Blacks fleeing slavery. Not in this land so beautiful in scenery and unselfish in character, a country that selflessly sends United Nations peacekeepers around the world so that others less fortunate can enjoy in their homeland the peace of Canada; the country that dispatches hordes of election monitors to any Third World country needing international certification that it is on its way to democracy. Unfortunately, the prevailing view provides no real answers to the questions associated with what it is really like to be black in Canada, to be a young boy or girl walking the streets of a major Canadian city, who live by the credo that despite their place of birth, they are really transplanted Africans first and Canadians second. Sometimes even Blacks unwittingly buy into this perception and can be shocked by the truth. We tend to forget how Canadian we have become, but that, alas, we might never be considered as fully Canadian.

Such was the case when I took my two eldest children back home to Barbados for the first time. I assumed this trip would be a family reunion and that I would simply be taking home these Bajans who happened to have been born abroad. The boys would simply walk into the family home, draw up a chair and fit right in, as if they were returning from a long journey. After all, they would be fitting right in with people who were just like them. And God knows, I had told them more than enough about growing up in Barbados, playing cricket, sitting with cousins swapping stories, all the good nostalgic things I like to remember, which I had hoped would smooth the road for them to make their way home.

The test of these assumptions came the very next day after our arrival back home. My sons joined some cousins and friends playing a game of cricket, or at least trying to play the game. Except, no matter how they tried, my sons could not get the hang of this game that I spent so many of my youthful days playing. When it came to their turn to bowl, they threw the ball the way a baseball pitcher would, which is illegal in cricket. When they were at bat, they instinctively waved the bat over their shoulders, just as they did in the Toronto school yard when playing softball. It did not feel natural for them to hold the bat on the ground, to tap it the way I used to when, at their age, I mimicked all those great Caribbean cricketers guarding their stumps. Instead, they took the most vulnerable stance possible in cricket—leaving their wicket unprotected. Of course, they didn't spend much time batting. "Who are these Canadians you have here?" my eldest brother finally asked.

Instantly, I felt sorry for my children. As I watched them struggle to come to terms with the game, with the nuances of the Bajan language other children spoke so excitedly in the heat of the moment, I realized the gulf into which I had dropped them. I realized that for my children, Barbados was simply a place to visit, but that home was elsewhere. And I realized that, because of my children and my wanting the best for them, but also knowing the alienation so many of us feel in Canada, I didn't quite have a home either. Perhaps, neither did my children.

But home is also a place of welcome, of automatic acceptance. Stephanie Daye is in her early twenties, a person who looks as if she could have been a recent graduate of the African-Canadian Heritage Association or one of its youth leaders. Working for a television network in Toronto, Stephanie has grown tired of the number of times she has been asked which Caribbean island is her home. "Actually, I find it quite disconcerting," says Stephanie. And she should, because Stephanie has lived all her life in Canada, her family having resided in Halifax for so many generations she has lost count. But Stephanie is not alone in the way she feels. Her girlfriend was born in Ghana but moved with her family to Atlantic Canada at an early age. She knows nothing about Ghana, except what her family and friends have told her. As far as she is concerned, Ghana is not home. Yet, most people she meets invariably get around to inquiring when last she was home in Ghana. Maybe it is the trace of her Ghanaian accent, she says, or simply the fact that it is still difficult for mainstream Canadians to accept that a Black can be Canadian. "You should talk to my grandmother," Stephanie says. "She can tell you quite a few stories."

Telling stories is one way members of the black community handle the built-in expectation of most Canadians that any black person encountered on the street or on the job is a visitor to the country. And it is the stories that keep the spirits up. These include the invocations such as those at the graduation of the African-Canadian Heritage Association. They also encompass the biting jokes such as those told to a Toronto lunch crowd by a Halifax comedian, Taryn Della. It is a painful story of how Canadians with thick Eastern European accents are likely to approach her in any major Canadian city and enquire, in all seriousness, when she arrived in the country. Or there is the story that the older folks around Toronto still tell about an event in the 1970s. An academic from England immigrated to Canada to take up a prestigious position at the University of Toronto. With him came the expectation of a stint in federal politics, so in a short while this immigrant was being touted as a possible leader of one of the major federal political parties. Several members of the Toronto black community were invited to meet this prime-minister-in-the-making at a reception at the university. While meeting the invitees, the guest of honour came to a young woman and, trying uncomfortably to make small talk, inquired: "Where are you from?"

"Toronto," she said.

"Yes, I know that, but where are you *really* from?"

"Toronto," she repeated.

"I meant, which island are you from?" he tried again.

"You are from an island," she replied. "I was born in Toronto." At which point, the potential leader of Canada moved on. Unfortunately, many of us immigrants did not find the welcome to Canada as generous as what was offered this immigrant from that fair isle called England. Still, it is worth remembering why some of us chose this country and the expectations that came with us.

These are the types of stories parents tell their children at our gatherings. Some of us can so quickly escape the tag of being an immigrant while others, several generations in this country, always have this *honour* forced on them.

* * *

From an early age, I knew that I would be an immigrant. It wasn't even as if I felt there was a choice. After all, from my earliest recollections there was always the hope, becoming ever more fleeting with every year, that I would live in England, where my parents had immigrated. In this respect, I was no different from thousands of Blacks now walking the streets of major cities in Europe and North America. I was no different from many more still living in the Caribbean.

As was the case of so many young people in the colonial Caribbean, the dream of self-fulfilment was built squarely on immigration. Even as the winds of independence blew out of Africa and raced across the islands in the late 1960s, they were not really intended for us. Independence was for those not so blessed with a chance to leave the region; the proclamation of sovereignty was to be an incentive for those left behind to make the most of what few crumbs they would get from life's table, but not for anyone with personal ambition. Even as we mouthed the words to the new national anthem, we never thought political independence was intended for the better educated among us, certainly not for those fortunate enough to have parents living in a foreign metropolis. It was not meant for us immigrants just waiting for the ticket to board the next plane or boat.

I can still recall how we felt whenever one of our friends announced he or she was leaving for another country. This gave them airs; it allowed them to boldly challenge teachers in class, to stop doing homework and to take on the more worldly pose of those plucked from among the wretched for good things. We were envious and wished that our time, too, would come soon. The older people of the villages doled out their blessings on them, invoking God's speed in their journeys and admonishing them to grab all the opportunities that were now bound to come their way. Immigration was a status symbol.

By the time I was a teenager, it had become clear that England would not be my home. Drastic changes to the British immigration policy, fueled by rampant fears there about race wars resulting from uncontrolled immigration in places like London, had slammed the door shut for many of us. More than that, Britain was suffering from the industrial malaise of decay, unemployment, low productivity and crushing debt. Thousands of Caribbean people, who previously saw this mother country as a new home, were bolting to Canada and the United States. Britain was no longer a place of hope. Years later, I would run into people like David Locker from Montserrat, who in 1958 jumped on a ship and went to London to attend technical college, but in 1968 realized England had no future for him. Someone suggested that he move on to Canada. Arriving in Montreal, he decided to stay there, making that city and Canada his home for almost three decades, working as a teacher and a leader of the Caribbean community in the Montreal area.

Or Dudley Thompson, who as a young man grew tired of working as a civil servant in Jamaica. Merely because his friends were going to England, he went along, too. But he didn't like England and was soon following his wandering instincts, ending up in Montreal and having three job offers. In almost 30 years, he has never been unemployed, he boasts, and has never once applied for unemployment insurance or welfare. Other young men from the Caribbean had turned their backs on England and set out for the United States via Halifax and Montreal. But with no clear destination in mind there, many of them never made it to the United States. The sheer natural beauty of the country, linking up with old friends and family, or the certainty of a job was enough to keep them in Canada.

About this time, people my age started thinking of going directly to North America from the Caribbean. Precisely, we were thinking of the United States. Coincidentally, changes in immigration policies about the same time were making it easier for people from Third World countries, long not the preferred types of immigrants, to get into Canada and the United States. Around us we could see signs of North American affluence, in the tourists arriving daily from the eastern seaboard and, of course, the very friendly French-speaking Canadians spending two or three weeks at some guest house on a beach near us. We saw it, too, in the Caribbean migrant workers returning home. They came back with valises filled with American clothes. They had American dollars in their pockets after spending time on contract cutting cane in Florida or picking fruit in the New England states and in Ontario. And they had the sophistication from living overseas, the finesse and poise that make young boys hunger to emulate them. Going to North America had become a rite of passage.

For the first time since 1924, when restrictive laws almost dried up a century of Caribbean migration to the United States, we, the fortunate generation coming of age in the 1960s, felt welcome in North America. We saw it as a chance to become all those things little boys and girls dream of when adults ask, "What do you want to be when you grow up?"

Simply going to North America would be the answer to our need for excitement, for our desire to take on greater challenges, to test ourselves with opportunities that were not available at home. Leaving home and making it in a new country would be the ultimate test of our lives. Even before we immigrated, it was horrific for anyone to think of not succeeding, of not fully integrating into our new country. We were confident of success even where others had gone before and failed. No way would we let the older folks back home, and the younger boys and girls of the next generation, think that any of us had squandered a chance to make good in an adopted country. Becoming antisocial and a drain on society were not badges of honour. Not only would we boast in minute details in letters back home about how we were succeeding by having a great time at restarting our lives, but we would also brag about our university and college degrees, about the freedom to travel and to rise to the top of our chosen trade or profession. And we would also show we were succeeding by our ability to send home regular money orders and barrels of food and clothes. With our noses in the air, we believed that any Blacks we met in the new country who were failures either were lazy or wanted to fail.

We could not wait to go abroad to be productive and to help those left behind. Our formal education system had taught—some would say brainwashed—us from early on that there were few callings higher than to be an immigrant. It had prepared us for going overseas and proving that although we were poor, we were as good and productive as anyone else in the world. Immigration has always been the safety valve to let off the social steam from a burgeoning population; it also was an economic force on the island, where in school we were trained to think that every dollar earned abroad and sent back home improved the standard of living. The money built houses and repaired roofs, bought school books to train more would-be immigrants, helped governments to provide pensions and other social services to those left behind. Simply put, it was a social and patriotic duty to leave the island; to take one more person out of the local work-force. And on a personal level, there was a compelling reason for leaving. We could go abroad, get a higher education, a trade or profession, save money and then return home to a comfortable retirement. In return, we would work as hard and honestly as possible to be productive and committed to the country accepting us. We would leave our homeland strongly holding the belief that, ultimately, we would be buried in the same place as our navel strings, but that we would die much richer and more worldly than we were born, than we would have become by staying at home. Immigration would leave everyone better off.

But the 1960s was the time of the Vietnam War and many young Americans were fleeing their country to avoid the military draft. Many who remained behind, including a future president, were in open defiance of their government. Ironically, many of us in Barbados welcomed the opportunity to get into the U.S. military. We were ready to sign up even if it meant the possibility of facing death in Vietnam. Our youthfulness made us feel that we would avoid a bullet or grenade from the Viet Cong. We were young and ready to take on the world and all its risks. The ads from the U.S. military that we saw in such magazines as *Time* and *Newsweek* were enticing, especially for those of us lacking the funds to go to university.

There was the time when Kenrick Taitt told us that he and his bigger brother were leaving for the United States to join their mother. Kenrick was a friend of my eldest brother and fancied himself as a singer. And where was a better place for him to become a professional singer than the United States? We all agreed. This was the home of Percy Sledge, Otis Redding, James Brown and all those fantastic singers from the Motown label in Detroit—all those singers that we heard on the local radio stations morning, noon and night.

Kenrick had no fear—at least none that he admitted to—about going into the U.S. Army. He was telling my brother that his joining the army was a certainty. The officials at the U.S. consulate in Bridgetown had told Kenrick and his brother that the first thing they would have to do on arrival in New York was to report for military training. They had to sign the relevant forms in Barbados when they went to the consulate to get their immigration papers. No problem, Kenrick told my brother. Anything to get into the United States. Anything to pursue his dream of becoming an internationally acclaimed singer.

So within days of getting his visa and draft notice, Kenrick was on an American plane headed for a life of opportunity in New York, with a detour via the U.S. Army. Within a year, he was back on the island, walking the streets in his immaculate olive-green, U.S. Army uniform, visiting

old girlfriends and regaling us with stories about life in the U
He was even speaking like a Yankee to boot, the American
status symbol, indicating which of us had graduated from wis
an immigrant to actually becoming one.

Kenrick had great tales to tell about the harsh boot-camp training in the army to make him combat-ready: crawling on his stomach while others shot over his head; crawling under barbed wire; handling guns and grenades; visiting Mexico with the army for training; changing his diet because of having undergone this tough, man-making training. Kenrick fascinated us by reporting that his diet was mainly fruits, mainly mangoes that he found plentiful in Mexico while on combat training and just as available in New York stores. As he explained, these were big, round and succulent mangoes that were so much juicier and had more flesh than the mangoes we knew in Barbados.

We listened in awe, perhaps seeing Kenrick as no different from all those home boys across the United States who were forced to comply with the draft, but who returned home to their neighbourhoods as heroes in the making. For us these stories were confirmation Kenrick was doing good, even if he had not found a band or a record contract for his love of singing. We all envied him and wondered when we would escape this blighted life and island.

Kenrick also told us there was a good possibility that he would be sent to Vietnam soon after his return to the United States. This was partly the reason he had come back home for a brief visit, to see his father and friends before shipping out. But that was a price any of us would have paid to get to the land of opportunity. And from the propaganda we were being fed, we knew that Americans were definitely winning the war against the communists. Occasionally, we heard of the odd demonstration by students around our age at American universities. But that didn't bother us. We saw the protestors as idle, rich brats already enjoying the luxuries of living in the United States. They had the time and needed the challenge and excitement from protesting. We were poor and wanted to get in and enjoy the American Dream. Also, the Americans had such heavy firepower and machinery, it was only a matter of time before Kenrick and his buddies in the army overran the enemy. Then Kenrick might have even greater stories to tell us when he got back.

And once he had served in the army, acquired a skill or profession, he could devote all his time to following the dream of becoming a singer. We expected any day to hear the local radio announcer scream with glee that he or she was about to play a record, hot off the press and all the way from the U-S-of-A. We anticipated the announcer telling us about that Barbadian singer, Kenrick Taitt, now doing so well in his adopted country. We could hear the dee-jay boasting about how this acclaimed singer never forgot his roots, never forgot the island of his birth, never forgot the people who nurtured him. This Harry Belafonte incarnate. We waited and waited. Kenrick returned to the United States and I never heard of him again, never heard one record by him, never heard if he survived Vietnam.

There were many young men on the island who felt the attainment of their dreams meant a detour through the military. Indeed, a generation before us, some Caribbean political leaders had gone abroad as youths and served in the British, American and Canadian militaries. Some actually faced combat in the Second World War. Some, like former Jamaican prime minister Michael Manley and the Vincentian leader, Prime Minister Milton Cato, and the late Barbadian prime minister, Errol Barrow, received military training in Canada. Barrow became the personal navigator for Sir Sholto Douglas, the air commander in chief of the British Zone of Germany.

These men were typical of Caribbean people who flocked to North America and Europe during the Second World War. One of the most outstanding was a Trinidadian barrister, Jack Kelshall, who left his homeland soon after the war broke out and became a squadron leader in the Canadian air force. But Kelshall's contribution was not only to Canada, but to the entire war effort in the British Commonwealth and the United States. He became one of the first pilot officers in the British Commonwealth Air Training Plan, the effort by the Allies to train some 200,000 pilots and navigators in a mere six years. The success of this training would win the war fought in the air over Europe, North Africa and the Pacific.

Kelshall joined the Canadian air force in 1941, and "[B]y the middle of the war, he had become both a leading instructor and a leader of men," wrote Canadian journalist Ted Barris in *Behind the Glory*, a book about the BCATP. "His ground school lectures about morale and duty were inspiring. They showed his students not only what they were doing but why they were doing it."

An example of Kelshall's ability to inspire others is evident in one of his speeches to an early graduating class:

> We must realize that in Europe and in Asia and the Pacific, men, exactly like ourselves, feeling and hoping just as we, are being done to death in all manner of painful, degrading, bestial ways. Yes, and the women and children also. We must stop thinking of this air force as an organization in which we can make a big salary without having to do too much work. We must quit thinking that here we are learning an interesting profession at which we shall be able to earn a good living when this war is over. We must stop acting as though the ultimate aim of all this training is to make us pilots or navigators, and realize that its real aim is to make us efficient in the various parts we are to play in a desperate struggle for survival. In short, we must look beyond the training itself to the aim behind the training.... The golden rule in every case should be to act in the way best calculated to help conclude this war quickly and successfully. Nothing must be allowed to detract from this main aim. No self or public interest, no personal inclination, no private benefit or gain.

When the war finished, Kelshall returned to Trinidad, where he became active in politics and the trade-union movement in the Caribbean. He died in 1991, at the age of 78. Four years later, when Canadians celebrated the anniversary of the end of the Second World War, nobody bothered recalling the vital role played by Kelshall and others like him. Neither did they bother celebrating the efforts of all those black and Caribbean people who contributed to the international war effort. This omission was not missed by several people in the Canadian African community, many of whom were soldiers who fought for this country.

Months after the official celebrations, the slight still stung the black and Caribbean community. The issue was raised auspiciously during the introduction of the former Jamaican prime minister, Michael Manley, a former member of the Royal Canadian Air Force. Manley's speech at York University in Toronto was sponsored by the consular corps of English-speaking Caribbean diplomats in Toronto. His job was to talk about Caribbean and Latin American integration. Introducing this Caribbean statesman was the then-chair of the Caribbean consular corps in Toronto, Burns Bonadie, a diplomat from St. Vincent. To loud applause, Bonadie wondered how the Canadian media could have overlooked the efforts of Caribbean people in the war. "If others are not willing to blow our trumpet, then we must do it ourselves," Bonadie said.

But obviously the attraction of the military for Caribbean boys and girls did not stop with the end of the Second World War. The same attraction we felt for the military in the Caribbean, the way we saw it as an exit out of a dead end, might have been no different from what took someone like a Colin Powell to the top of the U.S. armed forces. Powell, the son of Jamaican parents, and like Kenrick, a Vietnam veteran, was the former head of the Joint Chiefs of Staff. Powell pushed to its limit the dream that brought many of us out of the Caribbean.

"My parents let me and my sister know that we were twice blessed—as Americans and, every inch, as Jamaicans—children of the Caribbean," Powell said in a 1994 speech at the University of the West Indies in Jamaica. Powell had retired from the military a hero for his leadership of the allied troops in the Gulf War against Iraq. When he gave the speech, there was speculation that both the Republican and Democratic parties were courting Powell to be a high-profile candidate. They wanted him to become the African-American equivalent of a General Douglas MacArthur, Dwight Eisenhower or Harry Truman, all of whom parlayed a successful military career into a political pursuit. Some Republicans saw Powell as a winning presidential candidate, while the Democratic White House, seeing potential trouble on its hands, offered him the post of Secretary of State on the tacit understanding that he should not battle the incumbent Democrat in the White House. Some of the black and Caribbean publications I read out of New York suggested that a life of politics seemed a good idea for the good soldier, a crowning recognition of the contribution of Caribbean Blacks to North America.

Powell travelled to Jamaica where he was made an "honourary

Jamaican" and given the Order of Jamaica and an honourary degree from the University of the West Indies.

> Jamaica was always referred to as home. Fifty years after leaving, a visit back home to Jamaica by one of my relatives was called going home. I was raised with images of a place that I had never seen, but knew so well.... My extended family was spread from Jamaica to New York to Miami to Toronto to London.

This is the same type of speech members of Caribbean extended families tell their children. This is no different from what the children in the memorial hall in North York for Canada's fighting men and women hear from their parents, the same kind of thinking behind the several levels of consciousness we continue to face.

Although the majority of us wanted to go to the United States, some of us started to head toward such places as Vancouver, Montreal, Toronto, Edmonton and Calgary and Winnipeg. I would come to Toronto.

It was near the end of the last term at Harrison College, when the history teacher, Ralph Jemmott, asked the graduating class about our plans. One by one, my fellow students talked about the applications they had sent to institutions of higher learning with such names as University of Toronto, McGill, McMaster, University of Western Ontario—all of them in Canada. These were new possibilities for them. A generation earlier, most graduates would have inundated universities in England, particularly Cambridge, Oxford and the London School of Economics, with applications.

Jemmott, a graduate of the Jamaica campus of the University of the West Indies, seemed to be encouraging us to apply to foreign universities, even though only the well-off members of the class could afford this extravagance. Black and poor students, like Jemmott was when he was graduating from Modern Six form at Harrison College, had no choice but to go to the University of the West Indies. I applied to the law school at the University of the West Indies and was accepted. But at the back of my mind was the notion that this was not good enough. This was only a fall-back position until I sorted out my possibilities abroad. I still wanted to leave the island.

I was emulating others on both sides of my family by wanting to be an immigrant. By sometimes wishing I had an opportunity to join the U.S. Army, I was no different from my father who left the island a year after I was born to join the British army, the military being the only chance he saw to fulfil his dream of becoming an internationally recognized musician. My dream of joining somebody's army might have been fuelled anew every time we received a postcard from places like Addis Ababa, a letter from Frankfurt or some other exotic place where the British army had sent my father, where he played the clarinet, saxophone, trumpet and drums for his regiment.

Although my parents had gone to England in the 1950s, the United States had always been the natural choice for members of the family. One of my grandfathers spent his time between New York and Barbados. Every so often, especially when I noticed his house boarded up for long periods, I would ask where grandfather was. "He must be back in the States," was the typical reply. My father's father, like so many Caribbean young men of his time, had first gone to the United States to provide the cheap labour needed in munition plants. This was a time when U.S. plants brought in Caribbean migrant workers to help overcome an acute labour shortage.

Many migrants had to endure the worst of the Jim Crow laws in the southern United States and the disdain of the established black community, which felt the new arrivals were lowering standards and selling out by accepting cheap jobs. This was a combination that made them feel less than the human beings they were in the Caribbean. Some of them stayed and militantly rebelled against Jim Crow. Others stayed and for generations their families, although black, never fully integrated with the Blacks they found. My grandfather stayed on, eventually starting his own store-front church in Yonkers, New York. He never saw the United States as anything less than racist and unfair to Blacks, particularly Caribbean Blacks.

And there were others in the family who had gone to the United States and apparently had done well. There was the story of Clarence, my grandmother's brother. We heard how Clarence, in search of adventure, left Barbados for the United States. While there, he didn't keep in touch with anyone back home. Then, one morning, according to the story, he got off a boat and showed up at his mother's home, his pockets bulging with American money. Clarence decided to use this money to buy land, perhaps falling prey to the immigrant dream of always wanting to own a piece "of the rock" back home as a retirement investment.

The story goes that Clarence bought a large tract of land and left it in the trust of his mother, my great grandmother who we all called Gran. Then, he literally disappeared into the United States, where he must have died. Nobody ever heard of him again. One day, when I was about eight years old, my grandmother took me to a place called Clapham. We traveled by bus to get there, for Clapham was the site of a mill used to grind corn into meal, or cornflour as we called it.

During the lunch break, we left the baskets and their contents with the mill owner and Grandmother took me walking in the area. We ended up on a hill. Below, we could see all the way to the horizon, past the bluish green waters of the Atlantic Ocean, past all the splendour before us, the land spread out with the green sugar-cane stalks, corn fields, all gleaming and shining beautifully in the midmorning sun. "That is the land my brother bought and left for Gran to keep for he," Grandmother said to me. "And to think my brother got all this land and I have to be paying all this money that I ain't got to Ashby to rent a spot o' land to put a house on." Even as a child, I understood about freedoms that came with immigrating, with making money and sending it back home so my grandmother could buy a spot of land and not have to pay rent.

Grandmother's disappointment would become even deeper when Gran died, well past her hundredth birthday, and the land passed out of the family either because Gran willed it to someone else, or simply died without a will. We never knew what happened to the ownership of the land. Parts of the land are now tenantries for low-cost housing. Other parts have been developed by the more well-to-do residents on the island. Sometimes, I wonder if this story wasn't just a part of the immigrant lore on the island. Whether true or not, I believed it and wanted to repeat this success.

When the time came for me to think seriously about leaving, I went to have a chat with my grandfather, who was back home with his American-born wife, perhaps a sign that he had integrated. My grandfather was having a late breakfast when I turned up, unannounced. He asked his wife to add a plate for me at the table and after some small talk I got down to the real business of the visit. Could he sponsor me as an immigrant to New York? The answer came back right away.

"What about going to Canada?" he asked. "It's better there for black people, especially people like us from the West Indies." Then, my grandfather talked about the violence and hardship in New York, about his dislike for the place and how he would not encourage anyone to go there. This distrust extended to the food. "Take this breakfast we are eating here," he said. "This is real food. Not like in the United States where they are always injecting something or the other into the food. The eggs over there are like powder, not like the real eggs we got in Barbados." Canada would be a better place, he promised.

I never got the chance to speak to my grandfather again. And he, a preacher, apart from the advice to stay away from the United States, gave me what he thought was the only thing he had of any worth, the only thing to guide me in some strange country as I headed out into life as a man. He placed his hand on the crown of my head and prayed, loud and long, that God should guide my steps. For I was a young man seeking my way in the world, inevitable as an immigrant. We sat down to eat the scrambled eggs and bacon, me feeling queasy and disappointed. Queasy because at that stage of my life I was self-conscious about such open displays of religion. Disappointed because of what he had said about New York and the United States.

The next time I thought seriously about immigration, New York and the United States were no longer in the picture. My brother, Errol, had immigrated to Canada. I decided to find out if what my grandfather had said about the country was true.

Canada was a member of the British Commonwealth, just like the emerging nations in the Caribbean and Africa. Canada had decided to become a "big sister" to the English-speaking and French-speaking Caribbean, and it was seen as nonthreatening; it had no colonial designs, unlike Britain, and it was not a military power seeking to dominate the region, unlike the United States, with its military bases scattered all over the region. And Canada was seemingly a virgin country, with none of the violence we heard about in New York, Detroit and other major U.S. centres. As far as we knew, it did not have Jim Crow laws. And just around this time, Canada had tried to ease the unemployment in the Caribbean by agreeing to take in a small number of women on a domestic program.

My grandfather's fondness for Canada might have come genuinely from his knowing people who immigrated to Canada after the First World War. This was one of the earliest waves of Caribbean people to come to Canada this century. These immigrants settled mainly around the Halifax area in Nova Scotia and in Winnipeg, Manitoba, and some western provinces. In places like Halifax, they joined with the Canadian Blacks whose families had lived there for at least two centuries, but the presence of the two groups produces tensions that, even now, generations later, still linger. These were descendants of the United Empire Loyalists who had fought for the British in the war for American Independence. These were the same Loyalists who were promised good land for rising up against those republicans in the American states, but who found empty promises once they arrived in Canada. These were the same black Loyalists who helped create provinces like Ontario, New Brunswick and Nova Scotia. And some of them were the descendants of those slaves who had taken the Underground Railroad to escape into Canada.

Previous to this wave of Caribbean immigrants, Canada had also been tied to the development of the Caribbean. Dried codfish from Newfoundland and other Atlantic provinces has always been part of the staple diet of Caribbean people, to the point where a national dish of Jamaica is ackee and salt fish; in Trinidad, salt fish and callaloo; in Barbados, salt fish and cou-cou. The Caribbean and Atlantic Canada also have strong financial ties. At least one leading Canadian bank opened branches in the Caribbean before it decided to expand across Canada. And Canada had become the dumping ground, at least once, for early West Indians trying to overthrow the slavery system. In 1796, a group of Maroons, rebellious slaves in Jamaica, were loaded onto a vessel after a battle against the British military and exiled to Nova Scotia.

So Canada was viewed as a good place for Blacks, even though at times Canadian officials tried to dissuade Blacks from immigrating by arguing they were unsuited to survive the cold weather.

But the image of Canada as a refuge for Blacks was strong and enduring. About a decade before I had asked my grandfather's counsel, none other than Martin Luther King Jr., the black civil rights leader, was extolling the virtues of Canada. "It is a deep personal privilege to address a nation-wide Canadian audience," King said in an address to Canadians in 1967.

> Over and above any kinship of U.S. citizens and Canadians as North Americans, there is a singular historical relationship between American Negroes and Canadians.
>
> Canada is not merely a neighbour to Negroes. Deep in our history of struggle for freedom, Canada was the North Star. The Negro slave, denied education, de-humanized, imprisoned on cruel plantations, knew that far to the north a land existed where a fugitive slave, if he survived the horrors of the journey, could find freedom. The legendary Underground Railroad started in the south and ended in Canada. The freedom road links us together. Our spirituals, now so widely admired around the world, were often codes. We sang of 'Heaven' that awaited us, and the slave masters listened in innocence, not realizing that we were not speaking of the hereafter. Heaven was the word for Canada and the Negro sang of the hope that his escape on the Underground Railroad would carry him there. One of our spirituals, 'Follow the Drinking Gourd,' in its disguised lyrics contained directions for escape. The gourd was the big dipper, and the North Star to which its handle pointed gave the celestial map that directed the flight to the Canadian border.

This was still the romantic image of Canada, held by people, including immigrants, in the 1960s: a place of pristine snow and streams, a home of tolerance, a country in the forefront of racial harmony, where Blacks first crossed the coloured line in North American professional baseball. This happened in Montreal in 1947 when the legendary Jackie Robinson broke into the Montreal Royals of the International League, the farm team of the Brooklyn Dodgers. Robinson did so well in Montreal, where he took top honours in his first year, that he was soon called up to the major leagues.

Annette Goodridge remembers arriving in Vancouver for a vacation in 1964 and thinking it was the most beautiful place on earth. She had arrived from Barbados and had spent the summer travelling in the interior of British Columbia and Alberta. She was totally enthralled by the beauty of the Rocky Mountains, the foothills and plains of Alberta, and the rugged coastline as she travelled into Washington state. She found other Caribbean immigrants living on the West Coast and discovered other black communities in Washington. Four years later, she returned to Canada and settled in Vancouver where she has lived ever since, eventually becoming the consul general for Barbados.

Goodridge was following in the footstep of another Barbadian who turned up in Vancouver in 1885 and became quite a local character. I first became aware of Joe Fortes while eating at a Vancouver restaurant in 1986. On the walls was a picture of this sizeable black man from Barbados whose claim to fame was that he had saved countless people from drowning and that children loved him.

Joe Fortes was born in Barbados in 1865 and worked on sailing ships before ending up in Vancouver. Once in the city, he worked variously as shoeshine boy, a hotel porter and bartender. But Joe Fortes loved the sea, and during the mild months, he lived in a tent on the beach. According to the local history and material published in the Joe Fortes Library of Vancouver, he "devoted all his free time to teaching children to swim and to patrolling the beach. The self-appointed unpaid guardian continued to support himself by working odd jobs until, in 1901, the city appointed him its first official lifeguard."

Fortes seemed to be quite a character. "His contemporaries referred to him respectfully and lovingly as 'Old Black Joe' or 'English Bay Joe.'" According to the official count, Old Joe rescued 29 people from drowning, but "it is believed that the number is considerably higher." When he retired in 1910, the city gave him a gold watch, a cheque and an illuminated address as appreciation for his public service. And when he died in 1922, mourners crowded the cathedral to say "farewell to a brave, kind and modest friend." A flat stone, simply inscribed "Joe," marks his grave in the Mountain View Cemetery in Vancouver. In 1927, the citizens of Vancouver dedicated a monument to Joe Fortes in Alexandra Park. It carries the inscription, "Little children loved him."

The same experience that was pulling people like Goodridge to Canada was also attracting thousands of immigrants from Haiti. Canada, particularly Quebec, had become one of the primary stops for them in North America. Unlike residents on the French-speaking islands of Martinique and Guadeloupe, the Haitians did not have easy entry into France. Fleeing decades of poverty and dictatorship, many of them headed for Montreal. The Quebec government was also recruiting French-speaking immigrants, so the welcome mat was put out to Caribbean people who spoke French.

But Canada's new policy wasn't all altruism. From the 1950s on, it saw the Caribbean as a pool of cheap labour, primarily for women who could become baby-sitters, child-care givers and who could look after the sick and elderly. Many young women across the Caribbean took this opportunity to escape. The former Canadian prime minister, John Diefenbaker, took great pride from saying over the years that his domestic servant was from Barbados. Many other wealthy Canadians raided the labour markets in Jamaica, Grenada, St. Vincent and Trinidad to find domestic help.

Canada did not intend that these visitors should stay. Primarily for this reason, the immigration policy was carried out so that only women were recruited. And they had to be young women, ideally unattached romantically and without children. If they were, the spouses and children were left behind. The reasoning was obvious: if these workers had no family ties in Canada, they would not want to stay in the country. They would work, save money and return home. Canada was deliberately structuring an immigration policy different from that of Britain and the United States. In those countries, the rule was to get the men to immigrate and to leave the women behind to take care of the children. But Canada was different: it went for the women almost exclusively. What Canadians didn't consider was that these Caribbean women had more on their minds than remaining as visitors. They wanted to live and raise families in Canada. And whether or not the Canadian government wanted the men and children to follow, they would come anyway, many of them illegally.

Canada did change its immigration policy in the 1960s, moving in step with the United States to an open approach that welcomed people equally from all over the world. This made Canada a more attractive place for many of us growing up in the Caribbean, for those of us who had heard of all those lonely women from the islands living in Toronto,

Montreal, Winnipeg and Vancouver. In the 1960s, young people simply got on a plane and headed for Canada on vacation or to attend school. Later, they wrote back to say how they had changed their minds about returning home and were staying on in Canada. They said that jobs were easy to get and there wasn't the overt racism so prevalent in the United States. They would encourage others to come and visit this pristine land and to stay. In the late 1980s and into the next decade, the last major wave of Blacks arrived in Canada. They were mainly refugees from Somalia and other African countries, coming to start a new life and to escape from famine and political repression at home.

Such acceptance, as my grandfather had attested to, wasn't always the case in the United States. Newly arrived Blacks didn't only have to deal with white Americans, but from the earliest times there have always been rifts between Caribbean Blacks and those born in America. This was what my grandfather was alluding to when he also cautioned that some of the biggest problems for West Indians were from American-born Blacks. It was common for American-born Blacks to refer to the immigrants from the Caribbean as "King George Negroes." This disparaging remark signaled that until they immigrated, the newcomers were loyal subjects of the British monarchy. Naturally, some of King George's Negroes felt they would be more readily accepted in a country where George and his heirs were still king. Equally, because the number of Canadian-born Blacks was relatively small, and concentrated mainly in Halifax and a few smaller Canadian centres, a good wave of Caribbean Blacks could inundate these cities. This happened in the 1930s in Halifax and the Cape Breton area and once again from the 1960s on. In addition, the Caribbean immigrants went mainly to urban areas. Once they arrived, they simply used their numbers to take over the black agenda. They were more interested in such issues as assisting family reunion, helping illegal immigrants, helping family back home, finding a first home or apartment, finding out about social services and, for the first time, coming to terms with open racial discrimination.

Canadian-born Blacks had developed methods for dealing with racial discrimination in housing and employment; the immigrants had to devise a strategy for themselves, had to first come to terms with the shock and anger from this discrimination. They had arrived at a level of appeasement with the wider society. Segregation was a part of this understanding. Caribbean and African Blacks arrived not expecting or even contemplating having to deal with these issues. After all, they knew of Canada's international image. There would be no prescribed boundaries for them, no limits on their imagination. Unlike them, the established Blacks knew that perception was for foreign consumption only. The arriving Blacks and the established communities saw Canada through different ends of the periscope.

Many long-held issues, such as fighting for inclusion, for promotions, to be represented in all levels of society—issues for which the established black community had been fighting—were put off until a later date. Until the immigrants had set down roots. Until they started worrying about more than finding a first job and apartment. Until they started worrying about job promotions and how they could find the money to purchase their dream home.

Now, generations later, the differences appear to be melting away as the two groups assert one thing they have in common: their black skin, their Africanness. Caribbean and Africa-born Blacks have come around to joining their Canadian brethren and sisters in having to accept some level of appeasement. As they look on their children, the first Canadian Blacks in their family, they too must decide how much this appeasement means to the setting aside of dreams and whether the social acceptance that comes with benign segregation is tolerable. And it is for these reasons that we continue to meet in memorial and school halls. This is why we explain to our children that although they are Canadian, they must still lay claim to their inheritance in the form of all black achievements around the world; why we are steeling them for a future based on making choices about attempting to join the Canadian mainstream.

The answers to the questions we pose about our children's future go to the reality of what it really means to be black in Canada.

CHAPTER 3

TWO SOLITUDES

The bright floodlights illuminate a packed parking lot as I turn off the highway leading to the All Nations Full Gospel Church of Toronto. I look at the clock in my car and notice the time is well after one o'clock on what is now Saturday morning.

At this hour, most Torontonians are in bed. By now, most businesses are closed for the night. The traffic snarls that plague the nearby highway during the day are gone. Everywhere is the feel of a therapeutic let-down at the end of the traditional work week as the normally bustling city rests.

Except for the ever-present doughnut shops, even the fast-food restaurants have called it a day. Most churches gave their final benedictions hours ago. The doors to these dispensers of spiritual food are now bolted shut—a frequent occurrence these days even though the numbers of homeless people increase daily. The nearby high-rise apartment buildings are almost in total darkness, except for the odd light or two shining through the windows. The same is true for the detached and semi-detached houses, the town houses and the offices and warehouses in this working-class area.

But this is not true for the All Nations Full Gospel Church of Toronto. Indeed, this is not true for significant segments of the city's black community in the Greater Toronto Area who move to a different rhythm from the majority in the wider Canadian society. Somehow, these two communities never appear in sync—psychologically or socially. While one sleeps, the other organizes, plans the next move and even consults its god. On any given night, one thing is certain for many Canadians: many choices are available to them, often extreme choices that add up to the experience of being black.

The All Nations Full Gospel Church, with a membership of more than 1,000, claims to be one of the fastest growing churches in the city. Pictures on the walls of the church depict what appears to be a microcosm of the entire black experience, what with members drawn from 31 countries, mostly from Africa and the Caribbean. The flags from all the nations, including Canada, flutter in the breeze atop the church building, which to passing motorists might trigger an image of the United Nations headquarters in New York.

People turn up for service in an array of various cultural dress that includes anything from the traditional but drab business suit to the traditional but colourful African dress. These images provide snapshots of a community of different faces, sizes and cultural paraphernalia—the only thing in common for the worshippers is the predominant colour of the faces.

The gathering at the church, which is both a spiritual and social assembly, is one example—perhaps a passive illustration—of how the black community copes with the challenges of living in Canada as a minority group. It also symbolizes one of the main issues facing us Blacks.

As long as there have been Blacks in Canada, there has been a church at the heart of the community. Across Canada, there are several churches, in all denominations, trying to keep a community humming. For decades, the Canadian black community was almost solely defined to outsiders by its churches. A white politician wanting to test the mood of the community would contact the preacher or pastor; a young couple needing advice would seek out the minister; the newspapers looking for articulate spokespeople in the community would turn to the churches. The church is a long-standing venue for marriages, baptisms, funerals and all other celebrations and commiserations along the way. The church is a place for organizing the social picnics, the barbecues, the songs of service, the moral suasion that keeps everyone in check, that safeguards and protects the members' cultural garb and icons, whether they are from other countries or from the Canadian experience. The church imposes order on its community.

But our community has changed and, of late, there has been much criticism by black secular leaders of the role of these churches: Have they lost their way? Are they numbing the experiences of a congregation living in a dream-sapping society by concentrating too much on salvation of the soul and not enough on the maintenance of the body and of fulfilling the dream for a better here-and-now? Have they abdicated their leadership role by not speaking out on the many issues taken up by militant black-advocacy groups? And why are the black church leaders so silent on issues like police shootings of black men or the wider problem of black-on-black violence in some nightclubs, booze cans and other illegal businesses?

At the heart of this discussion is the question of whether the black community in Canada has changed to the point where the church and what it represents to black and white societies alike have become largely irrelevant. Does the church still represent the black population as a whole and, if it doesn't, is this a direct result of what has happened to the black Canadian community in the past three or four decades, as the community itself changed and evolved?

To a greater extent, the image of a strong black church is borrowed from the United States, where the church has a long history and deep roots in a population, black and white, that has been around for centuries. The church grew with, and established, a community, its role clearly defined. This is not the case in Canada, where the majority of Blacks recently arrived from various parts of the world, all with different expectations and religions. Many of them feel more comfortable in the traditional Canadian churches, as these were the churches they grew up worshipping in, in their homeland, where an Anglican, Methodist or Roman Catholic church might have the official blessing of the state.

The power and influence of the American black churches were on display during what has come to be known as the Rodney King riots in Los Angeles in 1992. Then, every television camera across the United States and around the world seemed to be seeking out a member of the black clergy to explain the violence that erupted in the streets of Los Angeles, for some evidence that the church can still rein in the anger of the community. Indeed, Americans have come to accept that their nation is most segregated at eleven o'clock every Sunday morning, when Blacks and Whites go their separate ways into different churches. And this point is further illustrated by the spate of bombings and destruction by fire that have always been visited on black churches by racist Whites striking out at the black community.

The influence of the black church was also on display in the final days of the double murder trial of O.J. Simpson in the fall of 1995. Camera crews descended on the churches and sought out the leaders in their pulpits for profound comments. In the final hours before the trial, some churches threw their doors open to invite people to hear the verdict, and according to the church leaders on TV, to allow the church to help curtail the fury that everyone was expecting with a guilty verdict. And when the not-guilty verdict came in, the churches became a place for celebration. So that when Simpson's lead attorney, Johnnie Cochrane, turned up at his usual place of worship the Sunday after the verdict, 300 people in the congregation gave him a standing ovation. Cochrane was called forward by the pastor of his South-Central Los Angeles church to testify to the power of prayer in helping to deliver O.J. Simpson from the hand of the ungodly—perhaps no different from how members of All Nations Full Gospel Church of Toronto celebrate rather privately for less publicized victories—and to rally the African-American community against all wrongs against them. "This case transcends just O.J. Simpson," Cochrane testified at the Second Baptist Church just days after all of North America appeared to be divided along the lines of race.

Blacks toasted the verdict as a long-fought-for vindication; Whites, for the most part, branded it as a miscarriage of justice and refused to accept the verdict as an exoneration of Simpson. "What it talks about is the justice system in America. It talks about how we as Americans see things so differently," Cochrane said in a quote from his testimony that was published in newspapers across North America. The expectations are the same when presidential, congressional, gubernatorial and mayoralty candidates make their pilgrimages to the pulpit of black churches so they can speak to the African-American audience.

Black clergy are not sought out by the media in Canada. For example, during civil unrest in Toronto, disturbances that took place at the same time as the Los Angeles riots, nobody in the Canadian media put members of the black clergy on television to plead for calm. And during election campaigns, unlike in the United States, rarely do you see Canadian politicians rolling up on their campaign buses, television cameras in tow, to address the congregations of black churches—although these politicians do drop in on Canadian synagogues, mosques and temples of other minority groups. Too many times I have gone to political rallies where the politicians from mainstream parties mouth that they are reaching out to the black community, where they suggest with a straight face that it would be so much easier to know what Canadian Blacks really wanted if there was one specific group that spoke for this community. These Canadian politicians wish the church could play the same role in the black community as it does in America, in order to make the black vote more "deliverable" by buying off the leaders and having the community vote accordingly.

Several attempts have been made by Blacks in Canada to form umbrella groups, such as the NAACP in the United States, but these attempts have always failed. While Canadian Blacks have long recognized some advantages of having a group to speak on their behalf, there has always been a fear that this would make life too easy and predictable for the wider society. All the politicians would have to do is win the leadership of this group over to their way of thinking. Then, all that would be required for the community to be kept in check would be for the politicians to get the blessing of the church leaders. As a result, everything would fall into its natural order. Life in the black community would therefore be predictable and more acceptable to society at large. The leaders would return to the community mouthing the thoughts and ideas of the wider community while essentially still leaving Blacks without a strong voice. So instead of having one voice, the Canadian black community has always relied on many voices speaking out on issues, sometimes some of them not even in harmony.

The All Nations Full Gospel Church asserts that its growth and vibrancy come from speaking to the needs of a largely black immigrant community, particularly for a specific segment of this population that is steadfastly law abiding and long suffering, but equally as anxious as the community militants about prospects in this country. Its approach is based on the notion that gains will be made through quiet acceptance and a bit of agitation, but not enough disquiet to produce revolutions and never enough turmoil to produce strident defiance. Typical of the black churches, its message is that it is better to integrate and conform. To this end, the church preaches the same Judeo-Christian values of the wider community: an appreciation for law and order; an emphasis on the traditional nuclear family; the adoption of all values and material indicators by which the wider society judges success. A belief in the power of hard work and sacrifice. No defiance is counselled.

The church tries to provide services that are not available elsewhere, not so much to challenge the wider society, but to make the black community more self-sufficient within the existing society. On Sundays, for example, two of its daytime services are in the Twi language of Ghana. Many who might have difficulty with the dominant culture and language can find refuge in this church, where their culture and language flourish and are important at least once a week. And all night from nine o'clock every Friday night, the church throws opens its doors to anyone needing a quiet moment for prayer, an opportunity to get their lives in order, a chance to reflect on the challenges of living in this country. Just as important, by opening its doors, it offers black youths a chance *not* to be elsewhere, *not* to be in other places still open at all hours of the night, *not* to be in those places that expose them to temptation.

In the case of the All Nations Full Gospel Church, fate—some members would say God—appears to have had a hand in deciding its location, as if intending to provide a contrasting testimony to the experiences of black survival in Canada, as if aiming to starkly demonstrate the extreme choices Blacks can face in this country. The church is located on 4.4 acres of land adjacent to the busy Highway 400 in the northwest of the city, putting it in easy reach for most Blacks in the Greater Toronto Area. But it is also at the edge of one of the largest black areas in Metropolitan Toronto, a neighbourhood which has had its share of clashes with the law.

A few months before I turned up at the church, one of these clashes had made its way onto the pages of the Toronto newspapers. It was also a late night event, when most businesses—and churches—had closed for the night. But this venue in question, a newly established nightclub, was preparing to minister to the secular needs of a population looking for some means to get through the night. On the program were some of the hottest deejays and reggae and dance hall musicians from around Toronto. Crowds flocked to the nightclub. When it became clear that everyone would not get in, pushing and shoving started. Someone called the police and a mêlée erupted.

The next day, the nightclub was branded in the media as a booze can. Although a legitimate business, it never overcame this stigma and closed soon after. The nightclub was on the same street as the church, symbolically with only the straight and narrow path of Highway 400 separating them. Although separated physically by less than half a kilometre, the church and the club were worlds apart, a perfect contrast of lifestyles and stereotypes of Blacks in Canada.

* * *

I am turning up at this church to find out what attracts people, many of whom have spent a week in tiring labour, to spend a night in this intense ritual of prayer and fellowship instead of resting at home.

"How long is this session likely to go?" I ask a man sitting on the edge of a table inside the doors to the church.

"It depends on the preacher and the needs of the members," he responds. "It could go to three o'clock or longer."

I push my head inside the doors leading to the inner sanctuary of the church. A man in a business suit is standing at a microphone talking to the congregation. I quickly close the door and rejoin the man, who is apparently taking a respite from praying with the others by sitting at the bank of glass doors. Several people—all black, some with pre-teenaged boys and girls—appear to be taking a timeout from the prayers. They are hanging around in knots or leading their sleepy children to cars in the parking lot. Occasionally, someone comes out from inside the church. "Shush. Keep the talking down. The noise is coming inside the church," one man says and promptly disappears back inside the church.

The man sitting at the glass doors is James Agyemang, a 34-year-old Ghanaian who has lived in Canada for nine years. At this hour of the night, there appears to be no sleep in his eyes. And perhaps seeing me as a potential new member, the chance to win a soul for his saviour, Agyemang responds eagerly when I strike up a conversation. This church, he says, is a haven for the wounded and alienated soul. But it caters to more, he says, to helping members survive in a new and hostile country.

And then he tells me his story, volunteering a tale of tribulation and alienation in a strange land, a personal testimony of how crucial the church is to his maintaining his sanity, to helping him overcome the vagaries of an uncertain future in this country. As it would turn out, Agyemang's story is a poignant reminder of the ambivalence so many of us feel as we try to bridge the gap between the solitudes of living in a familiar culture consisting of people who look and act like us, but who compromise heavily and change in order to work and survive in an alien society—one we call Canada. People like Agyemang are the answers to those who ask on talk shows and other media why those people don't try to conform to the Canadian way of doing things or go back where they came from.

Before leaving home, Agyemang was a radio technician at the Ghana Broadcasting Corporation. He has certificates from the City and Guilds examinations in London, England to show his competence. But he has never found a job as a radio technician in Canada. "I am hoping to go back to school to become a technician," he says. Somehow, after all the rejections, the years of having to survive by working in a factory making tools, living and working below the levels he expected before arriving in Canada, he has not given up hope.

Agyemang's hope is fuelled by being in fellowship with like-minded members of the church. This is where he gets his spiritual and psychological sustenance. Apart from addressing his spiritual needs, which he admits is paramount for him, the church also helps to keep him going. "Sometimes, it is so hard to be an immigrant. This country has a lot of opportunities but it can be so difficult. And when you tell other people [immigrants] that you want to go back to school, they ask what for. Why try?"

But it is different in the church. Agyemang tells stories of how the church helps others like him. Every member of the congregation is part of what the church calls a "cell." This is a kind of buddy system, with members responsible for keeping an eye on one another. This could include a telephone call to find out why a member is missing services. Or it might be to provide counselling on marital and financial matters, to help a student come up with money to pay school fees, to pray for the sick, to give a loan to members in financial need, or for employed members to whisper to other cell members about job openings in places where they work. And in many cases, it could be the endless hours of prayer for God's intervention in a personal matter like a refugee application. In some cases the intervention comes and just in time to stop a family from being deported from the country—an accomplishment the entire church celebrates.

The church also provides wider counselling, bringing in experts to discuss such things as how to set up and manage a small business. "This is good for those of us who don't know how to invest our money," he says. But often, what the church offers is comfort to the community, and the assurance of knowing that there will always be someone to listen to your problems, to let you know that all the members are facing the same problems and obstacles, that collectively and without disrupting the rhythm of the host society these problems will quietly and triumphantly be overcome. Ultimately, it is the personal successes, the salvation of the soul that binds members into something more than a church—into a special community as well.

Agyemang tells me the story of another Ghanaian, who was a doctor in his homeland. When he arrived in Canada, already in his forties, he had to take some medical examinations before he could be granted a Canadian licence to practise medicine. He failed the first two attempts at the examination, but the immigrant spirit persevered. He prayed to God, sometimes at the all-night sessions, and he commiserated with friends in the church. Finally, deliverance came. The man passed his examination and is now practising medicine in another town.

Agyemang says that undoubtedly God reached down and delivered this immigrant, but he also agrees that much of the help came from church members who were in a similar plight regarding their own profession. They understood what the Ghanaian doctor was facing. They banded together to make sure this medical student was successful and then they shared in his achievement, holding it up as a standard no different from what they are trying to achieve, which they will accomplish despite the difficulties and obstacles that face them. And they will reach their goal without running into conflict with the wider society. It is the success of this doctor that allows Agyemang to feel strong enough to return to school, even when detractors would put to him the question, "Why bother?" And because the doctor succeeded by working hard, complaining little and accepting the reality of being black and an immigrant, others like Agyemang can then use the same approach and probably be successful, too. They do not have to be revolutionary to succeed. Instead, they remain determined, while accepting that change will come slowly, if at all. In any case and for an added bonus, as their ministers promise, the real reward will come in the next world.

Padmore Tabi Gyansah—"everybody calls me Uncle Tabi"—was only days in the country when he was invited to worship at the All Nations Full Gospel Church. An immigrant from Ghana as well, Tabi says he has found a home in worshipping and working with the church. His main task is helping in the nursery that looks after the children while their parents attend the church services. "You must come and see my children. That's why everyone calls me Uncle Tabi." There is a broad smile on Tabi's face.

"I will want to remain here at this church until I die," he testifies.

"What about if you were to go back to Ghana?" I ask.

"I would find a church there," he answers. (All Nations has established five branches in Ghana and says it is laying the foundation for an outreach ministry in Nairobi, Kenya. There are also branches in Orlando, Florida, and Inchon, South Korea.) But obviously, he is not thinking of returning home. "In Canada, I have found a home here. At this church." In Uncle Tabi's eyes, if Canada is not quite Heaven, it could be the last stop on his journey there.

Churches like this provide only one example of the tone and timbre of life in the black community in Canada. But a church like this is only one of the all-night establishments available to this community. The competing establishments are very different from the churches. They are not as willing to compromise to the so-called Canadian way of doing things. And their clientele is much more defiant, looking for short cuts that might lead them out of the daily rut of living among the underclass of the Canadian society.

* * *

As the last call approaches, I check my watch and drain the last of my beer. I nod to the woman behind the bar, asking her to "fix me up" with the bill for the drinks. That is when the man at the corner of the bar makes his move. He gets off the tall stool and begins dancing, ostensibly to the pounding reggae, but unmistakably moving in our direction.

In his hand is a beer bottle, held casually between his third and fourth fingers. For most of the night, he had sat at the bar, talking to other barflies and occasionally glancing at the door when someone entered. This is our second time in the bar. Each time, we have arrived to find him sitting at the bar and have left him in the same spot.

"Me buy yuh a beer, brother," he shouts over the music. I nod in acknowledgement of the gesture. He signals with his head to the woman behind the bar. Quickly, another of my favourite brand of beer is on the table and a rum-and-coke for my friend. "Respect, brother," he says.

"Nuff respect," I answer, echoing the trendy words binding the more angry members of the Canadian black community. "Respect due." The man, in his late forties, dances back to the bar to resume talking, his job complete. My friend and I return to our drinks. It is now well past the time that alcohol can be legally sold. Yet, as this man is assuring us, there is no need to rush, no announcements of a last call, no concern for time. Here, we are among friends, family almost. Here, we abide by a different set of rules—practices that are definitely not the norm in the wider society.

On the surface, what I am witnessing is not unusual in most bars. Two strangers walk off the streets a few hours earlier, and a "regular," no different from an Agyemang at his church, makes them feel invited by offering drinks. But there is a big difference here, one marked by the open defiance and public bravado so prevalent in sections of the black community, an attitude that stands out in stark contrast to the spirit of benign acceptance at the church.

This is the life in the illegal booze cans, or in the quasi-underground black restaurants that can only survive economically by stretching the regulations, by remaining open and selling alcohol long after the law stipulates they should close for the night. Although some members may choose to pray and hope for deliverance from the daily job of lifting boxes for their daily bread, others choose a different living: maybe selling booze after hours; selling a little dope on the side; selling drinks and food that are unavailable in most Canadian restaurants; selling dreams of self-sufficiency. And while others might take great care not to draw attention to themselves by so openly defying the norms of the wider community—for despite their actions they still hope to some day become and be seen as a part of the wider community—the regulars at bars like this one exhibit more defiant attitudes. They want to stand out, to appear different, untamed and unsullied. They would not for one moment want to appear soft, to abandon themselves and all that they know, just to be conformist, just to appear Canadian. So they want to remain outside the pale of society, and boastfully so. Remaining outside will be their hallmark, their identification. It will be what makes them what they are, what keeps them whole and identifiable in a society in which they have given up hope of becoming a meaningful and contributing member. They are not prepared to pay the price of mixing.

Like the churches, these businesses also claim to be flourishing. They might be operated in apartments where someone holds a dance for the rent money; in house basements converted to illegal restaurants or nightclubs, and top floors transformed into gambling parlours; or in restaurants that are more than their appearances suggest.

Sitting in that darkened all-night bar, I could just as easily be in a rum shop in the Caribbean. Not just any rum shop, but one of those hard-core country establishments catering almost exclusively to cane cutters, fishermen, banana growers and hawkers—the regular Friday night crowd "pooling drinks" and "ol' talking." It is the kind of rum shop found way inland and off the beaten track for foreigners, not one of those coastal boutiques diluting their fare and clientele in a compromise to attract tourists. It is the watering hole where men retire for drinks as soon as they receive the weekly pay cheque on Friday, where they settle debts for food and drink from during the week, where they "lick out" what other pocket money they can afford to splurge in fellowship and ol' talk.

The ambience in this Toronto bar is the same as in the ones I knew in Barbados, watering holes with the men inside drinking and I and younger friends sitting on the steps listening to the talk. Apart from the rum and beer, the men would be consuming several cans of imported corned beef or sardines, the meat crushed in a plate and generously seasoned with diced onions and with very peppery hot sauce. This they ate with crackers.

In this bar, like the rum shops back home, tables are tightly packed and there is a long bar that people lean on. There is no art work or Blue

Jays banners except, ironically, for a poster of a scowling Hulk Hogan, the blue-eyed, blond "beefcake" of professional wrestling. This is no fashionable downtown Caribbean eatery going mainstream, prominently decorated with flags from Canada, Jamaica or Trinidad, or with African paintings and sculptures mounted on the wall. This bar knows who it serves, whose laws it respects and it doesn't feel it has to assert its cultural signature. Neither does it even try to camouflage its true intent by appearing to be Canadian—in this case, to be what it isn't.

On the walls over the bar are the appropriate Liquor Licensing Board permits and Fire Marshall certificates. At the risk of closure and possible financial ruin for the owner, it chooses to remain open beyond the normal business hours and continue to sell booze. Long after most drinking holes close, young men and women stream through the door, buy liquor in bottles and glasses and head in noisy groups for the car-park, right next to the busy highway cruised by the police.

Inside, couples dance under a reflective ball to music from mammoth speakers, the latest reggae and calypso and Caribbean favourites of yesteryear. Most youths are dressed in jeans, running shoes and T-shirts with messages venerating Malcolm X. Of all the faces in this room, not one is white. Unlike the more liberal black churches, integration is not counselled here.

Some two hours after the sale of alcohol should have stopped, the waitress makes a concession to the laws of the land by handing out plastic containers for the beer. This way, we do not have to keep the beer bottles on display and flout the law as openly. When we leave, the first of the sun's rays welcome us. People are still arriving, some for pickups of food and alcohol for consumption elsewhere, where despite the late hour, there is time for play. Even at this hour, there is no need to go home. Other places and gambles beckon us. After all, most of Toronto is still sleeping, so why not make the most of this time?

* * *

I am down to my last three quarters when I decide to chance it all. The machine accepts the coins with the musical chime of contentment. Before pulling the handle, I look at the sign on the wall above the bank of slot and other gaming machines:

> *These machines are for amusement not for gambiling* [sic].
> *Play at your own risk.*
> *No pay out.*

Obviously, "No pay out" is intended for those who don't know better. The owner is playing another machine, trying to convince us the games aren't rigged. A very friendly man, he doesn't fit my perception of anyone running an illegal gaming house. Others are playing the ponies, putting quarters in machines, selecting their odds and hoping the horses deliver in cash.

To one side, young men are playing dominoes, while older men in their late thirties and forties dance to the juke-box and drink beer and white rum. It is after three o'clock in the morning. Often there is a loud buzz overhead. The woman working the bar runs upstairs and escorts new entrants into the basement. Obviously, this business is doing well. The number of people coming through the doors and the fact the owners can hire a waitress or two are signs enough of a good business.

"One guy came in here earlier and with his third quarter hit the jackpot," the owner says. "I had to pay him five hundred dollars. The third time he's hit me so far."

I yank on the handle and almost immediately three red cherries line up under the bar. The machine spits out 20 coins into the metal container.

"Reminds me of Las Vegas," I say, the memory still fresh in my mind from a *fam* trip by a travel agency. "The odds on the machines seem to be the same."

"That's where they're from, Las Vegas," he says.

By the end of the night, I have returned all the winnings as well as twenty dollars of my own. Defiance, self-help and black business take on new meaning as I walk up the stairs to find my car among several in a make-shift parking lot. On this summer's morning, Toronto seems blissfully asleep. It is almost as if we are awaking from a midsummer night's dream of romping in the Caribbean to emerge into another world. And like so many people spending the night in prayer or in the all-night clubs, we are emerging from the familiar into a society that makes us feel uneasy, where we cannot be ourselves, where we feel, at the most, partially fulfilled but, very often, extremely empty. Why are these feelings so strong in the black community after so many centuries in this country, after a rush of black immigration in the past three decades? Indeed, why in our minds do we have to symbolically run *back home* when only a short while ago we were so anxious to run away, to escape from the lands of our birth, to fulfil the mission of our lives and calling, to live and prosper in a foreign country?

Like the churches, these businesses have always existed: old-timers tell of surviving in the 1950s when an illegal rent-party was the only way to raise money or to pay university tuition. Today, it is different. As in previous decades, these businesses are a testimony to how some immigrants settle in this country. The black community has its own rules, a ritual of acceptance that might be no more than showing up at a specific site, of supporting a given cause. It is still possible for people to be socially ostracized in the black community by being considered a sell-out, an "Oreo cookie" or whatever degrading term is used to show that brotherhood and sisterhood are more than just the colour of skin. The type of people that would not be welcome or accepted in the illegal businesses, the way my friend and I were by our new friend at the bar. Acceptance, indeed, is based on the company you keep.

On the other hand, just being in a specific setting can be a prerequisite for membership. Showing up is the same as displaying an understanding, appreciation and identification with a certain way of life. Just as showing up at the church is enough for the members to invite me to join, enough for Uncle Tabi to call me at home weeks later enquiring what has become of me and whether I have found a place of fellowship and worship. Just as patronizing a bar more than once is enough to gain acceptance.

Today, these businesses and social clubs are receiving greater attention from police, local politicians and other segments of mainstream culture. The criticisms are obvious: they are un-Canadian, defiant, thumbing their nose at the wider society. And, perhaps for the first time, these businesses are now drawing the condemnation of some in the black community, people who in earlier times might have held an illegal party themselves, might have frequented a booze can or two, played the regular hand of illegal poker, who just might have been willing to turn a blind eye.

The difference now is the violence that happens so often in these places. A deadly subculture inhabits these businesses. Shootings and stabbings prevail. And then nobody sees or hears anything. At least, no one will cross the gulf from one community to an alien one, especially if crossing over means co-operating with the police and a judicial system that belongs to "them" and not to us. So a level of violence is inflicted on the very patrons the businesses and clubs are supposed to help and rely on for their business.

But there is a deeper issue here and one that the black community must face. It is a concern that goes to the heart of the question of what the black community is and whether it can ever become a part of what is now viewed as the wider society. For despite the very obvious macho attempts by some members of the black community to appear to be *different*, nobody can deny that most of us in the black community are law abiding and want the same successes as the wider community. The vast majority of us are immigrants who once saw Canada as a Promised Land. The rest of us have for generations claimed this country as ours and have struggled, often against great odds, to find our place in this society. Yet many Blacks, particularly the youths, turn to illicit means to survive in this country. This was not our intention when we immigrated here; this is not what we dreamt of for our children. This is not what generations of Blacks who fought and died for this country would expect to be their legacy as we head into a new millennium.

Despite our dreams, we must face the reality that many who choose between institutions like the All Nations Church with its program of integration and the booze can with its open defiance choose to live by illegal means. Not because they want to, but because it might be the only thing left that makes them feel important, that makes them feel they can get attention and influence in the wider society. For when there is a killing in a booze can and a police man-hunt, perhaps for all the wrong reasons this is the time when the wider society pays attention to those considered society's outlaws. And if these nonconformists can bamboozle the wider community, if they can drive the police and newspaper columnists to distraction by not co-operating with the guardians of society, if they can draw attention to themselves by being the "bad boys," it gives this segment of the community a sense of power or control. As black youths explain, it gives them respect. Such is the reward for defiance, for rejecting compromise and integration at any cost.

And in many respects, this is just an example of how we are all so impoverished when, as immigrants, we look back on our time in Canada and wonder what went wrong. Why didn't things pan out the way we expected? After all, we, as immigrants, were selected by a system intended to pluck from elsewhere the very best and smartest. We were among the chosen, those most capable of adapting almost overnight to the Canadian society, to becoming contributing members. We felt we had the most to give and we expected so much in return. But what have we ended up with?

In one generation many of us willingly switched from being law abiding and socially adaptable into becoming the pariahs of the society; when symbolically so many of us choose the culture of the booze can over that of the church. This choice reflects the frustrations so rampant in segments of the black community. This frustration flows from a bitter resignation, born of well-entrenched beliefs, that Blacks in this country have always faced seemingly insurmountable obstacles, hurdles that prevent us from attaining mainstream status and acceptance. So that, in the end, the effort of trying to integrate is not worth the fight, is not worth the rejection. If you are going to be rejected anyway, why not glory in the rejection, why not make it a kind of status symbol?

Sometimes, we do not even have the choice. The society simply tells us who we are and what it expects from us. So if the wider community sees us as a community, that is what we become. It does not matter how much we protest; how much we might wrap ourselves in the Canadian flag and sing the national anthem. For, as is generally the case, when most Whites see Blacks in Canada, they see visitors or people who have not graduated to becoming fully accepted citizens. And often this is a perception that even those Blacks achieving the highest levels in Canada are forced to confront—that although they may want to see themselves as simply Canadians, they are viewed as coming from a group of people that, even though they are living in Canada, are suspect.

* * *

Donovan Bailey should have been at the top of the world in the summer of 1995. Only days earlier, Bailey had raced to the tape in 9.93 seconds to win the 100-metre dash at the World Track and Field Championships in Sweden. During his victory lap at the stadium in Göteborg, Bailey wrapped himself in a big Canadian flag. Joining him in the celebration in Sweden was another Canadian runner, Montrealer Bruny Surin, who was nipping Bailey's heels as he crossed the finish line. The last thing on his mind should have been the question of his nationality, whether or not he was just a Canadian who just happened to be world famous.

Many of the children who belonged to groups like the African-Canadian Heritage Association had a new hero. Here was someone who grew up just like them, someone to be invited to their annual celebrations, a Canadian to be added to their list of role models. For the second time within a decade, Canada could claim the fastest man in the world. In fact, for the first time Canada could claim to have the two fastest men in the world because of Bailey and Surin. Canadians could look ahead to the next Olympics and dream of big things.

National public radio is calling to talk to Bailey. In setting up the chat, Paul Kennedy, the host of the respected *Morningside* national program on CBC Radio on this particular morning, takes great pains to explain Bailey's achievements, but also to pin some small disclaimers on this man who wrapped himself in a Canadian flag in front of the eyes of the world. For obviously from the tone of the introduction, and the subsequent interview, Bailey is not quite your typical Canadian. He is not the small-town boy who went out to conquer the world and will always be remembered as a hero, the embodiment of the dreams and aspirations of all Canadians. His victory should be celebrated, the host seems to be saying, but perhaps from a distance. Listeners should make allowance for the shock of the morning after, when they might wake up realizing the experience was a dream, a trick played on a gullible nation. After all, those black runners have a history, don't they? They have been tainted before, haven't they?

Bailey appears to be enjoying the first moments of the interview. There is the usual prattle about how he felt before and after the race, about what he describes as awkward flaws in his running technique, how it feels to be called the world's fastest man, how good it looks on Canada to have taken first and second place. There is a possibility of icing on the cake, Bailey says, if Canada's top four sprinters win the 100-metre relay in a day or so at the same World Games. Only then, Bailey says, could he allow himself the pleasure of personal celebration. Until the relays, there is a job to be done, a job of winning gold for Canada.

Then, abruptly, the tone of the interview changes. So, says the host, I guess we can't have an interview about a Canadian becoming the fastest man in the world and not talk about "you-know-who."

"You mean Ben, Ben Johnson," Bailey snaps. For the first time there is annoyance in his voice, the obvious frustration of having to carry this albatross. With the frustration and tediousness of having to discuss the subject growing with every word, Bailey carefully explains that it is only the Canadian (and here he might have meant white) media that is so obsessed with this question, with this man, that they dare not even mention his name on national radio. As Bailey explains, he and other black athletes have done their darnedest not to have to be confronted with this boogeyman. But because they are black like Johnson, they must confront it constantly. And becoming the world's fastest man means Bailey is forced to run in the footsteps of the other black man who once took a Canadian flag under the pretence of being the world's fastest man through natural ability. Other Canadian athletes have been caught using banned steroids. But the next white Canadian rower, weightlifter, boxer or runner isn't automatically assumed to be tainted, to be cheating. And even if they are, it doesn't seem to be as much of a national disgrace, as if all Canadians have been tricked into letting their guard down, into believing these athletes could be trusted. Often, the offending individual is offhandedly dismissed as an errant person, not a representative of anyone or anything.

Apparently, not so for black athletes. My local community newspaper, *The Liberal,* celebrated Bailey's victory with a cartoon on the opinion page. Taking up about three-quarters of the panel is a jar of the household detergent, Mr. Clean; in smaller type across the bottom of the jar are the words, "Donovan Bailey." The picture on the jar is of a smiling, muscular man holding a Canadian flag, a huge gold medal around his neck. In the upper part of the panel are the words: "The best way to cleanse our memories of the Ben Johnson Affair..." At least, this cartoonist could name the albatross, the you-know-who, for all Canadian black runners.

As is well known, Ben Johnson, who arrived from Jamaica a little kid with a speech impediment, but went on to set world and Olympic records in the 100-metre dash, had become an albatross for all Canadian black athletes. His is one of the most telling and tragic stories of what it means to be black in this country. I remember the night Johnson dashed to victory at the Seoul Olympics. I had kept my then six-year-old son up well past his bedtime to see a black Canadian conquer the world. When Johnson took the tape, all black Canadians were with him in that stadium. All West Indians were with him. In our petty insular way, we even celebrated that he kicked the butt of that *mouther-man* American Carl Lewis, who, coincidentally, was not a Caribbean Black. On the modern battlefield of nations, Canada had been assured of at least one gold medal. Every black person in the country wanted it around his or her neck.

And what a medal—the most coveted in modern track and field. That medal was placed around the neck of a Caribbean immigrant who stood proudly in place of every one of us for the playing of the Canadian national anthem and the hoisting of the Canadian flag. A black immigrant had done this for Canada and Canadians. For at the same time that the prime minister of Canada was going on national television to speak to Johnson by phone—to tell him how a white Canadian prime minister and his family were screaming so loudly at this victory by a Canadian that they awoke the family dog, to tell Johnson all Canadians were celebrating—my brother was calling me from Barbados. This time he did not ask, "Who are these Canadians?"

This was a moment to be proud. This was the moment to be black in this country. Here on national TV was the fulfilment of the dreams of all those Caribbean and African parents who believed Canada could be home for their children, the pay-off for all those forgotten soldiers who fought for this country and got nothing in return, the reward for the perseverance of the descendants of the United Empire Loyalists and the modern immigrants struggling to keep the dream of acceptance and achievement alive. This was proof that if fully integrated in the Canadian system—whether in schools, jobs, boardroom, police and armed forces, in any facet of Canadian life—we could be winners. We could be an integral part of Team Canada. An American might argue that the military has been the most successful example of how to bring together ethnic groups and dreams. For us in Canada, sports would do the same job, whether it is Jackie Robinson breaking the colour bar in baseball, a virtually all-black Toronto baseball team gearing up for a World Series championship run or a Ben Johnson sprinting to gold. And it was also pay-back time for a long-suffering community. This was the moment to walk into the boss's office and ask for a raise; to ask the school principal why there are no black teachers in the classroom; to greet a policeman in the street and say, "What's up, man? Did you see Ben last night?"; to see a fellow Black on the streets, in the bus, in the parking lot and to just smile, a knowing smile that only another Black understands. This was the moment, and it had to be stretched out for as long as possible.

But just as quickly, the bubble burst. The urine test showed the use of prohibited steroids. Johnson and his entourage—most of them black and Caribbean—were banished from the Olympic village and from the hearts of mainstream Canadians. They were back where they seemingly belonged—black and outside the mainstream. All black athletes were suspect, symbolically, just the way we remember the banner that some Canadian—probably white—hung from his window in the athlete village in Seoul condemning all black Canadian athletes. All black people felt the chill. It was no different from when a police department puts out a bulletin describing a suspect as black, Jamaican, African or Caribbean, or *sounding* Caribbean, and violent. All Blacks know the chills and stares. It is time for black mothers to keep their sons off the streets; for young black men to feel the shadow of the security details in malls or to hear the footsteps of the store owners following them around while these potential suspects worry over such things as which brand of candy or pop to buy.

The national inquiry into Johnson, which masqueraded as an investigation into cheating in sports, further humiliated us. When Johnson took the stand, many of us were sitting right there with him. We felt his loneliness and frustration as he stammered and tried to explain the unexplainable, to come clean and ask forgiveness from a country that had turned on him. And when he cried, many of us in the black community wept with him. In the barbershops and elsewhere we cussed the judge holding the inquiry, the Canadian government for doing this to us, the black athletes who turned on Ben, the failure by whomever to find and validate our unshakable beliefs that there had to be legions of conspirators so envious of Ben, a Caribbean black man, that they must have set him up.

For in our bid to rationalize this tragedy, we questioned how this could happen to one of us when it is taken for granted the world over that every successful athlete, not just a black athlete, uses performance-enhancing drugs. We cussed the hangers-on who deserted him. And we cussed the Ben Johnson in all of us. We understood what drove this young immigrant to succeed, to want to buy the big house in the suburbs for his mother, the fancy cars, to defeat the feeling of always being an outsider even at the peak of achievement. And we knew that he was paying the price for the so-called double burden of being black: that you can rise to fame as an individual but you crash back to earth as a representative of your race; that several times Johnson had mounted the medal podium as a Canadian hero, but when the medals were stripped from his chest, when the world records were erased, he was merely a Jamaican, reduced in the eyes of the mainstream to his most common denominator, to his base.

Between the fame and the disgrace, he had been diminished in the eyes of the wider public to being the little boy from Jamaica who fooled Canadians into opening up their hearts to him, who tricked them into setting a place at the table for him, only for them to find out, with the world looking on, that he was a fraud.

Now, Bailey is being asked, in essence, if Canadians can trust him. In Bailey's entire career, there has never been a hint of any subterfuge. But just to make sure he has not become this decade's boogeyman, the media consider it fair to ask him if he is Mr. Clean. Without putting it so bluntly, the host is asking Bailey if his victory is simply another ruse to set up Canadians for another disappointment, whether he should not just come clean on national radio and spare the country the pain and expense of another inquiry. For after all, Bailey was born in Jamaica and immigrated to the Toronto area in 1980. He has seemingly come out of nowhere, won a place on the Canadian track and field team and is now the fastest man in the world. Gosh, the interviewer seems to be saying, is this possible? Does lightning strike the same place twice? What more similarity to Ben Johnson does the world need? And wouldn't Canadians be well advised to celebrate, if they must, but to be ready just in case?

So the frustration and anger become even more apparent in Bailey's voice. The questions are clear in his tone, in the nervous laughter: What can he do? Why these expectations for him? Can any good come out of Galilee? Why? It's only the Canadian media that keep bringing up the spectre of Johnson, Bailey says. Somehow, I feel that even Bailey finds this explanation inadequate. Somehow, Bailey must have a greater appreciation for Ben as he stammered and stuttered before the inquiry, on national television, reaching for the elusive perfect answer.

So, the interviewer ploughs on: Can you say without any difficulty you are a Canadian? The loaded question that probes the inadequacy of the answer, the unstated question every time Blacks begin a meeting with the anthem "Lift Ev'ry Voice and Sing." It is the question that must always be answered by the young woman whose ancestors have been living in this country for centuries but is automatically a visitor; the French-speaking Zairian who wants to wear his national costume in the St. Jean Baptiste parade in Quebec but is told to conform to a nationalistic dress code or take a hike; the young boys and girls attending celebrations by the African-Canadian Heritage Association and searching for their place in this country; the world's fastest man across the ocean in Sweden phoning home to boast how he has conquered the world for Canada.

"I'll always be a Jamaican, no matter what," Bailey answers, the nervous laughter explaining it all. The interview moves on. But both Donovan and the Canadian public have staked out their ground, their expectations, their reality and their limits. The world's fastest man knows that after the euphoria, after the celebrations, he must return home. He might remember the inspirational world of the other "national anthem" that he didn't hear played when he got his gold medal for Canada.

> *Sing a song full of the faith*
> that the dark past has taught us;
> Sing a song full of the hope
> that the present has bought us;
> Facing the rising sun of our new day begun,
> Let us march on till victory ... is won.

For it is in moments like these that parents hope their children remember their teachings, remember what it really means to be black in Canada.

If Donovan did, he would know what are the expectations of him back home, how he must guard himself not to have too many flights of fancy, not to run and jump and be carefree like most Canadians for too long. "I'll always be a Jamaican, *no matter what.*"

But as the African national anthem says, there is still a long march before final victory. And for Bailey it was to anchor the winning team in the relays. With him would be Surin, born in Haiti, Glenroy Gilbert, born in Trinidad, and Robert Esmie, born in Jamaica. In the summer of 1995, this was the fastest relay team in the world. And it was so typically Canadian, standing in front of the big red and white Canadian flag with the red maple leaf while photojournalists of the world snapped away. Should this glory disappear, should acceptance in Canada come with a question mark, *"I'll always be a Jamaican,"* said a foreigner in his adopted homeland.

CHAPTER 4

HOW MANY BLACK JUDGES?

Sitting in his oak-panelled chambers, you cannot but feel a sense of power and accomplishment. This must be what it is like for a Black to survive and make it all the way in the Canadian mainstream. This has to be the ultimate dream of independence: to be your own boss; to have some of the brightest minds in the country reporting to you; to know that your thoughts and directives have a profound influence on an entire nation. To be a real-life pioneer.

Here we are, sitting amidst the paraphernalia of achievement and respectability, the accoutrements of having exceeded the benchmarks and boundaries set by the wider society. The sweet rewards in the form of personal satisfaction, of having achieved a lifelong dream, of not selling out your principles or silencing a sharp tongue on the way to the top. Just being an integral part of this society, of feeling a sense of belonging and achievement, being valued and accepted—isn't that for all of us the ultimate dream?

Until Julius Alexander Isaac took on the garb of his office, all the status and power associated with it were the exclusive domain of white Canadians—not for a rank outsider. Not for someone who is black and has the background of a Julius Isaac. And what is the evidence of achievement? On the wall of the spacious office are various scrolls from the prime ministers and governors general of Canada. There are the shelves of legal texts and, on the walls, parchments from various universities conferring law degrees and awards. Waiting outside are the chauffeured limousine, law clerks, secretaries, bored security guards hovering at the entrance of a building so quiet you can hear yourself breathing.

Beyond this imposing building are the seats of real power in Canada: the House of Commons, the Senate, the Office of the Prime Minister and Leader of the Opposition, the Supreme Court, embassies of various nations—all within shouting distance. So this is power and achievement! The sign of an important man well ensconced. And is there a way for more black people in Canada to get their hands on more of this power and prestige? To achieve in the mainstream? Perhaps the answer lies, as so many Blacks believe, in how well we educate ourselves, band together, acquire political clout and live up to our family and community responsibilities. In how we prepare ourselves for acceptance. Perhaps.

As Chief Justice of the Federal Court of Canada, Julius Isaac is the highest ranking Black in this country's legal profession. And this is a profession, as the Chief Justice is wont to note, that has not been too kind to Blacks in Canada.

"Generally speaking, in the history of the legal profession in Canada, the fate of black lawyers is bound up with the prevailing attitude towards Blacks as a group," he told a meeting of black law students two months after he was appointed chief justice. And what is this attitude? "That black lawyers should be limited to servicing the needs of the black community and that small segment of the larger community that interfaces with it," he explained. In other words, it was once inconceivable that a black person would become a full-fledged lawyer, far less a chief justice.

Indeed, as the Chief Justice told the students at their meeting in Toronto, it wasn't too long ago when his friend and mentor, a top criminal lawyer and black activist named B.J. Spencer Pitt, commented in the 1960s that he would consider it a personal achievement if a single black person were to be named a judge during his lifetime. He died without achieving this dream.

This was the kind of attitude that required an act of the Ontario Legislature in 1884, authorizing the Supreme Court of Ontario to admit one Delos Rogest Davis to practise law, providing he passed an examination set by the Ontario Law Society. This would make Davis the first black lawyer in Canada. It was only through the enactment of this legislation that there was any hope of overcoming the obstacles thrown in the way of Delos Davis. Until this special act, the Law Society would not admit Davis as a lawyer because he could not complete his articling. And he could not article because no attorney or solicitor would have him "because of his colour and descent." Davis passed the special examination and was called to the bar in 1886.

For most of the next century, even after this breakthrough by Davis, black lawyers were forced to restrict their practices to black businesses. Just like the black community in general, they were marginalized in the wider society. There were more opportunities for black lawyers in the 1960s and 1970s because of the influx of immigrants, mainly from the Caribbean, but the opportunities were still limited.

"Liberalized attitudes in the society and in the profession made it possible for some fortunate few to obtain excellent articles and thereafter to enter practice on a competitive basis with contemporaries," Julius Isaac commented in his speech. "The majority, lacking that advantage, were restricted to practising as sole practitioners. The result, generally speaking, was that despite the increase in numbers in the 1960s and 1970s, black lawyers, as a group, were unable to have any impact on the profession or their ability to service fully their traditional constituency."

Chief Justice Isaac believes it is important that black lawyers, and the community in general, understand this history of discrimination and denial. The legacy of this history, he says, is the current economic and spiritual crisis among Blacks.

"Understanding the past is important because it provides perspectives and informs the future. But in charting a course for the future, it is well to remember that progress comes not from ideas alone, but from their application to concrete circumstances."

Therefore, it is understandable at a time when we are still looking for role models and holding up as examples those who survive in a white environment, why the black law students—still among the cream of the black intelligentsia—would celebrate the achievements of Julius Alexander Isaac at their very first annual meeting as an association. And it would also be understandable why the new Chief Justice, true to form, would deliver a speech like this—a call for these lawyers, and the black community in general, to understand what they can achieve through self-reliance and co-operation.

His calling the black community to arms, to empowerment through self-reliance and the making of money, can be heard in the dozens of speeches he has made to various black and Caribbean groups across Canada. Never one to shy away from a controversy, in his speeches Isaac sounds no different from many of the more politically minded activists across this country. Indeed, if you were to ask the Chief Justice, he would argue most fervently that too many Blacks are still going into law and other professions. There isn't enough professional diversity for his liking. "We have placed too heavy an emphasis on the humanities and the professions and not enough on business. I think that's changing now. In the larger context, one recognizes that the people who matter are the people in business."

But Issac's influence goes beyond the legal profession he has conquered, a conquest he is apt to say, publicly, resulted largely from the privation experienced by all the black lawyers since Delos Davis, and the war they waged. Indeed, Isaac is probably the highest-ranking Black in any profession, in all of Canada. Not bad for a little boy born on the Caribbean island of Grenada in 1928 and who grew up dreaming of becoming a successful lawyer, of literally becoming a chief justice—just like the chief justice he saw being driven to and from work in the lap of luxury, in the trappings of office and power, every day in his childhood Grenada.

Even now as he talks, he can still picture the chief justice of the Eastern Caribbean driving home in the back of his car, reading the newspaper. Young Isaac decided early to be like this man lolling in the car, or to be like the much-talked-about criminal lawyer, a Mr. J.B. Renwick, who reputedly never lost a murder case, a hero in Grenada and the Caribbean. These men had power and status. They were role models.

And his status isn't bad for an immigrant whose first job in Canada was sweeping the floors at *The Toronto Star*, the country's largest newspaper, while he was studying law at the University of Toronto. Eventually, he graduated to the then-illustrious glass-ceiling job for Blacks, a railway porter. Well into the 1960s, the porter's job was the ultimate in aspirations for many black men. Many of them supported their families on the salary of a railway porter, all the time stifling their ambition, unable to achieve any of the dreams that must have swum freely in their heads as boys—dreams that were snuffed out as soon as they realized they were black and that acceptance into the wider society, which had the influential and powerful jobs, was therefore off limits.

Not Julius Isaac. He moved on, stopping along the way to be a volunteer advisor to the union representing sleeping- and parlour-car porters on the Canadian National Railways. He was also the top lawyer at the Ontario Securities Commission, the largest stock-market regulator in this country. Before that, there were stints as a senior magistrate in Grenada and in private practice in Ontario and Saskatchewan. Then, on to a brilliant legal career in the Federal Department of Justice where he was a Crown prosecutor and an assistant deputy attorney general. Ultimately, he became a judge in the Ontario Supreme Court in 1989. Three years later, he was appointed Chief Justice of the Federal Court of Canada.

Along the way to realizing his childhood dreams, he became a member of the Negro Citizen Committee, a group established to fight for the improvement of immigration laws so that more Caribbean people could come to Canada. He was the founding member of the West Indies Student Association at the University of Toronto, an association that would become a refuge and a respite for the thousands of Caribbean students who felt the sting of racism and experienced culture shock in coming to Canada.

Even now he is the co-chair of a Black Studies program at Dalhousie University in Halifax, and is a distinguished patron for Canadian Artists Network: Blacks In Action, a Toronto-based organization representing black Canadian artists. Personal and community achievements must go hand in hand to be effective, he argues. This is his philosophy, one that has governed his activities in law and as a community activist.

Yes, I suggest to him, this office of Chief Justice and its holder are living proof that dreams do come true, that there are ample rewards for the dedicated. Or do they come true? Our chat is to probe this assertion. From the lap of his power, from amidst all the exhibit of status, Julius Alexander Isaac looks out across the land and finds a crisis in the black community that is getting worse. A crisis, he says, that one man, one appointment here and there, can never rectify. A crisis that Blacks themselves will have to band together and change.

* * *

The Chief Justice loosens his tie and relaxes with his ever-present pack of Craven A cigarettes. It's been a long night and day for him, he says. A law clerk he is supervising has been working on some decisions and he, himself, was up until about four o'clock the previous morning. Now, it is late in the evening and until now he has not had much time for anything but work.

But even as he explains the situation, there isn't any sense that this Chief Justice is unhappy with the long hours he must keep and the constant travelling. Neither does he appear uncomfortable with the burden of knowing he is a role model for hundreds of thousands of people across the country. His concern is that people, immigrants and blacks, think that he has real power. Indeed, there is a reason for this opinion. After all, there has never been a black chief justice of the Federal Court before him, and that achievement certainly must count for something.

Chief Justice Isaac begs to disagree over exactly how much his appointment is worth in the overall scheme of things. Blacks in Canada have no real power, he says. They will not be taken seriously politically, they will not see legislation passed to benefit them specifically, until they have economic clout. Until they are present in boardrooms and at shareholders' meetings, until they can hire and fire, receive and declare dividends. Until they own the places that hire them, that sell them the goods and food they eat, until they create a sound internal economy in their community.

When he talks like this, the Chief Justice sounds like any black economic nationalist, not only in Canada but in such places as New York and Los Angeles. But this should not be surprising. Isaac sees the black experience in the Americas as the same. The country or language doesn't matter. In his youth, he identified with what he calls the progressive movement in the United States, the leftist and socialist camps whose "interests were bound up with the interests of black people. I was connected with a number of American Blacks in the left movement, [people in] political events." Among these connections were progressive writers in New York and California.

His philosophy is from the same school that says black people must create the infrastructure to liberate themselves. Others go further and say that not only must Blacks own the stores and shops, but they must produce the goods and spend their money among Blacks. This is the thinking behind such groups as the Nation of Islam with its black-owned businesses and restaurants, with its call for Blacks to support black-owned business on their day of atonement. It is a message that obviously resonates across the North American continent—and as Chief Justice Isaac hopes, throughout the Western Hemisphere. In this solitary case, it resonates in the corridors of judicial power in Canada.

Progress will come only through economic independence, the Chief Justice argues, because only then will Blacks be free of the control of other groups. Only then will they be beyond hoping that some politician will appoint one of them to some top job, even as chief justice. Blacks will start having clout only when they take greater pride in their identity and work together, when they stop being distrustful of one another because they, too, might have bought into the negative stereotypes other groups have spread about Africans and their descendants.

"There is a complete absence of influence in matters that affect us as a community, as a people. An inability to lend a helping hand to brothers and sisters in need," the Chief Justice explains in the interview. Julius Isaac chooses his words carefully, pondering every question and occasionally pausing mid-sentence to reflect on what he is saying. "The last time I was in Toronto, I met a Jamaican fellow who told me that he owns a factory where he employs about 50 West Indians, and I thought that he is a unique individual. That is the sort of thing I am talking about: to have the ability to help and to influence the matters that affect our lives. We are at the mercy of other people in the community. You look around at the way in which the society is organized, and for want of a better word, you realize that it is organized on a tribal basis and that each tribe is vying for economic stability in order to ensure that matters that concern members of that tribe are disposed of in the most advantageous way. We are not able to do that. That is the nutshell of my thinking."

Part of the problem rests with society and the way it is organized. But Blacks must also take their share of the blame, he says. "We do not have the sharpened, acquisitive instinct. If it is sharpened, it is in a very marginal way that affects a family or an individual. We haven't been able as a community in Canada to acquire significant pools of capital to put at the disposal of the community for its development. I think that is where the focus should be."

Isaac says that he really became aware of the powerlessness in the Canadian black community in 1979. A political coup in his native Grenada had sent several former cabinet ministers and public servants into exile in Toronto "without resources to sustain themselves for very long."

"They appealed for help to those of us so-called pillars of the community, who lived here for some time. Based on their Caribbean experience, they thought that we should be able to help. Big shots are supposed to have clout!" he recalled mockingly in an address to the Grenada Association of Toronto in 1992.

> What I found was that except for short-term loans, which most of us could ill afford, a meal or two and comforting words, we were unable within the community to help them. We owned no substantial businesses; we did not command pools of capital; members of our tribe were not in positions of power; we had no influence, whatsoever, with people in power.
>
> Since that time I have looked at the black communities in other parts of the country as I travelled. I have found that the situation is the same in each province. I concluded, I think correctly, that the black community across the country was helpless to look after, in any meaningful and significant way, those of its members who are in need. Always, we are obliged to reach outside the commuity for significant help.

Yes, he told his audience, some of them might earn a decent living in a trade, profession or small business. But they are the exceptions. In any case, their so-called success has not resulted in the bettering of the material and spiritual condition of the black community. "Black people as a group are probably the most vulnerable in the Canadian society and the vulnerability is increasing," Isaac said.

Few Blacks could honestly disagree with this assessment and indictment of ourselves. How vulnerable the black community is can be seen in the daily hardships of the thousands of professional people who have spent the last while walking the streets of major Canadian cities looking for jobs. None of them seems to have a résumé good enough to get them the job they deserve; most of them protest about how they always manage to come up short because of someone with connections who jumps ahead of them because of a special relationship with the person hiring, because of a special position in the network.

In Toronto, for example, there has always been the disparaging joke that the city has the most highly educated taxi drivers in the world. You can never tell if the person behind the wheel of the taxi was a doctor, politician, engineer or lawyer in his or her native country. The ranks of these underemployed have been bolstered of late by many Blacks who hold degrees from Canadian universities and have experience in the Canadian workforce—two important qualifications that distinguish these Blacks from foreign doctors, lawyers and accountants who are driving taxis in a new country.

The vulnerability can also be seen in how the small black middle-class that started to emerge by the 1980s has taken a battering. Federal, provincial and municipal cutbacks have exacted their toll, as have the cuts at such quasi-government institutions as universities and hospitals. The restructuring to the Canadian economy caused by free trade with the United States has also thrown many of us into the ranks of the unemployed, especially those Blacks who worked in manufacturing and the hospitality industries. The cutbacks at the hospitals have been vicious, especially for the thousands of immigrant women who arrived as long ago as the 1960s so eager to work as nursing assistants. Now, as they near retirement, they face the uncertainty of not having a job, an income or an adequate pension to fall back on. Those who managed to acquire a home have watched the bottom of the real-estate market fall out at the same time their jobs started disappearing. So much for the plans to eventually sell the house, take the tax-free proceeds and spend them educating the next generation or retiring, possibly back home, with some security.

This is why it is troublesome to hear some Blacks in middle-management positions talking about attaining success. In most cases, this can only be inspirational talk, somewhat like daydreaming. One is often tempted to ask, success at what? Or could it be that we put the bar for measuring success so low that merely to survive or, at best, to live comfortably is to be successful? For this success can easily be wiped out by losing a job or by a prolonged sickness. For this reason it would appear wise for the string of black business and professional associations across the country to stay clear, certainly for the next while, of this idle talk about the business and professional successes among their membership. As the Chief Justice says, few members of these groups have any clout. This is not to say that there isn't a need for these groups. There is. What is not needed is all the chest thumping about mythical or low-grade successes. Indeed, much hasn't changed since Chief Justice Isaac had to come to terms with this vulnerability and economic helplessness in the black community in the 1970s.

After 40 years in the country, Julius Isaac sits at the pinnacle of what could be seen as acceptance beyond his own community. In the eyes of many, he is proof that by working hard, picking the right profession and staying out of trouble—in essence, rejecting the alternatives in the black community to the mainstream—any black boy or girl can transcend skin colour and rise to the greatest heights in this country. Even a leftist lawyer, who spent so many years working with trade unions; even someone who spent so much time as an activist outside the wider society. Even a black man who does not attempt to hide his belief in Pan-Africanism and who is always so quick to quote Aime Cesaire, the father of Negritude thought, Toussaint L'Overture, Franz Fanon, James Baldwin, Brazil's Benedita Sousa Dasilva and the Jamaican reggae star, Peter Tosh, about the oneness of the African experience the world over.

"Our past is also informative and inspirational. No one who has surveyed our accomplishments on this side of the Atlantic since Middle Passage can fail to be amazed and stimulated by the sheer will to survive that the record discloses," he says.

To students celebrating Black History night at Vaughan Secondary School in Thornhill, Ontario, he had the following comment in 1993:

> A starting point in our acceptance of our identity is the recognition that all our ancestors started life in the New World deprived of all those features of social life which promote unity and progress. They were deprived of language, of culture, of religion, of familial bonds, and they were required to live in the most inhumane conditions imaginable.
>
> That is our history in the United States and Canada, in the Caribbean, whether Cuba (Spanish), Santo Domingo (French

> and Spanish), Jamaica or Barbados (English), Brazil (Portuguese) and so on. Regardless of location, our history as victims of massive violations of human rights is the same.

Obviously, there can be little doubt that the Chief Justice of the Federal Court is important, the occupant of this office says. In this position he is president of the entire court and has rank and precedence over all other judges of his court. A good barometer of this status beyond the chambers of the court is the number of invitations to social events from the Ottawa diplomatic corps, especially the representatives of African and Caribbean countries. Even the black diplomats take pride in seeing a high-ranking judge that looks like them. The only possible improvement to his status would be for him to be appointed to the Supreme Court of Canada, or even to become the chief justice of that court.

Definitely, the Chief Justice of the Federal Court isn't something to sneeze at. Here is a man who presides over the hearing of appeals and is responsible for the management of a court that is made up of 24 judges. This court deals exclusively with federal laws, and while it does not handle cases like divorce, murder and break-and-enters, it spends a great deal of time "civilizing" the federal executive and the bureaucracy to enhance the administration of the laws of Canada. It deals with matters that touch the lives of Canadians in a very basic and fundamental way. This is true, whether it is reviewing the administration of the agency that sets telephone rates and regulates the country's radio and television stations, or whether the court is correcting past injustices by ruling on important land clams by the Canadian First Nations people. Complaints of unfairness or illegal conduct by members of cabinet or federal government employees come before this court, as do cases on such things as immigration and refugee rulings, complaints about the Canadian Human Rights Commission or the implementation of the federal government's employment equity program.

And, of course, there is the exclusivity of being the first Black to hold this office. This appointment is the kind of thing that, at the very least, will be included in any book on the achievements of Blacks in this country. History has its place for all pioneers. But there is also the uniqueness of another sort, the international recognition of being numbered among only three people of African descent to have risen to such legal prominence in all North America. This exclusive club includes the civil rights activist Thurgood Marshall, a fearless fighter who helped to make giant steps in civil rights for American Blacks, and Clarence Thomas, who appears bent on turning back some of these achievements.

With this in mind, I ask Chief Justice Isaac if there is a club for black jurists like himself, with an opportunity for him to network with his black peers, when black judges can meet, let the mask they show to their white colleagues slip, and talk about the plight of the Blacks they see streaming through their courts. For when he was on the bench in the Ontario Supreme Court, he must have seen the growing numbers of Blacks being sentenced to jail terms, and how they were disproportionately populating Canadian prisons. Is there such an opportunity for these judges to meet and talk, perhaps to reflect on the issue of Blacks and the law?

"How can there be?" he answers quickly. "How many judges of African ancestry are there in this country?" Point made. His mentor, B.J. Spencer Pitt, must still be rolling in his grave. We move on quickly to the next question. No need to name the handful of black judges in Canada, a number so small as to be virtually insignificant, not unless we want to talk about them strictly in terms of being pioneers, the first in the tradition of Delos Davis to lead where they hope many others will follow.

The Chief Justice's assessment is a blunt indictment of Canadian society. If there aren't many judges, then obviously there isn't much influence from the black community in the administration of justice, which, as an important study in the province of Ontario shows, disproportionately affects Blacks.[2] So that the appointment of one man, the anointing with limited powers and the provision of a spacious corner office, isn't much in terms of the advancement of a people. Now, we are onto a subject that pops up very often in speeches by Chief Justice Isaac.

One of his concerns is that Blacks must start flowing into the mainstream, availing themselves of all the rights and privileges of Canadians. There is nothing to be gained by staying in small, isolated communities, he argues. But just as important, the wider society must start making room for Blacks, so that their appointments will become automatic, and that eventually there will be so many appointees that they will make an

[2] *A Report of the Commission on Systemic Racism in the Ontario Criminal Justice System.*

impact on their communities. Otherwise, the symbolic elevation of a black person here or there will have little meaning, will be of little incentive for Blacks to march into the wider society. And that is true, he intimates, even if the appointee is the Chief Justice of the Federal Court of Canada.

We are now discussing a subject that goes to the heart of whether the Canadian black community has gained anything with the appointment of people like Julius Isaac to high-profile positions. Do all these trappings of power, lavished on one Black, mean anything for the hundreds of thousands of Blacks struggling to gain acceptance in the Canadian mainstream? Indeed, many have argued that the single appointment has had a negative effect; it is no more than placing an individual under the spotlight, raising hopes elsewhere in the black community, aspirations that an individual can never fulfil. The result, inevitably, is frustration for the appointee, who feels powerless and sometimes even guilty for enjoying the fruits of his or her achievement, but knows it is impossible to live up to the wider-held expectations; and disillusionment for those with raised hopes that will be dashed. Isn't it better, many ask, to remove all the systemic barriers to a people moving as a group into the mainstream? A century ago, the Ontario Legislature had to use the club of legislation to break down all the inbred discrimination working against Delos Davis. This resulted, albeit too many years later, in the appointment of the country's first black Chief Justice of the Federal Court. Isn't this a good precedent? But isn't it still necessary to use the law of the land to establish some minimum standards for fairness of employment in this country?

Perhaps, as late as today, we need legislation to cover the fairness of opportunity in the workplace, the biggest single test of a group moving into the mainstream. This could be a law passed, not for an individual like the first black lawyer in this country, but rather for an entire community. Added to this is the notion that these appointees are often represented as an elevation for the black community, the few people the mainstream has deemed good enough to promote into its ranks.

With such weight on their shoulders, with no power to do much, is there any surprise that many appointees feel paralyzed by the double burden of being black? That anyone can rise to prominence as an individual, but can only fail as a representative of the race or community? The burden is to make sure that you never fail, because your race will be failing as well. And this is a burden that the white appointee, maybe only a desk away, does not have to carry to bed at night and take to work every morning.

Chief Justice Isaac believes that in the final analysis the individual appointments really amount to hollow victories. Yes, there is the sense of personal pride and achievement. But for the wider community, so far they have amounted to very little.

Soon after his appointment, Chief Justice Isaac dealt with this issue head on. At a speech to the Grenada Association of Toronto, an association that he had helped to found, the newly appointed Chief Justice seemed to be warning fellow immigrants and Blacks not to expect too much from a single appointment, even if it was his. After all, the event was a celebration of how one of the association's founding members had scaled the heights of success, proving that there is room in the mainstream for others like him. Yet, he appeared to be trying to temper the celebratory mood.

Chief Justice Isaac reminded his audience of a speech by the then-prime minister Brian Mulroney, who at the opening of the black exhibition in the national capital patted himself on the back for appointing a number of Blacks to prominent positions. "As Prime Minister, I have been privileged to appoint African-Canadians to top positions in the decision-making process of our society: Julius Isaac, Chief Justice of the Federal Court of Canada; Donald Oliver, Senator; Lincoln Alexander, Lieutenant Governor of Ontario; Gil Scott, Commissioner of the Public Service Commission of Canada; Emerson Mascoll, Director of Canadian National Railways; Glenda Simms, President, Advisory Council on the Status of Women; and many more." So boasted Prime Minister Mulroney.

But obviously, this Chief Justice wasn't too impressed by this record, even if he was the beneficiary of one of the appointments. And in his typical outspoken way, he tried to put the appointments in a context of what they mean to the black community—not necessarily to the chosen individuals or a politician trying to score partisan points.

"I want to be very careful here," the Chief Justice said, "because I do not want you to misunderstand what I am about to say. All the people mentioned in that quotation, except me, are distinguished people indeed. About myself, I say, well ... I dunno! And their appointments to high office are achievements of which all of us as black people can be justly proud. Good role models, everyone shouts! But, and this is my point: Not one of that crew has any clout that means anything substantial to the community. And what is more, their appointments to high office have not made any significant difference to the condition of vulnerability of the community.

"In my considered view, it would have been infinitely more beneficial to the community as a whole if the prime minister could have dusted off and held up six individuals who were engaged in pursuits that gave the community an economic base, individuals who could, in their enterprises, provide employment to members of the community, and thus reduce their vulnerability."

Power, influence and all the perquisites of high office are meaningless if lavished on only the individual. Of course, this is assuming that most people think, as he does, that most Blacks assume that one of their tasks is to make life better for the downtrodden, for people like themselves. If the aim is purely personal aggrandizement, then the appointment of an individual means something, but only to the individual. If the aim is to send a message to the black community that they can achieve in the mainstream, then the appointment is useless without the conferring of real power over matters that are of vital interest to the community.

In this respect, a chief justice cannot provide jobs and help with the creation of an economic base that would lead to self-sufficiency and lower unemployment among Blacks. Yes, he may become a role model; but what does a role model mean to a black youth unable to find a job? So that while some Blacks will hold him up as an example of personal success, until he can help change the circumstances of their daily lives, then it is questionable how much the community benefits from having a black chief justice. The question, then, is how do we impact on the mainstream in large enough numbers to make a difference in our communities?

"Given our circumstances as children of Africa in the New World, I suggest that our survival demands no less, demands that we co-operate and support each other, regardless of place of origin, regardless of language or culture; regardless of station in life," he said in a 1992 speech to the Spice Island Ladies' Cultural Association in Montreal.

"I operate from the premise that, as a group, we are without power or influence in this society and that our survival requires that we have both." This means Blacks must recognize and accept their identities—*our negritude*—and they must organize in groups and co-operate to build a strong economic base within the community.

In a speech he gave in 1991 at the annual dinner held in Ottawa to celebrate Black History, Chief Justice Isaac said, "Individual accomplishments, unconnected to group power and group influence, are largely ineffective, viewed in terms of group development and consolidation of group power and influence. To put it another way, to matter, individual accomplishments must yield net benefits both to the individual achiever and to the group."

Finally, Isaac's philosophy of self-empowerment calls on Blacks to stand up and fight for their rights as Canadian citizens. We must not settle for less than the full enjoyment of the rights and privileges that flow from the Canadian constitution.

"I have no doubt that when that happens," he told a meeting of the Afro-Caribbean Association of Manitoba in 1989, "an appointment such as mine will no longer be national news or a significant event. It will be taken as a given that people from our community, like those from any other, with aptitude and abilities, will have aspirations to hold *any* office in the nation, including judicial office."

* * *

Juanita Westmoreland-Traoré, Ontario's commissioner of employment equity, thought her appointment would make a difference. It would pave the way for many more Blacks and minorities, women and the disabled to follow her to success in Canada. Basic issues of employment for some 60 percent of the work-force in Canada's largest province would become routine.

Now, as we talk in her office, she isn't too sure. A provincial election campaign is in its last days and the government that appointed her appears headed for defeat. Worse, the party leading in the polls has declared Westmoreland-Traoré and her program of employment equity as target number one. Every night, the leader of the Ontario Progressive Conservative Party, borrowing heavily from the rhetoric of the U.S.

Speaker of the House, Newt Gingrich, is on television promising that the employment equity legislation Juanita Westmoreland-Traoré holds so dear is history.

For Mike Harris, employment equity is an attempt to inflict on Ontario all the perceived ills of affirmative action taking place in the United States. For Harris, the legislation stems from the kind of socialist policy and social engineering that dares to disrupt the free market. As he moves around the province, Harris appears to have tapped into a vein of disenchantment among mainstream workers, those who do not like how Canada and Ontario have changed, who do not like minorities and other outsiders apparently making the same claim on jobs the members of the white society long accepted as their exclusive preserve. It is a feeling that appears to be fed by events in the United States, where another form of employment equity, affirmative action, is under attack and its supporters appear in retreat.

This is the same legislation Westmoreland-Traoré has spent the last five years chaperoning in its various stages through the provincial legislature. To hear her explain it, all the legislation does is try to make clear that everyone gets a fair chance at jobs available in the community, and a fair chance of promotion within business.

The legislation, according to a publication from Westmoreland-Traoré's office, is based on a few common principles:

•Members of designated groups (minorities, women, Aboriginals and the handicapped) have the right to be considered for jobs, hired, retained, treated and promoted without having to face discriminatory barriers.

•Every employer's workforce, at each level and in each job category, should reflect the representation of designated groups in the community.

•Every employer shall make sure that its employment policies and practices are free of systemic and deliberate barriers which discriminate against members of designated groups.

•Every employer shall put in place supportive measures to help recruit, hire, retain, treat fairly and promote members of the designated groups; these measures will also benefit the workforce as a whole.

To this end, the management and unions of the affected companies would establish a timetable to achieve specific goals. The government's role would be to monitor these goals. This is the gist of the controversial legislation. As we talk in her office, all that is needed is for the provincial government to announce regulations and the employment equity legislation will be law of the land. This cannot happen, however, until after the election.

Westmoreland-Traoré is nursing a bad cold that forced us to cancel a couple of earlier interviews. Her voice is raspy. These have been very bad days for her physically and emotionally. Of late, she has been the target of personal attacks by a public exceedingly hostile to her and the employment equity legislation. Only a few days before we meet, *Share*, a Toronto black newspaper, has carried a story of an angry confrontation between Westmoreland-Traoré and a group to whom she was explaining the legislation. At one point, the story says, the debate got so heated and personal that a white woman went to the microphone and screamed at the employment equity commissioner, threatening to sue Westmoreland-Traoré for discriminating against able-bodied white men if the legislation is ever implemented.

Yet, despite the growing hostility, symbolically on a day like this when she is hoarse and the political odds seem so overwhelming, Juanita Westmoreland-Traoré ploughs on. She, too, is committed to self-empowerment of Blacks and other minorities. She understands the economic argument that Blacks must get into business and have economic and political clout. But it isn't possible for all Blacks to own businesses, she reasons. For one thing, there is the question, which Chief Justice Isaac raised, of acquiring the necessary pools of capital, and that cannot be done overnight. She knows it is not desirable that Blacks remain outside the wider society in employment—people equate their importance with having a job and enjoying their employment. They are happy and productive when they believe they can succeed in the workplace. When they do not have a job, or cannot find one to match their education, experience and potential—simply because of their skin colour—people start to drop out of society. Then, everybody loses.

Westmoreland-Traoré also knows from personal experience something else, something that is very significant to Blacks. For decades, Blacks, especially immigrants arriving in this country without significant capital, always saw a job in the civil service or the professions as their entry into the middle class. This is particularly true of all those Blacks who populated the mid- and entry-level jobs in the civil service and major corporations. This is particularly true of all those immigrants who were schooled in the humanities and other disciplines in their native country; they were prepared to be good clerical workers when they immigrated. It is particularly true of all those mothers drilling into their sons and daughters that they must acquire an education to better prepare them for the workforce.

The employment equity legislation would be uplifting and give them hope, make them feel that everyone is playing by the same rules. They would feel confident that their chance of getting a job, a promotion or a bonus is not contingent on who they know, on their ability to break into the exclusive circle of friends that *network* about jobs and promotion. And with the force of law protecting them and their job, they could get on with the other things in life, such as raising a family or preparing for retirement. The legislation she is championing would provide a channel through which Blacks and other minority groups could vent their frustration at the system, rather than just dropping out and becoming alienated and unproductive, rather than endangering the social peace.

As we talk, there is an unmistakable sense that Westmoreland-Traoré is a driven woman, someone who believes in the righteousness of her work; her cause is employment equity. This is a woman who sees the implementation of this legislation in personal terms. Implementation will be the crowning point in her career as a law professor, a human-rights commissioner and a jurist—a career she put on hold to work on something in which she believes passionately. Like Chief Justice Isaac, she has first-hand knowledge of how the legal system works and of its imperfections.

Before taking this job, Westmoreland-Traoré was a former commissioner of the Canadian Human Rights Commission and was the immediate past president of the Conseil des communautes culturelles et de l'immigration du Québec, an agency that looks at immigration policies in the province. At different times, she was member of the Quebec Civil Liberties Union and the International Relations Council of Montreal.

Growing up in Canada, and working as a human-rights commissioner, she has firsthand knowledge of how employment discrimination can hurt people. She says she knows how frustrating and denigrating it is for members of any group to fight discrimination case by case. And she wants to do whatever is possible to remove the traditional inequities of the workplace.

During our conversation, she speaks slowly and softly, answers every question in excruciating detail, as if making a case for a client she knows to be innocent of all accusations, but who is facing a stacked jury of public opinion. Occasionally, she touches the tips of her trademark braids, which are pulled back today and held with a bow at the back of the head. Employment equity is an initiative that cannot fail, that cannot be allowed to fail, she indicates. She will do her utmost to save the employment-equity legislation.

This battle is also a personal one for Juanita Westmoreland-Traoré, a fight she is waging on behalf of her community and women's groups, that she can't lose lest she let down the side. For her, the implementation of employment equity would be one example of the appointment of a black person to a high-profile position in Canadian society making a difference. Employment equity would ensure that some of things people like Chief Justice Julius Isaac talk about, happen: that there be clear rules for employment, so that Blacks and other minorities, women and the disabled will know what is expected of them, and what they can expect of an employer when they apply for jobs. So that there will no longer be a need for the symbolic appointment of an individual here and there. "I think that now we have come to the realization that we need not only to look at the individual approach, but the systemic approach, and we need to see that workplaces have a planned approach to eliminating discrimination," she says.

But the signs outside her office are not good. The opposition has the government on the run. The man who wants to become premier of Canada's largest province says his first act in office will be to do away with employment equity legislation, with what he calls—to thunderous applause from crowds of white voters—the quotas that would make employers hire more minorities, women and the disabled. Even though Juanita Westmoreland-Traoré and her supporters try to explain that employment equity is not the same as quotas, nobody appears to be listening. So Westmoreland-Traoré is obviously frustrated. She knows that some people believe that black people cannot afford to fail at anything they attempt in the mainstream. Is she just another victim of the double burden of being black, I ask, of having to be successful in the mainstream because so many people are watching and in this case rooting her on? Suddenly, it appears that I have penetrated the darkness. She lets more of her real self show through. In the end, this is what it really means to be black.

"It's true," she says after a moment of thought, an admission that even now she is still uneasy accepting. "I do think that if you are a minority person, a Black ... you do have to be always aware [of this burden]."

And this burden impacts in many ways, but primarily by hanging like an albatross around the neck, an omen of what would happen with failure. "You do always have to think twice and you do have to be very well prepared. I guess that is obviously an additional burden....you are vulnerable, so you always have to be aware of [your vulnerability]."

Indeed, this is what many Blacks call keeping your eyes on the prize and not getting side-tracked by criticisms and obstacles. "If you do have a sense of being able to bring about some small change or some medium-term change for significant groups of people, I think it is worth it," she says.

Of course, there is always the sense of being just another foot soldier in the battle for equity, in the war to make it easy for other Blacks coming after you to attain and surpass your level of achievement. "I am proud to be a woman of African descent in Canada. I am Canadian. I benefit from many different achievements that have gone on before, both in my group and in other groups. I am part of a human rights program in Canada. I have that confidence and self-esteem and I want to share it with many people because I believe that often there is a projection, an underestimation of qualifications and the dignity and the competence and leadership skills of many people in our communities."

But no matter how she tries to explain it away, at the end of the day she is still confronted by the notion that as a high-profile Black she simply cannot fail. There is just too much at stake for others who are counting on her to lead the way. "I think that [succeeding] is one of the main things I have to do besides my daily work. I have to do that and I try to do it and plan it into my work. It means it takes more time [to complete a job], but I think it is very important because of the image that is often projected."

But why does she feel so driven?

"It's a series of events that have taken place in my life," she says, explaining also what gives her the strength to continue in the face of such opposition from the mainstream. "But a large part of it has been education by my family. You know that my family, and a lot of the families we grew up with, didn't accept second place. They overcame discrimination and barriers the likes of which we still have difficulty really grasping. It was 'This is your place and no matter what your training is, this what you will do.' People were very arrogant, and obviously for people who wanted to be doctors, who trained and wanted to be teachers, this [career path] was just cut off for them. When you are living with and trained and educated by these people who have such great depth and insight, and who were obliged daily to cope with discrimination and racism, and still lead a valuable life, and raised their children and achieved as best they could, you learn many lessons."

Westmoreland-Traoré says she also learned from watching how difficult it was for individuals to break into various professions. The problem was that the professions had to be integrated one at a time, never a collective decision by society to do away with the barriers. "So there is that influence on my life. It so happened as I was continuing my studies, I did meet with people from all over the world who were involved either in liberation struggles, or civil-rights struggles, or to defeat sexism, people of great mettle and leadership, who have made great sacrifices, and I also was able to work with some. These were people that weren't very easily discouraged. I believe that working as a professor brings you in contact with a lot of young people who obviously have an image of how they would like the world to be, and that is refreshing. You don't get onto a beaten track. So I think I would be dissatisfied, I won't be fulfilled basically just accepting the status quo."

The election did turn out as the polls predicted. And as promised, the first task by the new government was to close down the employment equity office. Juanita Westmoreland-Traoré was out of a job. A few months later, the new citizenship minister, Marilyn Mushinski, officially scrapped the legislation, opting for what she called a return to the merit principle in employment. "We do not feel that we should be in the business of telling the private sector how to restore the merit principle back in hiring practices." For many Blacks and minorities, with this act, mainstream Canada was once again closing the doors on integration and acceptance. They would have to remain on the outside looking in a bit longer, until Juanita Westmoreland-Traoré or a successor began the fight for equity all over.

* * *

Although it's early morning, Dudley Z. Laws looks tired and older than his 58 years. His body is lean, ramrod straight, his beard white and his head covered by the trademark black beret.

His office is sparsely furnished, files thrown around. Pictures of Bob Marley, Martin Luther King, Malcolm X and of a younger Dudley Laws hang on the walls. So does a poem Dudley composed and gave to Walter Sisulu, deputy leader of South Africa's African National Congress, at the University of Toronto in 1991.

Brave warriors of South Africa,
No man, no river, no mountain can stop you now,
You have created a mighty bastion,
Like tempered steel, it will never bow,
March on and create your African Nation.

This poet's task is to create a strong black community in Canada. This poet faces, at the grassroots level, many of the issues people like Chief Justice Julius Isaac and former employment equity commissioner Juanita Westmoreland-Traoré agonize over in a more abstract form. Dudley Laws and his supporters get to see what happens when the legal system and government fail to embrace Blacks, when there is no longer any confidence in their administration, no longer a dream of making it in Canada.

Just like the country's first black chief justice of the federal courts, Dudley is a disciple of black pride and self-help, a latter-day follower of Marcus Garvey, who like him was born in Jamaica. Dudley lives his philosophy every day, in his personal life and as head of the outspoken Black Action Defence Committee, a group that started as a watchdog for how the police and justice system treat Blacks, but which now has an impact on just about every facet of community life. This group is best noted for calling on the government to lay murder charges against police officers who, supposedly in the line of duty, shoot and kill Blacks.

To the white community, Dudley is the epitome of defiance, a so-called self-appointed leader of the Toronto black community, or so many white commentators claim. Throughout the criticism, Dudley remains as defiant as the name chosen for his organization. For this group is simply known as BAD-C, with the emphasis placed firmly on the first syllable. This is a group that has long given up on integrating Blacks into the wider society. Dudley Laws has risen to leadership level by steadfastly refusing to be co-opted by the mainstream.

"My phone was off a couple of days and I'll tell you, it was really a rest," he jokes. We are meeting early in the morning in Dudley's office. Since I entered the room at the back of the building, the phone hasn't stopped ringing. Already, a stack of telephone messages awaits Dudley's attention. "I'm feeling a bit tired but it's not too bad. Everything could be worse."

Is the system grinding him down mentally? I ask. Dudley has had several recent brushes with the Canadian and U.S. police. In a sting operation that involved the connivance of several law agencies in Canada and the United States, he was convicted of smuggling illegal immigrants into the United States, a charge that Dudley and his supporters claim was a police set-up. And he was arrested for wife battering, and still later, charged with having assaulted a woman about two decades earlier.

Just around this time, Dudley had opened his hydro bill to discover a message from someone promising to get him. It was signed by the Ku Klux Klan. The hydro company confirmed the letter was sent from its offices. A promised investigation by the company turned up nothing. The belief that Dudley is a marked man for the police was given some credence when a document was released during one of his trials showing Metro Toronto police had a list of so-called trouble-makers in the black community. On this list was Dudley Laws. Just as important, Dudley's supporters always wondered whether it was a coincidence that whenever the police were arresting Dudley, the news media were always on hand to snap belittling photographs of the man who unceasingly calls Canadian police the most racist in the world. So I want to know if all this pressure is distracting him.

"It's both physical and mental," he says. "It never stops. Every day there is something new, a new situation, a new case. And it's not just policing, it's all different levels, like housing, schools, people fired from hospitals and all that. It's the multiplicity of the problems the black community is experiencing at this time."

Any black person—simply by the colour of the skin—is a member of this group, whether or not he or she knows it. Members are expected to throw a few dollars the committee's way every now and then. As part of its self-help theory, BAD-C relies solely on members, financially. "Sometimes it can be hard to meet our expenses. That is taxing to me. It means pressure."

At times, the thought of leaving the struggle and taking care of himself and his young family, and starting to plan for financial security in retirement, is very inviting but, "It's hard to say no when you're being called upon every day by different people."

He is not optimistic about early retirement. "I see it getting worse [for Blacks], especially in the area of policing and employment."

For many Whites, Dudley Laws is an enigma, a self-appointed spokesman ready to ruin their beloved city and country. For many Blacks, he is the opposite. As he says in his poem on the South African struggle, he is to many Blacks a brave warrior selflessly challenging the Canadian society, leading the march for the creation of a strong, self-sufficient and respected black presence in this country.

"You have a lot of so-called black middle class who themselves have problems with policing, whose children have problems in the school system and still are afraid of coming up and saying, 'Look, the system is wrong, the system is bad. [They] are protecting their own employment or other interests.' I think you are not doing the community a service by doing that. I think we all have to speak out against injustice, whether it affects us personally or the community generally. I think we have that responsibility. Not only the black middle-class—but other black people who don't want to acknowledge the existence of racism, although they suffer from it every day."

* * *

To understand the accolades Dudley receives, people need to attend at least one BAD-C meeting to see how, and understand why, when all else and all others fail, the truly unfortunate members of the black community invariably turn to one man—Dudley Z. Laws.

Her voice choking, the woman pencilled onto the agenda as Alisha begins telling her story. "I need the support of BAD-C and the black community. I need them to turn out in the court to give support 'cause you know there's no justice in the courts for Blacks."

Alisha had arrived late for BAD-C's regular Wednesday meeting. Dudley is giving a speech across town at the Scarborough Campus of the University of Toronto and cannot attend the meeting. But even knowing that she might not achieve much in Dudley's absence, Alisha decides to push on. She needs help and she needs it desperately and quickly.

Alisha believes her only son was damaged in the womb when her doctor accidentally kept her on fertility pills three months after conception. When the child was about six years old, he developed very heavy nose bleeds, "as if his brains were coming though his nose," she says. Doctors told her privately this was a side effect from the fertility pills but, she says, conspired to keep her silent and to stop her son from getting treatment at various hospitals. Even the black media are part of the conspiracy, she claims, for they are refusing to expose her story. Now, she is fighting the dreaded Children's Aid Society, and evoking frightening images in the black community of these modern-day baby snatchers, in a custody battle. Children's Aid might be powerful, it might even like to take kids from their parents, but with the help of Dudley and BAD-C they will not get her son, she vows.

Several times, members of the group ask Alisha if she has a lawyer. While she doesn't give a forthright answer, she leaves the clear impression she has also lost confidence in lawyers and the courts. She is distrustful of all mainstream institutions. Only BAD-C can mobilize the help she needs, she argues. Only BAD-C can help, because when Dudley speaks, at least people listen and he gets attention.

"I'm not going to lose my son," she says defiantly. "How many of you are going to be there to support me in court? We need all the help we can get from BAD-C." Several volunteer, mainly out of solidarity, less so out of conviction. The chair of the meeting, sensing the dilemma, suggests the case should be examined privately. The meeting adjourns and the BAD-C leadership take Alisha into Dudley's office, awaiting his arrival and directions. Ultimately, Dudley will decide.

This scene is no different from the colonial Caribbean I know, a place that perhaps lives only in our imagination. But it is a place of strong leaders, militant people fronting the labour movement or outspoken groups; a place where you go to meet with an influential figure in the community to intercede on your behalf with powers that be. Dudley Laws is the old-fashioned type of Caribbean leader, from the era of pre-independence. Strong and determined, he is the right man to throw in the fray among groups with unequal power. Alisha, a single mother, unsure of the community she expects to help her, distrustful of the wider society holding her accountable by rules she doesn't understand, waits and waits for a strong messianic leader to throw off the imperial yoke. Her face shows all the anxiety of the single black mother feeling alone and up against forces she cannot confront and defeat on her own.

* * *

Alisha's case, and many others like hers, bring home one clear truth to many of us: despite how badly Blacks want to recreate the familiar, there is one reality we cannot escape. We are living in Canada and we are a minority. The question for the majority of us is how to make the transition and still remain true to our culture and spirituality.

The Caribbean communities we have established in Canada are old, based on a society that no longer even exists, and a model of life that is static. Ultimately, we must deal with the mainstream. Eventually, whether we are dealing with the police, the doctor, the media, the Children's Aid Society or the boss at work, we must come out of any cocoon that is our defensive shield and face up to this reality. And while some of us might try to limit the contact and reliance on the institutions in the wider society, we cannot do this forever.

Then there is this other dichotomy: most black immigrants did not come to Canada to live in a community that is cut off from the mainstream. To the contrary, how well we can integrate, how quickly we can be accepted as Canadian, how easily we can move between what we perceive to be Canadian and black communities are elements in our overall success. In a real sense, success is measured by the same benchmarks as those of the wider society. The wider society also sets the standards for us.

There are certain costs to transferring a lifestyle suited for one community into a society that operates according to different codes. Invariably, there will be problems from trying to deal with two different worlds, from deciding in which milieu to reveal the real face. So, it becomes a challenge for Caribbean and African-born people wanting to live according to the way they did back home and having to also keep an eye on the law enforcers, social agencies and the socializing efforts of the wider society. Problems can arise over such seemingly simple responsibilities as disciplining children. See any group of black parents together and notice how quickly the conversation turns to condemning the wider system for expecting black parents to use an alien form of discipline on their children. This is perhaps best illustrated in the question of corporal punishment. Many a black parent can swear that he or she was turned from a road of shame because of parental flogging back home. But floggings are not tolerated in Canada. (This is the country that charged a U.S. visitor for child abuse when he spanked his daughter in a public place.) Doctors, teachers and social workers are constantly on the look-out for signs of corporal punishment at home. And, of course, detection of the first welt can lead, ultimately, to a visit from the Children's Aid Society.

What we have here is cultural shock of the worst kind. It can be more than frustrating for the parents to face the taunt of some children promising to inform and bring the wrath of the country down on the family if the parent so much as raises a hand in the child's direction. Worse, such complaints, in the eyes of the parents, could lead to society taking the child away, or to the parent having no control over the child while the youth is still under the parent's roof. It could lead to a crisis like the one Alisha has with the Children's Aid Society. How do people resolve these dilemmas?

Obviously, these problems are symptomatic of the immigrant living one type of lifestyle but feeling measured according to the mores and standards of an adopted society. Take the courting relationships between men and women in the Caribbean, relationships that are not considered the norm in a country like Canada with its traditional emphasis on the nuclear family. As most historians and sociologists point out, the nuclear family is not the norm in the Caribbean. Neither does the relationship between a man and woman pretend to be one of equality. In the Caribbean, women are responsible for mothering and fathering the child, to administer the home, to plan for the future. It is not unusual for them to raise the children without the presence of the father, although members of the extended family are always on hand to help out. The father's role is primarily financial, and it might require the efforts of the courts to make sure the male keeps these commitments. The familiar society back home caters to the non-nuclear family, anticipating that the norm is for most children to be born out of wedlock and to be raised primarily by the mothers.

And there are specific roles for males and females in the wider community. In what is typical for the Caribbean, a study in 1985, for example, found that in Barbados males account for 84.5 percent of the top positions—jobs such as doctors, lawyers, church ministers, accountants, architects, police officers—leaving women the paltry remainder. This situation guarantees that the woman is even more dependent on the Caribbean male. However, the situation is virtually reversed in Canada. Although it is true that neither the black male nor female has much chance at the top employment positions, in Canada women still have better paying jobs than the men. A Caribbean man socialized to react to his wife or partner in one way is forced to make a radical adjustment in North America.

Other cultural traits obviously conflict with the Canadian norms. For example, it is usual for Caribbean people to marry when in their thirties, by which time they might have had several children and be involved in several relationships. Starting in their teens, they go through three types of sexual relationships. First, the man might visit the woman's home for extended courting that does not hold either one of them to a long-term commitment. Then, there is non-legal union, in which the man and woman live together in a common-law relationship. Ultimately, they might marry, but this happens only when the partners are fairly secure in life.

The branch of the norms of one society cannot be grafted onto the root of another. The average Black is likely to have to endure the worst of both worlds.

* * *

Ruth is 34 years old. She is tall and slim and speaks in whispers. A Caribbean immigrant, she is battling to stay afloat, to escape from the trappings of living the Caribbean way in Canada. This means holding down her government job, taking as many night courses as time permits in the hope of bettering herself through education, and taking care of a six-year-old son and four-year-old daughter. But it is caring for the son that is her toughest job. For as Ruth says, there are times when she feels like giving up, when raising a son without a father is just too much. As I speak to Ruth, she is almost in tears.

"It's very difficult [being a single parent] and a lot of times it prevents me from doing more things. Sometimes, too, I really feel that I can't do this because it is hard having the two kids. It's hard to attend evening meetings, workshops and whatever. But I don't have a choice. It's just something I have to do. I don't feel that I should have to give up, because I am raising two kids on my own. Sometimes I'm here [at work] and the day care would call, or the school would call, and I would have to leave. It's my first choice to look after my kids."

When we talked, Ruth had been a single parent for four years, having decided to leave her husband when she was still pregnant with their second child. To Ruth, her former husband exhibits all the bad traits of black men who do not live up to their responsibilities.

"I don't think they should be getting the kids and then disappearing. Raising kids should be a two-parent thing, but a lot of them don't see that it's really important, especially in my case. My ex-husband sees me as this person who doesn't really need his help, I can manage on my own. But I'm barely managing because it is difficult."

She has to rely on the courts to take automatic support deductions from his paycheque, even though, as she says, he has a good job. "If it wasn't for the courts, he probably wouldn't be paying support payments."

As a result, she says, her life is lonely and always pressured, with no mate to turn to for help. "I always have my kids. Sometimes I beg him to take them for a day just so I can have a break and he always has other things planned. So it gets to the point where I just don't bother [asking] any more."

Her biggest concern is for her son who is beginning to look for a male figure around the home. This is when she really misses the extended family in the Caribbean. "In the West Indies I think it's a lot different, because raising your kids there is like a community issue. But here in Canada it's so different, it's like you have your kid and you're on your own, because you don't have anybody else. Even if you have an extended family, they are too busy to help you out.

"Sometimes, I find it really tough because I don't work eight to four, or nine to five, and that's the daycare time. That means I would have to have somebody going to the daycare to pick up my kids and look after them until I get home. Sometimes it's tough, because I don't always have that extra money to pay out for child care, you know, considering that I pay daycare once a month and I only get paid once a month. Sometimes I do find it difficult that way. Sometimes there are workshops or educational courses that are being offered out of town, but I don't have anybody to look after my kids. It's really hard. There is no one you can actually depend on for help. And even if you have the money, it's difficult because you don't want just anybody looking after your kids. You don't know them. There are one or two people who look after them on a regular basis, and they might not be available."

Ruth also has another burden: she doesn't want anyone to think she is a welfare mother. So that even while help might be available to her, she shuns it. She is equally dismissive of those who would suggest that it might be better, certainly for her sanity, if she were to stay at home on welfare and look after her children.

"I would not think about that at all. I do not want to be at home on welfare. I was at home on welfare for two years when I was back in school. Of course, I wasn't happy because that's not what I wanted. I didn't have any self-esteem. I didn't want to meet any new people. I didn't want to go out, apart from going to school, because I was afraid people were going to ask, What do you do? I don't want to say I'm home on welfare because that's not me, really. I like to know I can get up in the morning, go to work and come home at night. Of course, a lot of people choose that lifestyle, but it just won't work for me."

The big problem for Ruth is how well she is preparing her son and daughter to participate fully in the wider Canadian society. She wants them to grow up ready to make something of their lives, to get the jobs and opportunities that she did not have. If this is a society in which jobs will be awarded on merit, she wants them to be qualified, perhaps even over-qualified. So she spends many sleepless nights wondering what more she can do, especially for her son.

"I'm afraid that I'm teaching them one way at home and they'll probably be taught differently in society and at school. I might say this is something we should value, this is important to us, but when they go to school or to daycare, they might find out that it shouldn't really be of value. So it scares me. I don't know what they hear or what they learn out there."

I ask her if she is trying to teach them to develop a strong work ethic for adulthood. "More or less. I'm teaching them to be a person, really, and not to think of the fact that you are black, and because you're black you're going to have problems growing up and in society. I remember one day my son coming home to me and saying, 'Mummy, my friend in daycare tells me I'm black and he doesn't like my colour.'

"I said, 'What did you say to him?'

"He said, 'I didn't say anything to him.'

"So I asked him what he could have said to his friend, and he said, 'I could have told him I love myself.'

"I said, 'Well, that's good. Next time you see your friend, you tell him you are black, you are beautiful and you love yourself. He shouldn't really have to tell you you're black. You don't need to be reminded, you know that. But it's important for you to be yourself, be positive in whatever you do. Be confident in yourself, go to school and study your lessons because it is important.'"

Ruth worries about what she is doing. For one thing, she is concerned that some friends might be right when they say she is pushing her son too hard, that she is putting too much pressure on him to excel academically, for he is only six years old.

"I'm always talking about my son. When he was in senior kindergarten, I realized he didn't know A from B and actually I panicked. His dad is not very educated and I panicked, 'cause I'm saying to myself, 'Oh my gosh, he probably has dyslexia,' which was really very stupid, he was only five then. I did hear of Higher Marks [an all-black private] school, but I wasn't sure if I wanted to send him there. In February, I sent him to Higher Marks and I started paying more attention to his school marks. He's doing very well. And he could only count up to 20.

"A lot of people said he's doing okay. Only two people have said he should be doing better. Everybody else is saying I'm pushing him. At home, I tell him he's not allowed to play at home. That's important for me. They are not supposed to play at home because they play at daycare five days a week. He goes to school half a day. So when they're at home, it's time to study their lessons or do something else."

If she is concerned she might be pushing him too hard, why doesn't she ease up, I ask. Is it because of a deep-seated fear that when her son becomes a man he will have to be so much better than his white competitors?

"Yes. This is the most important time for him to learn. People learn more in the first five years of their life, so I don't want his first five or six years to be wasted. Sometimes I'll see him there—it's like he's not doing anything, he's all spaced out—and I'll say, Close your book and get up now because I think you are tired. Especially on Saturday evenings, I do that a lot. He goes to school on Saturday. I do feel I am pushing him too much sometimes, but then sometimes I say, well, I'm doing it for his own good, and later on he'll appreciate it."

Ruth admits that she is simply grasping at straws, not sure of what she is doing, but hoping that her natural instincts are telling her what her children need to survive in this society.

"In a sense I'm scared of the unknown. I don't know what will happen, especially to him. Because sometimes he does get rebellious, not because he doesn't want to do his school work, but because his dad comes around occasionally. You see, things would be fine until the dad shows up. He'd show up and then things seem to be different. The things I was teaching them before he comes don't seem to matter any more. My son seems to be easily influenced and it scares me that way. Sometimes he would say, 'I don't have to do this because my daddy says I don't have to.' And I'll say, 'Well, your dad says that but this is what I'm asking you to do. I prefer you to do this.' It takes him a while to understand.

"So, their dad just breezes in and out of their lives. Then, they cry and get miserable. It's just hard to get them back. Sometimes he'd ask why his dad can't stay over, and I tell him he needs to understand his daddy is married to somebody else, he needs to be with her. Sometimes I feel they see me as the bad guy, especially when it comes to their daddy. It's frustrating sometimes because I feel I'm doing so much and then there are all these different forces."

* * *

At 31, Gregory is the type of black father Ruth is talking about. The father of an eight-year-old boy, he hardly ever sees his son, not because he doesn't want to, but because his poor financial situation makes it difficult. And like many other separated black fathers, Gregory argues that the mother of his child doesn't understand. She doesn't understand how tough it is for any man with self-esteem to be constantly unemployed, doesn't appreciate how shameful it is not to be a full provider, how tough it is just being a black male in this country.

The black males argue that North American and Canadian societies want it that way—employers see black females as less threatening than males, so they are more willing to hire them. And the men argue that black women are always capable of finding more and better jobs than men. Because they have jobs, they can bring home a bigger paycheque, especially if they work in institutions like hospitals, hotels and nursing homes.

All this economic clout makes black men feel useless. Many of them, like Gregory, remember the role played by black males in the Caribbean, primarily that of the bread-winner, of working outside the home and leaving the responsibility of rearing the children and the administration of the home to the women. But at the end of the week, there was always more than an equalization of power in the home. That was when a man was a man. That was when he handed over his paycheque for the next week's groceries, when he liquidated the debts owed to the village shopkeeper, when he provided the funds to fix up the house if it needed repairs.

In North America, the displaced Caribbean man finds that he does not even have the economic pull over the black woman. He sees the black woman as strong, intimidating and frightening, because without any economic clout he sees no reason for her having him in the home. More than that, he doesn't feel quite right in the home. Not when the females relentlessly push him to make a contribution.

This is the story some men will tell for giving up on relations with black women, for fleeing their responsibilities because they cannot cope, for feeling trapped, handcuffed by the expectations of a foreign culture, for feeling emasculated by a society that does not value the black male as highly as back home.

Gregory says that for several years he has been trying to land a steady job. First, he graduated from university with a degree in mechanical engineering, only to see the market for his skills collapse because of the recession and the devastating effects of free trade on the Canadian manufacturing sector. And he has another burden to carry—tens of thousands of dollars in debts accumulated as student loans. These problems make it difficult for him to become the father he says he wants to be, the kind of father he had hoped to become when he left Jamaica.

"I have a family," he says. "My mom. And I have a son. He doesn't live with me. He lives with his mother, out of the city."

Gregory says he tries to be a responsible dad. "I know what it takes to be a responsible father and I don't think I put in as much. It's not really my will. When they [mother and son] used to live in this city, I used to spend more than five hours or so during the week [with him]. On weekends, sometimes I would have him for the whole time. But they moved and it takes me three hours to drive one way for a visit. So I try to visit as much [as I can], there is a phone call every week, and I try financially, but that's the best I can do right now. Circumstances."

For Gregory this is not an ideal situation. "To me, my idea of having children, I want to be directly involved with their lives, ongoing from there, because when they reach teenage [years] it's hard. My grandmother always says, Try to bend the tree from when it's young. Right now, I'm losing in that department."

And how does he feel when his son looks for a male role model in the home? "He's too young to ask for it. But I can see that he needs it, and whether or not there is an indication, I know every young child, daughter or son, needs the female role and they need the male role. I grew up in a single-parent family. My mom was my mom and dad. She did the best she could. However, just the idea of growing up with a dad, it gives you a certain amount of responsibility. You see your dad get up every day, doing what he needs to do to make a living, it becomes part of your being, something to aspire to, and all of that. I don't know. Look, that is one of the biggest issues with us as a people right now, the issue of parenting. I know that in Jamaica—I came here when I was 17—growing up in Jamaica, people believed that as long as they can provide for their child materially, that's it. It doesn't stop there. There is so much to know. You never stop learning how to be a parent. For some people, they don't understand that, don't go to the parent-teacher meetings, they don't see the little silly problems of their children as important. You have to make your child believe that the little nonsense they are talking about is very important to you whether it is or not."

But Gregory fears he cannot give his son the kind of livelihood he would like. If he can't, he believes that he may as well stay away. "I think right now he has a better standard of living than I do. In terms of financial, that's okay. His mom, she has a pretty good job. Right now, I'm unemployed. However, I don't know about the future because, you know, your parents having a good standard of living doesn't really dictate the kind of future [you will have]. Right now I am thinking entrepreneurially, I'm thinking of developing something. I'm in the enterprise course sponsored by the YMCA. They teach you how to start your own business. I've been at this on and off. I took some courses on the side for international trade and all that stuff."

When Gregory says that the success or social status of the parent is meaningless for the progeny, he is tapping into our common perception that our community is perhaps the only one in which the next generation might be worse off than the current one. Alarmingly, Blacks appear incapable of replicating success. The sons and daughters of black doctors, lawyers and politicians are just as likely to drop out of school and to be harassed by the police as are the offspring of domestic servants. For many young Blacks, this situation is not acceptable. They are not buying into the dream that hard work and sacrifice will help them to gain acceptance and economic independence. So that ultimately the decision of whether we choose to seek integration quietly, or defiantly try to stay apart, will have meaning only in terms of the next generation. Every community worries about the next generation, what it is we're leaving, what standards we are passing on. And for many Blacks, it is frightening when they look out into the next millennium, into the next generation.

CHAPTER 5

LESSONS FOR THE LEARNING

In black gatherings across Toronto one summer, Aretha Franklin's song "R-E-S-P-E-C-T" was as popular, if not more so, than it was in the sixties. Black youths took to it the same way they celebrated other popular reggae songs that underscored their notions of self-respect and their differences from the wider Canadian community. The renewed popularity of this song was happening at the same time that we were experiencing a surge in violence: frequent shootings at the all-night clubs; murders on the dance floors at house parties and in the parking lots of black restaurants; shootings by Blacks in white mainstream restaurants. Could this be the sign of a community losing its way, of a community turning on itself with deadly results?

Chatty, chatty,
Can't live in peace
Everything I do,
Yuh run to police.

In its heyday, few songs were as popular as this ditty in which the singer admonished tattletales informing on such things as gun battles, illicit love affairs and illegal activities. Songs like this are almost never heard on mainstream Canadian radio. Yet, they touch the pulse of the youth movement in the black community. They give insight into how a crowd of black youths can witness someone drawing a gun and killing another over a piece of jewellery, and why nobody comes forward to help the investigation. It explains why a hundred customers at a black nightclub will remain silent when the police ask for witnesses to a murderous gun battle. Underlying this silence is a deep distrust of the police.

I see this questioning attitude among Blacks armed with their pagers and cellular phones. They are openly in the employ of what they call "the illegal business." The mere fact they no longer refer to their work as selling drugs but, euphemistically, as the illegal business indicates how much they really think their livelihood is no less important than anybody else's, only that a hypocritical society brands their retailing of the business illegal. But for them, this is the same dominating society that sells Blacks the drugs, thereby exposing Blacks to persecution from the police and prosecution from the courts, while allowing the brains behind the business to escape untouched by the law.

"We got to get control of the distribution in our community," a university student says to me in all seriousness. "We do not have the means to bring the drugs into our community, so if the white man is going to bring it and sell it to us, we may as well get control and make some money, too."

These words seem straight out of festering ghettoes in New York and Los Angeles via popular movies like *New Jack City* and *Boyz N the Hood*. Yet, I hear these words repeated so often—by men and women of all ages, but most frequently by people younger than I—that they must flow from a solid conviction that drugs are a problem in the black community only because they're profitable for Whites, because the lives of Blacks are not as valued and respected. So, the argument goes, there is a different morality to doing business in the black community.

One of the most frightening things about this conversation is that I am talking to one of tomorrow's black intellectuals, not to one of the 60 percent of black youths from the Toronto area who don't finish high school. This is how he feels our community will earn *respect*, something he says that will happen only when Whites realize that Blacks are serious about controlling the distribution of the illegal business, when Blacks show they can flout the law with impunity like anyone else; when Blacks show they are willing to get up off their knees and to achieve something, anything.

"When they see us with the pagers and cellphones, they freak out," he says. "That is teaching them to respect us." It is even worse when they know that the drug dealers are also armed. This, he says, is the first step toward asserting ourselves as a community. And this assertion starts with economic clout and independence, which in turn depends on Blacks spending their money in their community and setting up an economy of their own.

This difference in perception in how the white and black segments of Canadian society view the police is always boiling below the surface. One of the times it blew up into an open controversy was in 1994. It started when police answered a call to investigate a shooting at a Toronto booze can. When they arrived, some patrons were dead and the scene was relatively deserted. The police put out a call for witnesses, even offering protection to potential informers. Nobody came forward. This made some police spokespeople angry, wondering what the police have to do to get our people to co-operate.

About this time a reporter approached the only black member on the Metro Toronto Police Service Board—the civilian administrative body of the police—and asked why there was this reticence by Blacks to come forward. Arnold Minors, the outspoken black member, sparked a controversy by speaking the truth, by talking about a strongly held perception in the black community of a large and growing gulf between Blacks and the police. There is a thousand-year history of seeing police as an occupying army, Minors said. Minors might have been better advised to quote the lyrics of some popular songs and underground poems in the black community—it would have spared him the ensuing anguish. For although he was echoing the sentiments of the lyrics the black youths had danced and romanced to in the same clubs, he was misunderstood and pilloried in the media and government circles. Facetiously, the government of the day, on its last legs and wheeling from attacks for having appointed him in the first place, called an inquiry into Minors' conduct. The investigation subsequently cleared him of any wrongdoing. But for a while, Minors' job was on the line. One newspaper even trumpeted a front-page headline and story that Minors would be fired for his statement. Still, few people understood the point Minors was making. Instead of his answer helping to ease the tensions between Blacks and the police, instead of highlighting the polarity between these two groups, the statement was taken as effrontery to the upholders of the law, to the so-called Canadian way. It was used to aggravate the situation between the two groups.

But there could be no denying the truth in Minors' words, a reality that was perhaps best accentuated by the difference in reaction to the statement by the black and white communities. Few in the black community saw the "occupying army" statement as alarming. Many people had called the police such names whether they were discussing the issue in an illegal bar or at the dinner table. "Take care when you go out there, you hear. 'Cause you know them police, how them like to stop black people and thing." This is a common sentiment, shared by drinking buddies at a bar and a black mother admonishing a young black male to be careful. Seldom would they view the police as a friend.

But mainstream and powerful elements in the Canadian society are not attuned to, or ready to accept, this way of thinking. They do not readily see the colonial relationship in which this society holds most Blacks. Black culture is still exotic, the type to watch from a distance, to taste fleetingly in the name of a benign multiculturalism, not the brand of multiculturalism that shares power, not the multiculturalism that breaks down colonial walls. Imagine the reaction to Minors' statement from a city familiar with the songs and the defiant lyrics of the black population. How, then, would they react to the lyrics young black men and women were spouting in their poetry readings around the city?

Neither justice nor just us
Cuz their hour of power is sour
But it'll soon be over
As soon as you an' me yell: "Black Power!"
An mean it and back it up and bring it about
By any means necessary!

This is from a poem by Minister Makit Faust, then a 24-year-old student from Edmonton whose poetry deals with such themes as police brutality and black beauty. Oni, a 21-year-old Ottawa student of Haitian parentage, hit on the same themes:

Dead! A brother is dead from a pig's lead
A child needs to be fed families left in red
He ain't done no wrong to nobody
What about his family?
Morality! Hah! Most police ain't got none.

Or, we don't always share the same morality. These are the voices of a marginalized people, bubbling with talent but feeling ignored by the mainstream. Many of them do not consider their writings to be part of a Canadian tradition that reveres a Margaret Atwood, Robertson Davies or Alice Munro. Rather, they lay claim to a proud tradition that produced international names like Derek Walcott and Bob Marley, some of the voices of the extended Caribbean society—a community that nurtures them in Canada.

* * *

Her eyes red from lack of sleep, she walked into the office and politely introduced herself. "I am Cheryl's mother," she said in her Jamaican accent. "And I would like to talk to you about the mark on her assignment."

I had seen this confrontation coming for several minutes and had delayed it for as long as I could by drawing out conversations I was having with my other students. I had seen Cheryl and this other woman arrive. They waited patiently in the hallway outside the office, the bespectacled older woman with her whitish fall coat and a black handbag and hat. Cheryl had beautiful braids down to her shoulders and was dressed, as usual, even more provocatively than most of her fellow female students, and that is saying a lot. Inevitably, the flow of students ahead of Ms. Bain and her daughter petered out, and I was facing the unavoidable.

"Cheryl's been very upset and couldn't sleep because she believes she deserves a better mark," Ms. Bain explained. "I told her there are always two sides to a story, and I want to hear your side, too."

Talking about Cheryl is absolutely the last thing I want to do, I thought to myself as I offered Ms. Bain and her daughter two chairs. I sat behind my desk.

Some meeting this will be, I thought, as we got comfortable; three black people who are probably going to end up screaming at one another and making fools of ourselves in this white-run institution. In my mind's eye, I could see the looks on the faces of staff walking by the office. I could hear their snickers, and that was not even taking into consideration the students within earshot waiting their turn in the hallway for a chat with me. And all this because of one of these black students who we always see hanging out aimlessly. All because of a bad attitude.

For me, this meeting had all the potential of a teacher's nightmare. But it would be more than that; it would force me to question many things I take for granted, particularly the role of black teachers. This meeting would bring home to me the dangers of what can happen when we lose sight of the individual because of our expectations and prejudices, even when our biases are well intentioned. When we, too, fall prey to the prevailing stereotypes.

My last meeting with Cheryl was a disaster. She wanted to get back an assignment that I had marked and had not yet returned. Now, not only did she hand in the assignment late, but she did not even have the courtesy to turn up in class on the day I had promised to return the assignments, on the day I had set aside to meet one-on-one with students to discuss their work and grades. Somehow Cheryl managed to miss that crucial class, as she had missed other important sessions throughout the semester.

From early on, there was no doubt that Cheryl and I were on a collision course. From the very first class, she had a way of getting under my skin. It might have been the way she strolled into class long after the lecture started, in my eyes undoubtedly to get attention, but succeeding only in disrupting the class. And that was *when* she showed up. Many times, she did not even bother attending. And most times when she did, she sat in the back by the bank of computers and whiled away the time playing solitaire, or completing some overdue assignment for another instructor.

So it might have been her attitude that turned me off from the outset. Or, it might have been the fact that she is black and I expected more and better of her. I expected that, being black, she would not simply presume that I would pass her just because we had the same colour of skin. To the contrary, I demanded more than just coasting if college life was supposed to be preparing her for the realities of life outside the classroom. Students like Cheryl should start their preparation for the wider society by understanding the double burden of being black, just as people like Chief Justice Isaac, Westmoreland-Traoré and Dudley Laws recognized this burden and made their choices.

When she came to see me recently, hours after she should have been in class like the other students, I wasn't in much of a mood to meet with her. Feeling that she was not even attempting to apply herself fully, far less showing any real commitment and zeal for the course, I proceeded to give her short shrift in our curt discussion. Needless to say, this pissed her off royally, just as I had been all semester, just as I wanted to send her a message that in life if you are lucky, you get back what you put in, and if you are black, your return is usually much less than your deposit. I would demonstrate to her the reality of this burden of being black, what every mother and father is supposed to instil in black children. There would be no coddling on my part. This would be a good dose of tough love, from one Black to another. I would play it straight and send her the signal that the world does not revolve around her. Too many black youths had this attitude, I thought, and this was why there were so many problems with their subculture. Too many of them believe everyone has to get in line to suit their agenda, to be on hand for them but only according to their timetable and wishes. Bad vibes, I thought.

When she showed up in the office for the first time, I was talking to another black female student named Dorene. Dorene was older, dressed more conservatively, and perhaps missed even more classes than Cheryl. Even though she was a poorer student academically than Cheryl, I had a better rapport with her. I felt she had a positive attitude, an outlook tempered by having felt the sting of life in a hostile country, from paying the price for having made one or two mistakes but was now willing to make amends; from being too busy just to waste time fruitlessly hanging out in groups. She was too busy, perhaps even too hard-pressed by the realities of life, to waste time and opportunity.

I didn't feel that Dorene was simply flaunting her good looks to get by, but that she was hampered by various circumstances that appeared to be getting in her way of fulfilling her ambition to become a television show host. Neither did I get the impression that being dressed in the latest fashions was that crucial for her. There were other important things, especially for a student on a fixed budget. For one thing, Dorene was a mature student, and each time she left a message that she had to miss class because her daughter was ill or a baby-sitting problem had come up, I was understanding. Attitude was everything. Dorene, despite some tough cards, was at least trying to play by the rules. Unlike Cheryl, she at least offered an excuse for missing class. I was willing to give her as much time as she wanted to complete her assignments and for discussion outside the classroom, even if on that day it meant making Cheryl wait a bit longer for her turn.

Cheryl, on the other hand, I thought, simply accepted that her good looks would sail her through life. I, for one, was determined not to fall into that trap. Also, as a black teacher, I felt that the white students in the class might very well be watching to see if I was more lenient to black students, although I never saw any evidence of this thinking. Yet, this suspicion was always nagging at the back of my mind, especially after the horrible experience of one of my friends at Ryerson Polytechnic University in Toronto, a man with whom I have had several conversations about black students and teachers in the Canadian educational system. He had taken a more interventionist approach to helping black students. He championed their concerns in the university's administration and ended up badly burnt. He was out of work at a time of drastic cutbacks in the educational system, and many of his fellow black teachers and professors believe he lost his job for standing up for black students.

I was wary of this happening to me. What added credence to this feeling—although it was said in absence of any real evidence—was a statement by Dorene how some of her classmates found me intimidating and unapproachable. "You just freak them out," Dorene said as we lapsed into our Caribbean vernacular, the sweet rhythms of her St. Lucian accent serenading and cautioning me, " 'cause none of them never had a black teacher before. And to have you, a black man, teaching them writing, it's like wow, man!"

This statement was confirmation of my suspicions that I had to be extremely careful and play everything straight and by the book. From time to time, I would have this suspicion reinforced in talks with other black teachers at various educational institutions in Ontario and Quebec, all of whom would vow not to take any chances in the classroom. There is always the fear that you could suffer from a slip or from some unintended slight to a student, perhaps the same fear that Juanita Westmoreland-Traoré recognized when she talked of being so circumspect in everything she does, of feeling that nothing should cause her to fail. Indeed, very often, we had discussed whether this mentality did not force us to be too unrelenting, to be too careful in appearance and action. Is this why we build up a barrier between us and the students we consider potential trouble-makers? Could this be why some white teachers keep their distance with black students—because of the fear of trouble and the worry over a charge of racism?

For me, Cheryl and a few black students like her would be my test. I would be as stringent and demanding with Cheryl as I would be with any student. And if Cheryl wouldn't put out her time and effort to see me during regular class hours, why should I set aside time for her? So, as I continued talking to Dorene, the two of us laughing and sharing stories, I noticed Cheryl standing and steaming, impatiently rocking on her feet, her face hard-set and her hands folded across her chest.

Finally, Dorene and I finished our conversation and I turned to Cheryl. A sudden frost descended on the office.

"I am here for my assignment," she said.

"Of course, you know that I not only handed back the assignments this morning but that I sat with every student who was there and individually talked about his or her story," I said, throwing the first punch in what I expected to be a brawl. By now, I had been transformed into a different person from the one who was talking with Dorene, from the concerned instructor and experienced journalist and writer who was encouraging her to be aggressive when going after job interviews. Dorene devoted much of her spare time to volunteer at a cable television station in Toronto; although she got lots of experience, there was no pay—something that she needed badly. I was always encouraging her to use this experience to go after jobs in the mainstream media.

With Cheryl, I would pull down the mask, I decided. I would be cold, clinical. By puffing out my chest, I hoped to become even more intimidating, putting distance between the two of us. Cheryl wouldn't get away with thinking that some talk of black solidarity would suffice. I would demand that she put out her best and ensure that she would not get a mark more, or a mark less, than any other student handing in similar quality work. As for her attitude, well, it was a good thing I couldn't find a way to penalize her, otherwise her mark might have been much lower.

Cheryl took her paper and quickly flipped to the last page for her mark: 19 out of 30. "Is this the best mark you can give me?" she shot at me, the anger in her voice obviously matching my sarcasm. "I want you to know that I worked darned hard on this assignment and this mark isn't good enough. And there are no comments on this paper."

"You might recall that I had set aside the entire class this morning to talk with students and to give them comments and feedback," I repeated, my voice even colder and deeper. "Now, would you like to sit and talk about it?" I asked, offering her a chair, going through the expected ritual of appearing to be open and sympathetic, but letting her know that I was doing her a favour by meeting with her during my unpaid time. She sat down and I took the paper from her.

Cheryl had written a story about a woman she thought to be exceptional and strong. This woman, a hard worker, continued to go after the dream that brought her from Jamaica to Canada, intent on being an in-house role model for her children. One indication of how exceptional she was, Cheryl had written, was the fact that at the age of 42, she had returned to school part-time. This was in addition to her full-time job as a nursing assistant and raising a family. She had enrolled in the nursing program at Humber College, hoping to eventually reach her life goal of becoming a registered nurse. This, Cheryl had argued, was part of a trend by mature people to return to school at a time when they might start to believe that they have achieved very nearly as much as they could in life. At a time when they might have their own children at college or university with them. Such dedication should be an example to younger people who might be taking their education too lightly, Cheryl had written. This exceptional woman was Margaret, and she was Cheryl's role model. More important, she was Cheryl's mother.

Like many students, Cheryl's writing had some flaws. She had difficulty switching writing styles from what we call hard news to soft news or features. In hard news, the emphasis is simply on providing the news—the latest information—as quickly and as unambiguously as possible. In news reporting, there is no room for drama, suspense and lengthy argument, and definitely no room for opinion. Generally, for example, nobody tells a good murder mystery by disclosing the solution in the first paragraph. Hard news is presented every hour of the day on radio and television and on the front pages of daily newspapers.

Feature writing is different. It presupposes that the reader has time, might be somewhat familiar with a specific news item, and needs analysis and background information about the development. So there isn't the same urgency of just delivering the news and all the salient points before the reader moves on. Features allow for a more natural or traditional way of telling stories and all that this entails. This means that, structurally, a feature must, for example, have a beginning, a middle and an ending. It must have a central theme, and even a few minor ones, and the feature must show authority and expertise on the part of the writer. Here is a chance for the writer to show his or her prowess with words, to argue convincingly through the marshalling of facts, information and opinion.

Many students, in their early days, tend to become fixated on one of the two styles. If they are good at writing hard news, they might have a problem switching to feature writing and vice versa. Cheryl's assignment showed she was really trying to write a feature using the hard-news model, but ending up with what was simply an elongated story of questionable news value and judgement. In essence, it was a fawning interview piece about her mother.

"Well, let's start with the introduction," I said to Cheryl. "First of all, you ..."

Within minutes, Cheryl and I were screaming at each other. I felt she didn't have a clue as to what I was trying to explain. She appeared totally unfamiliar with any of the key phrases and concepts I had used in the class, the very points I had announced to the students that I would be looking for in their assignments and evaluating accordingly. I felt that while she might be proud of her mother, she needed to do much more research if she wanted to write a better story about mature students returning to school. It would take more than interviewing one person to adequately tell this story and to talk authoritatively about the trends forming the basis of her article.

She felt that I didn't have a clue about the hard work she had put into the assignment. I was the only instructor making her life miserable because she was doing exceptionally well in every course but mine. She had no intention of accepting my mark. Then, she threw her biggest punch. She had noticed, Cheryl said haughtily, that I had no time for the black students in my class, especially for her and her buddy Ray, two of the four Blacks in that class.

This was the equivalent of throwing out the Duchess of Queensberry Rules. This was a low blow: to accuse a black teacher of insensitivity toward black students. That is something white teachers might do, and get away with, but not Blacks, not people who share the same experience, sensitivities and obvious commitment to the advancement of the race.

Somehow, I had expected a variation of this accusation: after all, this was the reason for her lax attitude, I thought. If I had gone along with a nod here, a wink there and the flicking of her long braids, I had expected that she would have taken another tack to make the same point. I had played the argument in my head. She simply expected me, supposedly a sensitive black instructor, to be aware of how tough it is to be a black student in a white institution, and to set lower standards for her. This is what I expected: a compliant acquiescence, not striking out angrily. She would want a double standard. And not only she, but her friend Ray. Her buddy had all of Cheryl's bad habits and, in fact, I could not recall the last time I saw him in class. Once, he showed up midway in the lecture, sat at the computer, proceeded to have a running conversation with his neighbours, while banging so loudly on the computer keyboard that I could hear him across the room. If you must be that disruptive, I had said to him, maybe you should leave the classroom. That encounter had obviously embarrassed Ray and set the tone for the rest of the session.

In the incident Cheryl was talking about, the two of them had handed me an assignment—it was already a week late—at the end of the class—technically making it two weeks late—and minutes before I was to start another class. I took their assignments and brusquely told them that I could not talk to them at that moment—my attitude was to make them understand that I could not accept why of the 30-odd students in the class, they always had to be the last to hand in assignments. Why do I have to keep impressing on them that punctuality is valuable?

Even as we talked about her marks, I was also looking forward to receiving Ray's assignment, which was even longer overdue than Cheryl's. I wanted to see how he could possibly write anything worthwhile after missing so many classes. Yes, Cheryl was dead right. I had no time for students who were not willing to put out the effort. Not for Cheryl or for her good friend Ray, who, as I found out, still owed assignments to one instructor from a year ago. This instructor had been quite forgiving when we discussed the matter, saying in passing that Ray is such a sweet and nice guy, if only he would buckle down and do the work required of him.

How Ray could hope to graduate without completing his assignments, I had no idea. How he could expect to get a job as a journalist in a very competitive field without graduating, or without having someone who can honestly vouch for his work habits and his ability to perform under pressure, was a puzzle to me. For one thing is important in the profession they were choosing: in the real world, journalists must produce the story or commentary by the set deadline. They just have to. No, the colour of our skin had nothing to do with it. I was just clinically demanding all those things the college's academic rules say we should demand in assessing the work of students. Or so I thought.

"Well," I said, still trying to recover from her frontal attack in place of the expected quiet whimpering, "if you are unhappy with my mark, why not find another instructor and see if he or she will mark it?"

"I know what I'll do. I am paying for this course," she shouted and with that she headed next door for the office of the co-ordinator of the journalism program. The end of that problem, I thought. Now I can get back to doing other things.

Now, first thing this morning, Cheryl was back, looking just as angry. And with her was her mother, this exceptional woman. The last thing I wanted on this Friday morning was to get into an argument with two angry black women.

From our first exchange, it appeared that my worst nightmare was happening. Ms. Bain wanted to discuss Cheryl's marks and how it was possible that I could return an assignment to her devoid of written comments. "How would she know how to do better?" she asked.

"Ms. Bain," I said, "I appreciate your concern but I have to tell you that I cannot discuss Cheryl's work with you. I am prevented by the provincial privacy act from having such a discussion."

This would be my dodge, and hopefully it would bring a speedy end to this matter. After all, I said, the college required us to abide by the law of the land and, I offered, if Ms. Bain were to call the registrar's office and request information about Cheryl, she would get the same answer.

To be truthful, I was surprised that Ms. Bain had shown up, not only because of Cheryl's age (she was a mature student), but because one of the knocks against black and immigrant parents was that they do not take the time to visit those who teach their children. I have attended countless community events where speaker after speaker has tried to motivate black parents to pay greater attention to what is happening to their children in school, to attend parent-teacher functions, curriculum nights and to pick up the phone and call to inquire about what is happening at school. Usually, the answer comes back that the black parent is too busy; perhaps he or she is working two or three jobs; the parents might be working shifts; or, as many educators and social activists believe, the parents might just be intimidated by the school and the institutions of a culture they don't fully understand. Ms. Bain was obviously not the norm, or, dare I say, the stereotypical black parent. She had worked overnight at her job at a nearby home for the elderly and, even though she said she was tired and her eyes were burning, she had decided to stop by to find out what was upsetting her daughter.

All of which I appreciated, I told her, but the law is the law and I couldn't do anything about it.

"But I am her mother," Ms. Bain pleaded. "And she is here with me. What am I going to do? Run out and tell people that you gave me the information?"

"I am sorry, Ms. Bain, but I can't discuss Cheryl's work with you."

At this point, it all boiled over. "Well, imagine this," Ms. Bain exploded. "I work all night and then I decide to come to talk to you, to find out what is happening to my daughter and this is the answer you give me. And to think you are a black man, that you would know better. Do you have children? Would you prefer that Cheryl be out on the street with a big belly or pushing a stroller instead of coming to school and trying to make something of herself? And you are a black teacher, who should be encouraging her."

By this time, Cheryl had once again fled into the office of the co-ordinator, who had now joined the meeting and was trying valiantly to lower the volume. This gave me a chance to take a closer look at Ms. Bain. And at that moment, I felt I had met her before. I felt that she was a creation of my imagination. Ms Bain was no different from a character in my novel *Sleep On, Beloved*. In the novel, I describe a scene between Ona Morgan, black handbag and all, and the principal of her daughter's school, with Ona squeezing the meeting into her lunch hour. This scene seemed too real and familiar. The only difference was that in my novel the unsympathetic principal was white. And even without her knowing, I heard in Ms. Bain's voice the words I had given to Ona Morgan to spout at the representative of the white establishment, to question whether life would have been any easier for her daughter if she had black teachers, to question the marks awarded her daughter, to protest the administrator's cavalier manner over holding her daughter's future in his hands while hiding behind seemingly impenetrable rules and regulations.

Ms. Bain, true to her daughter's description of her being a formidable woman, had struck me where it hurts. She was putting to the test something that I have argued extensively in newspaper columns and on radio and television: that black students need black teachers to inspire them and to be understanding. Now, here she was throwing back my assertions in my face. But she was also doing something else. She was making me question something that I occasionally discussed with other black teachers and professors: Do we tend to grade our black students tougher than white students; are we less tolerant and forgiving of black students because they are ... well, simply black like us? Are we ashamed for the race when a student doesn't live up to expectations? And if we do, are we caught in some time warp that faced black educators generations ago, but from which the presence of more of us in the classroom and so many successful black students still cannot free us?

Confrontating Ms. Bain and Cheryl, I had no answers. Indeed, my defence of hiding behind the privacy act was stripped away when the co-ordinator said that, well, yes, there is the question of privacy, but that she thought I was interpreting the strictures too harshly. She was sure that we could discuss the matter and resolve it amicably.

At this point I relented a tiny bit, but I was still leery of running afoul of the rules. I remembered my friend Winston. He had been a professor without tenure in the Geography Department when some black students approached him. They were feeling uncomfortable about another professor who they claimed spent a great deal of his time criticizing affirmative action and employment equity. They claimed that this professor had argued that affirmative action and employment equity were quota systems and that only black and minority, female and handicapped students should bother applying for jobs. Able-bodied white males were being discriminated against, he argued. The students said they felt uncomfortable because of the excessive discussion of this issue and the fact that the professor obviously had a closed mind on the matter. They asked Winston to raise the matter at an interdepartmental meeting. As it turned out, a member of the student body was attending the meeting when Winston raised the issue. For this he was found to be in breach of a technicality—that one professor should not criticize another in front of a student. He would have to be disciplined. The matter went to the highest levels in the university and to arbitration by the union. About that time, the Geography Department announced that, because of budgetary restraints, it would have to eliminate some courses. Naturally, the courses Winston taught were cut. When he applied to teach other courses that were available in the department, he was turned down. It is for reasons like these that black teachers do not take chances. Nobody knows when a technicality will arise.

"And I would think that as a black man you can teach Cheryl so much," Ms. Bain said. "If black people like you are not helping, then who will?"

Ms. Bain had not only inflicted a wound, but was digging it deeper with every word. I would not accept this load of having to carry a race on my back, I said, and besides, I have always spoken out for black causes. But I was in retreat, out in the open.

"Yes, mother," Cheryl said. "As I told you, I think I can learn so much from him, but he doesn't have any time for people like me or Ray."

"Why?" Ms. Bain asked.

At this point, the co-ordinator decided that perhaps I should take another look at the assignment as a compromise. She offered to shift Cheryl to another class in the second semester so she wouldn't have to deal with me. But Ms. Bain would not have it. As a black teacher, I should be more understanding, she insisted. At this point, I was ready to capitulate and to come out from behind the privacy act. The co-ordinator took Cheryl into her office and Ms. Bain and I agreed to stop shouting at each other and began to talk.

But even as we talked, I was still trying to wrestle with several problems that this case highlighted. Was I being too harsh on Cheryl because I didn't like the way she dressed and felt that, stereotypically, she was more interested in flaunting her good looks than in doing the necessary school work? I didn't feel I was, for there were other black students who were applying themselves and were scoring high marks. Indeed, there was one third-year black student I had taken to nagging on a weekly basis in the hope of motivating her to believe in herself, to apply for jobs, to apply her extensive knowledge about sports on radio or television. So far, I was not having much success with this student, who suffered badly from a lack of confidence. But I still had high hopes for her and would tell her what I thought, to the point where we had started joking about my nagging. Still, with Ms. Bain's admonition ringing in my ears, the doubts remained.

Another question was whether, indeed, the black students I met in my classes were on par academically with white students. This was really the raw nerve. In my experience at both Humber College and Ryerson University, I felt that the weakest students in my classes were black. That's not to say all black students were weak—many of them were top-notch. But the weak students that remain in my mind, the ones that I felt got by with a mere pass, were black. Now, this creates a few other problems for me. Could it be that I remember these students because they are black and I tend to be more dismissive of the weak white students? One member of Humber's faculty suggested this might very well be the case, because she could recall weak students of all races. If she was right, why do I single out black students? Could I indeed be afraid of falling into the trap of accepting a common stereotype that black students tend to be poor academically?

When anyone makes such a suggestion to me I am usually quick to jump down his or her throat. But could this quick defence mask an inner uncertainty? Whenever I have had to deal with this issue publicly, I have always argued that black or white should make no difference. Indeed, a short while after the meeting with Cheryl and her mother, I was on a talk show on a Toronto radio station discussing racism and its effects. One caller suggested that Blacks are generally weak academically because they find it cool to be failures at school. He trotted out the same old argument that black students create peer pressure to force a stream of failures. According to this argument, if a black student scores well in school, he or she is considered a nerd by other black students, or worse, is said to be selling out by buying into the white establishment.

I would have none of this argument, I told the caller. Even if I accepted his premise that some black students do not try as hard as they could, this might be more of a case of the school, and society as a whole not motivating them by rewarding black students for being successful. Where are the jobs to reward black students for doing well in school? I asked, pointing out that unemployment among black youths has traditionally been very much higher than for the general population. For indeed, the schools do not present these students with positive images and show them the way to success. And as I made this argument, I could hear Ms. Bain taking me to task. Could I have bought into the stereotype of black students, and was therefore using Cheryl and her friend Ray as test cases, when in fact I should see them as only two black students out of many in all of my classes, all others applying themselves, attending classes and doing well.

The questions go much deeper for me. Recently, educators in the black community have been pushing the idea of what is called Black-focused school. Over time, my opinions have swayed either for or against Black-focused schools, depending on how optimistic I am about race relations in this country and on the prevailing definition of what a Black-focused school is. When the idea was first coming into vogue, I had written a column in *The Globe and Mail* criticizing Black-focused schools as a backward move, as an attempt at segregation, and arguing that all segregated schools are inherently inferior.

I felt that Black-focused schools would not prepare students for the real world of living in a multicultural society and that, just as important, setting up such schools was putting too much of an onus on Blacks to adjust, rather than forcing society to make room for us in the schools, in the curriculum, in the teaching fraternity. Black-focused schools would lead to ghettoism, I argued, and in any case, why should taxpayers want to set up segregated schools?

The Globe article did not make too many friends for me in the black community. I received calls from acquaintances in the United States, one of whom wondered what madness I was writing. He said he had been talking to another friend in Toronto about what I had written and thought it necessary to call me from New York for a little chat, albeit well intentioned. He asked if I was aware that some African-Americans would not be caught dead at any other college than one of the traditional black universities. How would I account for the success of such places as Howard and Moorehouse universities, and a host of other black schools and universities he reamed off to me? Students learn best in situations where they are comfortable, he argued.

And even the kindest of critics argued that all I was doing was providing comfort to the enemy by joining them in attacking a concept that was not yet fully formed, but which was just one of many suggestions by the black community to come to terms with a staggering drop-out rate for black children in high school. Typically, in the Toronto area, 60 percent of black students do not graduate from high school. This is about three times the average for the general population. The drop-out rate for black males is even higher, if we account for the fact that black females perform somewhat better. But for black males, as a recent Royal Commission on Education in Ontario reveals, the results are woeful. It is interesting to note that the commission suggested that Black-focused schools might be a solution.

Indeed, it did appear as if there was some truth that I was giving comfort to the enemy when my article in *The Globe* was excerpted at length by fellow Caribbean immigrant writer Neil Bissoondath in his controversial book, *Selling Illusions*. Bissoondath quoted the article, not as an argument against Black-focused schools, but against multiculturalism, which somehow surprised me because I thought I had argued that a multicultural society would not need a Black-focused school. In addition, some critics had snobbishly suggested that I would change my mind about Black-focused schools when my children entered high school and started to encounter the kind of problems most black students claim pave the way for failure. It would be in high school that my children would miss not having black teachers and role models, they argued. That is why I had taken exception to Ms. Bain hitting a nerve by asking if I had children in the school system.

But what is a Black-focused school? Is it what Ms. Bain was suggesting: having sensitive black instructors looking after the interests of her daughter and encouraging and inspiring students like Cheryl and Ray? These days, it is hard to tell. I remember moderating a panel discussion of Canadian and U.S. educators and politicians on focused schools at a forum at York University only a few months earlier, and failing to get the panel and the audience to come up with a working definition of a Black-focused school. This failure had put an end to hopes by the organizers of the discussion to get panelists to provide a list of suggestions as to how a Black-focused school should operate. The most we got was a discussion from an educator from Detroit, who told us of the success he and his colleagues were having in all-black schools. But even then, we recognized that the Detroit model would have little use in Canada, if only because we do not have the geographical concentrations of Blacks to allow us to virtually elect a black school board and set up black schools. We do not have the concentration, money or votes to set up a similar system in Canada. In the end, we concluded by attempting to define the role of the black teacher as the community tries to stop a trend of many of our children failing in school. But as the saying goes, the devil is always in the detail, and the detail was defining what we were arguing about.

Depending on who you talk to, a Black-focused school could be an independent school in which all of the teachers and students are black. The curriculum would be black oriented, with emphasis on the achievements of Africans around the world: on achievements of Blacks and Africans in literature, the sciences, politics, history, culture—in every facet of life. Black role models would come to the school regularly.

This way, the argument goes, black students would have people to turn to who understand them, who talk like they do, who are outside the mainstream as they are and who can appreciate how tough it is to be growing up black in this country. The parade of community role models would inspire the students that they should aim for success in any occupation or profession. Under this plan, the administrators for the school would get funding from the educational boards, but only the administrators would have a say in the selection of staff and the setting of curricula. Except for the financial requirements, these schools would be independent. (I had argued in my *Globe* column that this was wishful thinking. Who as a school trustee would hand over taxpayers' money and not maintain some control or accountability?)

At the other extreme, some people think that Black-focused schools can co-exist with other schools under the administration of the existing school boards. These schools would be set up in an area where there is a sizeable black population, as in some parts of Toronto where 80 or 90 percent of the student body is already black. The difference is that the school would be tailored to look after the unique needs of the community. If there is a need for special role models, then the school would go hunting for them and might even have them on staff. It would also pay greater attention to the cultural and ethnic mores of the student body. And it would reflect the diversity of the student body in the curricula, textbooks and teaching body.

Indeed, some people argue that it might be necessary for the Black-focused school to also make room for other disadvantaged communities, such as the Hispanics, who are also having problems in the mainstream school system. And some people argue that discipline must be a big component of the Black-focused schools. Students would wear uniforms, spend their lunch hour in meaningful activity, and would not be permitted to listen to the vulgar lyrics from gangsta rap and the likes. School would be a place for students to be serious about studying, about preparing for life after school, for university and jobs. It would be a place where strong teachers exercise discipline, just like the schools the older black immigrants had attended in the Caribbean and Africa.

I don't think too many people can be against this kind of school, especially if such schools help to keep more black students in the classroom. This is what we all want. I believe the high school students when they claim they feel alienated in the school. They do not see themselves in the textbooks or read about African or Third World history. Who can they turn to when they have a problem of cultural identity? Perhaps we don't need independent schools to achieve this, I had argued, but just a few sensitive black teachers in the classroom or even on staff so that students can talk to them anytime. But we also need students to be conscientious.

While the system needs to be fixed, I also feel that the attitudes of many black students also need overhauling.

To my surprise, Ms. Bain appeared in agreement with me. In Jamaica and the Caribbean, she said, nobody fooled around when it came to an education. It should be no different for black and West Indian students in Canada. Sensing we were onto something, I threw caution to the wind and stopped hiding behind the privacy act.

For the first time in our discussion, Ms. Bain went silent. She folded her hands across her chest and started to relax. "Now I understand what is happening," she said. "Now I understand, 'cause I know something had to be missing from what Cheryl was telling me, because I don't see from what she explained to me about you why she should be having any problems."

I opened my binder to show Ms. Bain that Cheryl's marks were not out of line with those of the class for the assignments she had handed in. But I also pointed out to her that Cheryl and her friend Ray had not submitted all of the assignments, that they were always late or skipped class, and that I felt that they were not applying themselves as well as they could.

"Being black has nothing to do with it," I said. But I didn't think I had convinced Ms. Bain with this one.

The co-ordinator and Cheryl appeared at my door. "I have told Cheryl that she must understand how a teacher can feel disappointed when a student keeps missing classes or shows little enthusiasm," the co-ordinator said.

"So, Cheryl," Ms. Bain said. "Why are you missing Mr. Foster's classes?"

"I think that I only missed maybe one, or two, or three ..." Cheryl replied.

"And what about the assignments?" she asked.

"Well, I ..."

"You know, Cheryl, I always tell you that you have to apply yourself. Now, I understand what is going on. And I think you got to apply yourself more. Look at me. Although I am working, I never miss one class because I am coming to this college to learn. Even though I am tired. And I think you have to start showing Mr. Foster more respect and he in turn will help you."

"Yes, mother," Cheryl said.

By now I was breathing easier. But inside, I still had the nagging doubts. Was I discriminating against Cheryl and Ray because they are black, and was I holding them to a higher level of excellence than my other students? These are questions that would stay with me. Could I, too, be a victim of the stereotyping of black youths?

*   *   *

Not long ago, an old acquaintance was grieving over the loss of his 20-year-old son, an only child. Roughly the same age as Cheryl and Ray, he had been stabbed to death at a party at Carleton University in Ottawa by another black man. It was another example of senseless black-on-black violence, the kind of incident that seems to happen with increasing frequency when black youths are just hanging out.

The murdered young man, by all accounts, was a peacemaker and had been stabbed when he intervened to prevent an argument from escalating into physical violence. The man he was talking to apparently pulled a knife on the peacemaker and ended his life. None of the hundreds of students attending the dance was willing to co-operate with the police, and after some months the police had not made an arrest in the killing.

"What's going to become of our people, especially our youth?" a friend said to me when we discussed the situation. "So many of our people see nothing, hear nothing, say nothing. And what do the police do in a case like this? It's just another black man that gets killed by another black man. And if black people are not going to co-operate, then why should the police bother themselves? We got to be responsible, man."

We wondered why anyone attending a student dance would turn up with a weapon of any sort. And why would they use it? Must be some strange thinking abroad among the black youths, we commiserated. Maybe they deserve exactly what they get, if they are going to be so irresponsible and kill one another. Indeed, we wondered, what would become of our black youths, especially the ones who aren't taking life seriously, have no respect for others, are just interested in breezing through life with a minimum of effort, just interested in the latest clothes and the most expensive running shoes. Yes, we, too, have our negative stereotypes—or are they concerns?—about black youths.

I had served with the dead youth's father; as a director and then president of a community association, he worked tirelessly to make sure that young Blacks learn a greater respect for life, that they go to school and respect the law, and to help to get the community to pull together and help feed, clothe and educate those among us who are in greatest need. Now, this stalwart had lost his only son in a senseless murder and nobody was speaking up. Now, this man was grieving, was wondering why anyone should inflict such pain on him. What would become of our black youth? we asked, clucking our tongues.

Perhaps I am no different from most people who probably think they know better and want the best for the people with whom they identify. Black literature is replete with stories about this kind of behaviour. Recently, there was the movie *Stand By Me,* based on the life of a stern New York principal who would walk the hall of his school, bullhorn in hand, making sure that the youth of his race were disciplined. Then, there is the famous book by Ralph Ellison, *The Invisible Man,* in which Dr. Bledsoe, the principal at the university, was so hard on black students that he drove them away from the university, all in the name of saving the race. Does every black teacher have a part of Dr. Bledsoe in him or her?

> "Boy, you *are* a fool," [Dr. Bledsoe] said. "Your white folk didn't teach you anything and your mother-wit has left you cold. What has happened to you young Negroes? I thought you had caught on to how things are done down here. But you don't even know the difference between the way things are and the way they're supposed to be. My God," he gasped, "what is the race coming to?"

Obviously, I did not think I was anywhere near these people in attitude, nowhere near a Dr. Bledsoe who would punish a black student for being black and not acting the right way. But the thought did cross my mind as I talked to Ms. Bain.

And this remarkable woman must have understood my thinking. For before leaving, she apologized for coming down so hard on me for assuming that I would not want to inspire her daughter, that indeed I was attempting to drive her daughter out of school.

"This will not happen again," she promised. "Cheryl, when you come home, I will talk to you. We as a people must learn respect."

By this time, I, too, had learned many lessons and promised to sit with Cheryl and to be more patient with her.

"And another thing, Cheryl," her mother said, "I don't think you should change your class next semester. I think you can learn a lot from Mr. Foster. But you have to start showing him respect."

"Thank you," I said sheepishly. We shook hands and said our goodbyes.

Later in the day, I met with Cheryl. We agreed that we would never let the situation reach this level again. And we kept our word. Cheryl turned out to be a model student, seldom missing class and always asking questions. Ray, her friend, continued to stay away, but somehow he handed in surprisingly well-written assignments. Nothing I could do could change him. Not even when I flattered him that if his assignments were a true reflection of his ability, then he was shortchanging himself by not applying himself. But I guess that is a fact of life: you win some and lose some. And if you can make a difference in the life of an individual, then you have achieved something.

And Ms. Bain, I believe, remained a remarkable woman and an excellent teacher herself.

* * *

Talk to most people and they will tell you that the gap between the black experience and the wider Canadian society is widening. This does not augur well for either side: not for the black youths who are likely to find themselves marginalized and as frustrated as their parents; not for the wider community, which must always be wondering what price must be paid for social peace.

As we reach the close of the 20th century, there appears to be a mean-spiritedness on the Canadian landscape. It is a sourness aimed mainly at those who are less able to help themselves, at those who are not mainstream. So that the hurtful barbs of overheated political rhetoric and draconian economic measures are aimed at immigrants, no matter how long they have been in the country. We see the mean-spiritedness in the eagerness to dump such measures as employment equity and other pieces of social legislation intended to bring about some modicum of integration. Canadians have gone sour on reaching out to those who are not in their crowd. And because Blacks have not yet made it into the mainstream, this sourness affects us in a significant way.

But the reaction from the black youth, the ones to receive the brunt of this sourness when they are, for example, denied jobs because of who they are, is not likely to be dealt with the same way as it was in the older generation. These young black men and women are Canadian in their actions and thoughts, even if their inspiration is from the Caribbean. They do not want to escape into some place called "back home." They do not plan to run away, and some day go back to some country when the slings and arrows of living in Canada become too much to bear. More than that, the Caribbean model their parents established in this country is static: heck, it is not even like what the Canadian-born children see when they visit their grandma and grandad in the Caribbean. And because the youths have nowhere to run, they will have to stand and fight. For what is the alternative?

More than anything else, because they are Canadian, they know how the system works. For in the same classes where the schools teach our children not to accept corporal punishment, wider lessons on how the system works in general are also being soaked up by the next generation of black leaders. Unlike their parents, they will not be that forgiving. They will be able to fight for their rights within and outside the mainstream. They will not be content to limit their actions to praying all hours of the night or grumbling about their lot in life over bottles of beer. They will have those options and more.

But a confrontation, the so-called fire next time, doesn't have to happen. We can turn away from this polarization if both the black community and the wider society recognize what is at stake, and the consequences. We, as Blacks, must recognize that, while our culture might not be mainstream, that in just about every other thing we rely on the wider society for validation. We are not islands in the stream. So we must get our house in order, too; we must teach our youth to appreciate the wider culture, to see themselves in the mirror reflecting the Canadian mosaic and to eschew a penchant for violence and the illegal business. Yes, there must be some conforming, some integration. We must continue to take the best from the church.

At the same time, the wider society must realize that Blacks are in this country to stay and that we will not be happy living as a marginalized community. Just as other ethnic groups have moved from the periphery to the centre, so the black community will have to follow their lead. The wider community must make room for people they have not been used to dealing with as equals. So Blacks will have to start taking our place as our birthright in the boardrooms of the nation, in the classrooms as students and professors, in the media, in the church and in politics. And we will not be taking those places as offers of tokenism. Neither should the elevation of one man or woman be enough to appease an entire community. It must become possible for a black mother to tell her son or daughter that he or she, too, can grow up to become the leader of a national political party, the premier of a province, or the prime minister of this country. That he or she should have all the rights, privileges and expectations of all Canadian children.

CHAPTER 6

THE INTEGRATION GAME

Eventually, even without the shield of such mechanisms as employment equity, every person belonging to a minority in Canada gets to decide whether or not to play the shell game of trying to join the mainstream. In many respects, the decision is a charade, because few minorities ever get to wield power or to feel fully at home in the workplace or mainstream institutions. This might sound like a gross generalization, but you only have to look around and see how few minorities form powerful groups in the wider Canadian society. Take a closer look at the few and find out how many are in positions of influence or have any say even within those groups. Most of them are usually no more than window-dressing.

A good place to start is by looking at the media. See how many minorities are featured prominently in Canadian TV shows as news journalists or television personalities. Listen to the radio and play the game of picking out the so-called nontraditional accent. The dearth of minority personalities and accents is not exactly favourable testimony to the picture of Canada as a genuinely multicultural country. The reality behind the usual optics and mouthings about Canada becoming a home for all groups, all of them sharing equally in the gains and riches of this country, is easily discounted.

Better yet, take a good look at what happens at the parties, social events and company conferences. You will probably see a wide gulf: minority people in clumps and the white Canadians in others. If you look closer, you will probably notice the palpable tension and uneasiness when members stray into the wrong group. And, no, it's not because minorities don't like to mix. It is that very often they feel unwelcome even in the organizations they help build with their dues and their volunteer work. If you ask many minority workers, they will tell you how often they never hear of the after-work parties, of when the gang meets at the local watering hole for drinks, of the softball games on weekends. They can tell you of how they often return to work and stumble into a conversation about some social event that went on without their being invited. They can tell of how they are often reminded, indeed told by the actions of others, that they are different and not important. To socialize, the minority worker must not only seek out his or her own kind, but is often forced by the attitudes of associates and colleagues to do so.

On the other hand, if the minorities are of some usefulness to the group or association, as in being expendable or willing to compromise their principles, then that's another story. This is the reality of playing the integration game in Canada. Of providing the spice and flavour, the exotic in what is taken spuriously as integration, the making of a multicultural society in which diversity is supposedly welcomed and cherished. And for those outside the mainstream, those who are the proverbial fly-in-the-milk, it can be damn frustrating before they drown.

Often, this frustration leads to most minorities having to decide if it is better to exist outside the wider community, especially if their job or way of making a living is not dependent on integration, and if there isn't the force of laws or regulations to help smooth the path—nothing to sensitize members of the dominant culture to the needs and expectations of those long considered outsiders. It is so easy to ask, Why bother? Why even try?

Eventually, every person belonging to a minority group must ask this question: Is the pain and frustration of getting these institutions to make room for us worth the effort? Or is it better, as some black activists argue, to go out and form our own groups, have our own agendas and social pecking order?

When answering these questions honestly, Blacks and other minorities cannot but come to an obvious conclusion: groups reflecting the dominant culture have agendas and priorities different from those of minorities. Seldom do the dominant groups and the minorities see things the same way.

For decades, Canadian Blacks have bought into the notion that the best way to bring about change to their status in the wider society is to infiltrate mainstream groups and make changes from within. Here is the suggestion that you join the group, help shape the discussions and help sensitize the existing members. At the end of the process, after much diligent work and no complaining, and after having grown a very thick skin, you hope you have transformed the old group into a multicultural club of sorts that is noted for its new-found sensitivity to minorities. If changes can be made one group at a time, eventually, and without anyone looking, the entire face of the mainstream would change. It would be softer, gentler and kinder. Through some timely and colourful renovation, Blacks and other minorities would take an established structure and transform it into a home that is theirs, claiming right of possession to what was once a seemingly impenetrable ivory tower for whites only. That is one argument for going mainstream. Get inside a group and bend and cajole it into something more accommodating. Graft your agenda onto the existing agenda. The only other option is to stay on the outside, powerlessly wringing your hands and changing nothing.

But there are those who argue that infiltration is useless and frustrating at best. They contend that too often it is not possible to accommodate two different agendas in the same organization. This is true in political parties, unions, social advocacy groups, police associations, the military—in just about any association set up and defined by representatives of the dominant group, no matter how liberal and well-intentioned their desires.

Perhaps there is no better playground for this game of frustration than politics. This field is littered with many of the hopes, dreams and aspirations of Canadian Blacks. Over the years, these dream-makers thought that fighting within a political party could make a difference, that it would advance their causes and community. Usually, they were wrong and, perhaps, still are.

The reason for this can be found in the very nature of Canadian politics, which is essentially to serve the dominant group and to only appease those outside the mainstream. In Canada, the question of Canadian Blacks in party politics is largely an exercise in finding at what point the parties can buy off the black vote while safely ignoring the community's real concerns. The big question for the mainstream is this: What do these people want, and once we find that out, what would it cost to appease them?

Every time there is an election, the major political parties mount a concerted effort to find a place on their tickets for one or two high-profile Blacks. So far, the most successful of the mainstream parties, at both the federal and provincial levels, are the Liberals. For several decades, the Liberals have gone into every federal election knowing they have the Canadian black vote sewn up right across the country. This is a situation similar to the way the Democrats in the United States count on getting overwhelming support from African-Americans in the presidential, gubernatorial and congressional elections. Bill Clinton took a staggering 92 percent of the African-American vote in the 1992 presidential election, and this was even after he had picked a fight with such notable African-Americans as Jesse Jackson and Sister Soldier to demonstrate to conservatives that he had not sold out to minority interests. Clinton could afford to do this, because the obvious question was, Where else can African-Americans take their vote? To the Republicans?

This attitude is just as prevalent in Canada. The difference between Canada and the United States is that Blacks in Canada do not congregate in large enough numbers that, as the saying goes, would allow them to elect a dog catcher. Canada does not have the inner-city housing projects, populated in large numbers by African-Americans, as are those found in the United States. This means that the black vote in Canada, even in cities like Toronto, Montreal and Halifax, is very diffuse. There is no real clout. Even at the riding level, the total black vote is marginal. This difference is even more dramatic at the national level: whereas African-Americans make up 20 percent of the American population, African-Canadians account for less than 1 percent of the population.

But every political season becomes a strange form of employment equity, which the white politicians know how to use when it suits them—the message goes out for Blacks to put forward candidates. The one exception that springs to mind is the watershed Ontario provincial election in 1995 when the three major parties tried to outdo one another holding minority groups at arm's length. This was a campaign marked by an acute backlash against minority and equity issues, with the winning Conservatives campaigning successfully on the notion of returning common sense to politics by silencing what it called special-interest groups. This was undoubtedly a code for putting certain vociferous groups in their place and returning to simpler times when there was an expected natural order in Canada. Back to a time when everyone in every group knew what his or her station was in life, and the group's expected role in society. A return to a time when it didn't take that much to appease Blacks and other minority groups simply because they were politically invisible.

As the success of this right-wing agenda soared, the Conservatives obviously had no need for black or minority-group support and did not go out of their way to court it. The two opposition parties likewise tried to pick up some of this growing right-wing support as reflected in the polls. They started copying some aspects of the Tories' agenda. One way they chose to undercut the soaring Tories was by staying away from championing black and minority issues. In their worst moment of need, Blacks discovered how expendable they were—and are—to the political process and the established political parties.

Black and minority activists can only hope this campaign was an aberration. Many suspect it was not, and there is a very poignant reason. Blacks have paid a big price for their fidelity to a single party. First, it means benign neglect. The Liberals go into an election knowing they can count on these votes regardless of what happens. The same is true for the Democrats in the United States. During the Reagan years, while the so-called Reagan Democrats deserted the party, African-Americans remained faithful to their party. The same was true in Canada during the Brian Mulroney period from 1988 to 1994. Yes, the Tories did make a small dent in the black vote in Toronto and Montreal during those years when Mulroney was trying to appear as a Red Tory. But the gains were negligible and so were ignored.

Similarly, at times the New Democratic Party has managed to siphon off some black votes. But this is never to the point of threatening the Liberals' lock on this vote at the federal and provincial levels across the country. The Reform Party, the other major force in Canadian politics, has been so racist with its diatribe against immigrants and welfare recipients, and with its law-and-order agenda, that Blacks easily recognize that once they decipher the coded language in the Reform Party's political rhetoric, there is little room for Blacks in that party.

As a consequence of these developments, Blacks and other minorities in Canada are now caught in the right-wing backlash with no party to defend them. The parties running against the Liberals have recognized that they will have to win with or without—and the latter is more likely—the black vote. So, they can come up with policies that ignore Blacks, that pander, in fact, to an anti-black, anti-minority vote. Why? Because there is nothing to lose.

At the same time, the Liberals know they have the minority vote in the bag, and spend their time trying to court the mainstream. Why waste time and effort on what they already have, or rather, what nobody else really appears to want or to work hard enough to get? This could account, for example, for the reason the current Liberal government would bring in absolutely draconian immigration and refugee policies—everything from a distasteful head tax on new immigrants to a mean-spirited attack on sponsors when an immigrant needs welfare or social assistance—and get away with the measures. And this is a Liberal government that has the highest number of minority parliamentarians in the history of any parliamentary caucus. A government of a party that prides itself on making Canada officially a multicultural country.

The Liberals can get away with their ingratitude because they are simply trying to grab part of the anti-immigrant and anti-minority vote as well. They also know none of the other parties has anything to gain by standing up for what is basically a Liberal constituency. Such are the thanks Blacks get for their political fidelity.

One can only wonder what would be the case if, instead of thoughtlessly locking up their vote every election, Blacks were to vote strategically. What would happen if Blacks approached politics from a practical position based on the awarding of power by joining with other allies to reward the politicians who offer them the most? We can start working toward this goal of educating black voters to be emancipated from the chains of any particular political party. With such thinking, we might not even have to worry about whether infiltration works.

When the mainstream political parties seek out high-profile black candidates, they always leave in their wake the interminable question: But what can these candidates hope to achieve other than being mere window-dressing for the parties? It is not surprising that it becomes very frustrating for the elected politician from the black community and for Blacks who rally around members of their community, hoping that the election of a single member will make a difference. As the record shows, it is very difficult for Blacks to genuinely influence, far less shape, the political thinking in these parties. Instead, the parties try to remould the captured minority candidates, make them over in the party's image, and send them back out as representatives of the party to the black or minority community. Or the party simply imposes a ceiling on how high they can rise.

The limitation inherent in this attitude can only lead to grave disappointments. Blacks and the mainstream parties are now going after different, and often contradictory, agendas. Caught in the middle are the black politicians who run for office, sincerely believing they can make a difference, that their voices will present a different opinion and perspective when ideas and policies are debated and developed. Alas, history shows this is not the case.

Several examples support this observation at both the federal and provincial levels. Take the case of Rosemary Brown, a dynamic politician who immigrated from Jamaica as a young woman and decided that politics was an avenue for change. Politics, specifically the socialist brand, would bring liberation to the down-and-out minorities and women. A community and human-rights activist, she was also bold enough to make a run for the leadership of the federal New Democratic Party, making her the first Black to attempt to attain such a lofty goal in Canada. And she did this, for example, before Jesse Jackson made his much-heralded run for the presidential nomination of the Democratic Party in the United States.

Brown ran essentially a grassroots feminist campaign and from all reports had mounted, arguably, the most effective run for the leadership. And going into the leadership convention in 1975, it was widely believed that she was the outside candidate to beat. She had galvanized the feminist and minority groups into quite a force. And for Blacks, here was a woman who would not be held back by the colour of her skin, a politician and dreamer who encouraged Blacks of every political persuasion and economic status to think big, to believe that by working within the system they could achieve their dreams. For Blacks, just the recognition that Brown ran an effective campaign, that she dared to try to open up the establishment and her party, was an achievement. At least for the duration of the campaign, black people dared to dream and to wonder what could happen if only...

But, the backroom shakers and movers of the party felt embarrassed—

indeed, were quite frightened—over the prospect that a black woman could emerge as leader of the party. This would destroy the party, they whispered. A black leader would guarantee that the New Democrats, the perennial third party in federal Canadian politics, would never be put into power, because Canadians weren't ready for a black prime minister, they argued. Brown might be popular, able to stir up a crowd and address all the issues that are the bedrock of the party, all of which would be well and good if she were to remain just an ordinary member of the party. But to be leader, well, that was another matter.

This was the same argument that reverberated in the United States when Americans tied themselves in knots debating if they were ready for an African-American as president, for even an African-American vice-president. It was the same thinking that coloured so much of the discussion in 1995 whether U.S. army general Colin Powell should seek the American presidential nomination for the 1996 election. After a black and African presence in this part of the world for almost 500 years, as long as any other ethnic group, it is still debatable whether a black person can ever become a leader of a political party, far less the prime minister of Canada or the president of the United States of America. As we enter a new millennium, this, more than any other, is a startling commentary on the place of Blacks in the North American dream, whether it is the American or Canadian version.

In 1975, the NDP hierarchy felt it would have been suicidal to elect Brown as federal leader. Writing in her memoirs, *Being Brown*, Rosemary concedes that during the campaign she amused herself by thinking of what would happen if she actually won. So she imagined the wild and bizarre headlines that would announce her victory:

> "White Canadian Party Elects Black Leader"
> "One of the World's Largest White Countries Led by Radical Black Feminist Socialist"
> "Shocked Canadians Appeal to World for Help after Black Leader Elected"
> "White No More"
> "Brown Is Beautiful Says Black Leader to White Country"
> "Country Falls to Feminist"

And Brown says she recognized that while the prospects of her victory tantalized the media, which was so representative of the wider society, that the radio, television and print reporters

> were hoping that in the end the party would choose a staid, sensible leader in the Canadian mould. At the same time, it was obvious that the campaign was a challenge for them, as they bent over backwards to be critical of its content and style without appearing to be patronizing, paternalistic, racist or sexist.

So, in late-night meetings, the delegates looked for a different kind of compromise candidate. They decided that an arresting and exciting candidate wasn't good enough. They needed *less* than this candidate would offer. So they put their money and efforts behind a more prime ministerial candidate, Edward Broadbent, a university economics professor from Toronto. Broadbent went on to defeat Brown, partly because he was a man and white. Where is employment equity when you need it? So Brown returned to provincial politics in British Columbia.

This story is told many times over in the Canadian black community as an example of how integration does not work, of how the best often doesn't win when race becomes the ultimate factor. For it was not a question of whether Broadbent would eventually go on to be a good leader of the party—he obviously did—but whether he was the best candidate at the time.

In defeat, Brown, the woman who ran on the slogan "Brown Is Beautiful," a deliberate rip-off of the "Black Is Beautiful" slogan so she could be identified with all North American Blacks, scored a victory. "The one aspect of the experience that gives me the greatest joy," she writes, "is knowing that on July 7, 1975, all over this country, black people, children as well as adults, eyes and ears fixed on TV and radio, waited for the results of that final ballot and, for a short while, dared to dream the impossible." A victory indeed, but only if you believe it is still an achievement to show up at the starting line for the race, even if you know all sorts of leg irons and obstacles will ensure that you will never win. As we move into another millennium, just showing up for the race, just being a contestant and being willing to accept defeat purely on a question of race, is no longer good enough or acceptable.

As fate would have it, the question of whether a Black could become the leader of a major political party was once again put to the test when the NDP was looking for a leader to follow Broadbent. At that time, the party was concerned that none of the candidates that NDP insiders and stalwarts were talking about as frontrunners had any flair or charisma. There was one NDPer in the House of Commons with political flair and who could talk up a storm. That man was Howard McCurdy but, and here came the rub, he was black. McCurdy, the grandson of a Jamaican immigrant, boasted a long political history of fighting racism and working with unions, of toiling with the poor and the underclass from his days as a local politician in Windsor, Ontario. These were many of the characteristics good NDP members are supposed to possess. And in the political arena, few could out-class him in debate on the floor of Parliament; few could give a more impassioned speech on the political hustings.

I remember discussing with Nelson Riis in the early days of the campaign the possibility of enticing McCurdy to run for the leadership. Riis was the NDP's house leader, and one evening he had dropped by a conference I was attending in Vancouver. We spent a few hours discussing politics at the hotel bar. Riis was sure the time wasn't right for him to seek the leadership of the NDP. For one thing, he was concerned about talk that the Trudeau Liberals had asked him to cross over and join them in government. Even though he said he never had any intention of joining the Liberals, he felt that the mere rumours that he had been approached by the governing party—which was looking for a high-profile western politician and must have dangled a few plums in front of him—were serious enough to harm his candidacy. But looking at the slate of potential candidates, Riis wasn't too happy. Why doesn't the party be bold and do something to capture the nation's attention? I asked. Why not get Howard McCurdy to run? Instantly, Riis's eyes lit up. He would certainly encourage McCurdy to run because he would make a good leader, he said.

Perhaps Riis was just being a good politician in telling a stranger—who possibly got Riis's attention for so long because he was a reporter—what he wanted to hear. McCurdy did decide to run. Several years later, I was pleasantly surprised when McCurdy wisecracked that I had started all his trouble by having this talk with Nelson about running for the leadership.

Once again, the black community rallied to support one of its own. Rosemary Brown had been a kind of Moses leading the way. Now a Howard McCurdy could become a political Joshua, leading Blacks out of the wilderness, as far as the NDP was concerned. Blacks manned the offices, they did the lobbying and they opened a bank account to provide financial support. Letters went out to Canadian Blacks of all political persuasions asking them to dream of the possibilities if a Black were to win the leadership. A group of Toronto-area Blacks had held a weekend retreat near Niagara Falls to discuss issues and leadership. McCurdy gave us the keynote address, teasing us to watch him as he tried to bring some changes to the party, as he "kicked butt" trying to make the party more inclusive of minority groups. We all wished him well and promised to spread the word. Some of the people at the retreat played pivotal roles in the campaign.

Looking back, McCurdy recalls that he got into the leadership race to show that Canadian Blacks and other minorities cannot be ignored in the political process. He also wanted to broaden the make-up of the party so that more minorities and Blacks would be included. And he also wanted to bring some new ideas to the party. On the question of welfare reform, for example, he was among the first to argue that the party should advocate ways to give people a hand up—not a handout. He also wanted changes in research and development and wanted the government to find new ways to engage the country's youth.

On the hustings, where so much allegedly matters in the race for convention delegates, McCurdy outperformed all the other candidates. Watching his performance, even more people in the black community dared to think the impossible. Could it be that this black man from Windsor, a man who could trace his roots for several generations in Canada, could bind the newly arrived Caribbean and African Blacks and the old-stock Canadian Blacks into a force? Could he do it? we asked ourselves, praying that he might.

But others were noticing, too. As the convention drew near and McCurdy was proving to be more than just a fringe candidate, the question turned to what would happen if the NDP woke up the morning after the leadership convention and found it had a black leader. As McCurdy recalls, he was getting the best audience responses at the political debates and he remembers two particular incidents. One was in Halifax where the crowd was almost totally behind him, with people waving banners and rising to his political rhetoric. And in Ontario, in a session before the steel workers' union, McCurdy "blew away" all the other candidates, including the apparently anointed leader. And he remembers those two incidents for two primary reasons: not a word was mentioned in the mainstream press about his performance in Halifax; and although he out-performed everyone in the candidate debate before the steel workers' union, his so-called win did not translate into union delegates at the convention. From both cases, it appeared the fix was in.

Once in Saskatchewan, the home of traditional NDP support and some of the biggest movers and shakers of the party, McCurdy recalls that the audience was so taken up by his oratory that one listener gave him the ultimate compliment for a Canadian socialist by comparing him to Tommy Douglas, the grassroots populist who essentially founded the party. But then there was also the negative side of that swing through western Canada, such as when a reporter for *The Globe and Mail* condescendingly accused him of affecting the rhetorical style of the late U.S. civil rights leader Martin Luther King, Jr. "I told him that I am following a long tradition of speaking in the black tradition, of which Martin Luther King's style is only one."

The fact that McCurdy is black, something that has always been a source of great pride, began to work against him. Would Canada accept a black leader of a major political party, especially one who can be as fractious and is an amalgam of so many different social-interest groups? This was the year after Jesse Jackson had added some unusual nuances to North American politics by seeking the presidential nomination. Blacks across North America were pinning their hopes on Jackson. Canadian Blacks were just as anxious to "See Jesse Run; See Jesse Win." This seemed to be one of those rare magical moments in the black community, when the stars were aligned to favour us politically in Canada and the United States. For if Blacks in New York, Chicago and Atlanta had their Jesse, we in Toronto, Halifax, Montreal, Edmonton and Windsor had our Howard. For his campaign, McCurdy raised $85,000, with about half the amount coming from Canadian Blacks.

McCurdy's handlers thought of inviting Jackson to Toronto for a speaking engagement at Maple Leaf Gardens to boost the campaign funds. They had no doubt that Blacks from Toronto and the surrounding area, even Buffalo and Detroit, would come to hear Jackson speak. But they scrapped the idea, claiming that Jackson's fee would have been too high. In reality, they got cold feet, thinking that Jackson's presence would send a wider message, one that might undermine the new reality of McCurdy's campaign. For at this point McCurdy and his people were beginning to genuinely believe that with a base of popular response, they had a chance of winning the nomination. Therefore, his handlers didn't want McCurdy to appear to be "too black" a candidate by emphasizing the one most obvious thing he shares with Jesse Jackson.

"That was not the explicit response," McCurdy admits. "But that may well have been true." McCurdy says that he had met Jackson in Namibia some years earlier and that he doesn't think that Jackson is relevant to Canada. In fact, he regards him as "opportunistic and self-enhancing."

"Jesse is still fairly popular in Canada among Whites and Blacks. But it is just that I didn't think it would have done us that much good. I do not like having American black leadership coming to Canada as saviours and I don't think they will ever see Canadian Blacks other than as just marginal." So, according to McCurdy, although some of his people had reached out to Jackson, he nixed the idea.

Undoubtedly, the thought of McCurdy appearing to be a one-issue candidate—in essence caught by his black supporters and pandering to them by bringing in Jackson—was no doubt at the back of the organizers' minds. For going into the convention, the organizers were busy attempting to show that McCurdy was representative of the mainstream, was a consensus candidate, and that even though he was black and that black issues would naturally be of interest to him, as leader he would not be a black politician, but a genuine representative of all the various groups in the NDP. Funny, none of his competitors felt they had to make apologies for the colour of their skin.

Blacks in Canada are often placed in the position of having to compromise in the hope of reaching a goal. The question becomes how much of a compromise. Should a McCurdy accept any notion of de-emphasizing the colour of his skin in the hope of winning office, even if by winning office he might be able to do some good for Blacks? Is it better to compromise and get something done or to remain unflinchingly faithful to your views, remain uncompromisingly outside the mainstream, and succeed in achieving nothing? For many Blacks, there is another way of asking these questions: What price do you pay for your soul? McCurdy had to look at himself in the mirror and answer the question of at what point he could be appeased.

Going into the convention, McCurdy and his political advisors believed that the momentum was in their favour. McCurdy says that his campaign and those of his rivals had placed him in a solid third position with 385 votes. Their main rival was a first-time member of Parliament, who appeared very fuzzy on issues, did not perform well in party debates and was not considered an effective speaker. But this candidate was a woman and white, and with the feminist movement pushing her, the party establishment, including Nelson Riis, supported her. The highlight of the political convention was the speeches on the night before the vote. McCurdy produced a political barn-burner. Audrey McLaughlin bombed. Stephen Lewis, a stalwart in the NDP, who was commenting on CBC-TV that evening, was scathing in his assessment of McLaughlin's speech. There was no doubt that McCurdy, despite a bad cold which he says made him too passive and not as animated as usual, still produced the best speech, further adding to the notion of the momentum staying with him. His handlers were elated in the late night politicking as delegates professed to them how impressed they were with McCurdy and how they would vote for him.

Even at that late hour in the campaign, the whispers were intensifying: Would Canada elect a black prime minister? McCurdy people went into the vote confident of a third-place finish on the first ballot that would set him up for a run in later ballots. Several candidates had promised "to walk" to him on the convention floor and to bring their supporters. But the rumours were too much.

"There was a significant campaign out of Saskatchewan warning people that there was a deadly prospect that the party would end up with a black leader," McCurdy recalls. "That was when reality re-entered the picture. It just wasn't going to happen." On the first ballot, McCurdy got a heart-breaking 250 votes. He felt utterly betrayed by all those who had promised him the vote but did not follow through. And he knew the only reason he didn't get the vote was because he was black. McCurdy dropped off the ballot.

For a while, and perhaps to assuage its own disappointment and hurt, the black community was rife with rumours that McCurdy was agonizing over whether to quit the party. For many, this was another unmistakable case of how integration just doesn't work. Another example of how impossible it is to renovate the old house to make it a home for the traditional outsider.

McCurdy says that he never seriously thought of leaving politics, for he believed that he had scored a moral victory with his performance. He had influenced the campaign, had opened up the party to more Blacks and minorities, and in general had done much better than the party establishment and the national media had expected. Plus, there are those questions that would continue to haunt someone in McCurdy's position: Isn't it better to put aside your personal hurt and remain in politics? At least for as long as he was in the House of Commons, every black child watching the parliamentary channel, and occasionally the news, saw him when he got up to ask a question or to speak in Parliament. And there is so much a member of Parliament can do that an ordinary citizen can't. McCurdy could travel the country, speaking to black groups and inspiring them. For the next while, McCurdy would use his position in the House of Commons to raise some black and social causes, and to help in an ill-fated attempt to get Canada's black associations to form an umbrella group, somewhat like the National Association for the Advancement of Colored People in the United States.

McCurdy knows from firsthand experience how effective such a group can be, how it can speak with one voice for Blacks, how it can nullify criticisms that most black leaders speaking out on social and political issues represent fringe groups. McCurdy would know. Before entering politics, he was the secretary-treasurer of a group called the National Black Coalition of Canada, also patterned after the NAACP, which, until its demise from internal wrangling, was perhaps the most effective national black umbrella group in the country.

Audrey McLaughlin became the new leader. In return, she marched the federal party into oblivion. In her first election as NDP leader the inexperienced McLaughlin, still incapable of producing a rallying speech, led the party from 43 seats to 6. The NDP lost its official status as a political party in the House of Commons. McCurdy also went down to defeat. McLaughlin promptly announced she would not lead the party into another battle. As with the 1975 NDP leadership, questions arose in the black community. Would a black leader have done any worse than McLaughlin? Or to put a more positive spin on it, would a capable and more seasoned politician have done any better, even if he were black?

McCurdy seems to suggest that anyone with more parliamentary experience and competence would have done better. And in those two areas, he was way ahead of McLaughlin. "The whole thing is a manifestation of the pathology of the NDP," he says, in which the party becomes enthralled by an idea at a given time and simply swallows it. For example, the party had been convinced that Ed Broadbent should have been replaced by a woman. This was so, even though there was no woman in the federal caucus with the requisite experience.

"Audrey was just too inexperienced. She didn't light fires in anyone. I went to the steel workers' union and blew her away on the issues. Along the way someone must have noticed that [electing McLaughlin] was not going to work. Then, the people who elected her deserted her. They let her go down in flames and the rest of us with her. I ended up being one of the few caucus members that gave her sustained support."

McCurdy says that his biggest disappointment with the NDP and the Canadian Auto Workers came in the 1995 Ontario provincial election when the union decided not to support the re-election of premier Bob Rae. McCurdy says he thought of leaving the party because he realized that to the party establishment and the union, black and minority issues are dispensable. McCurdy also might have been speaking out of the hurt of knowing that the CAW had denied him the nomination for a Windsor, Ontario, riding by supporting a political unknown whose main job in the election was to embarrass Rae for ripping up a number of contracts the government had signed with public-sector unions. The labour movement had decided to punish Rae for imposing his social contract on the unions. McCurdy says that the CAW decided "to do a job on the party," no matter how much he tried to point out to them the good work the Rae government had done for Blacks and minorities.

They had introduced employment and pay equity; there were many more Blacks in positions of influence and many in the civil service and near the seat of power. "The CAW completely ignored all of this to focus only on the issue of the social contract. It didn't for a moment consider the sacrifice that was going to be imposed on minorities." As this case shows, the interests of the dominant group will always override those of the minorities in the political arena.

* * *

Jean Augustine was the first black woman to be elected to the House of Commons in 1993, although Blacks have been in Canada for generations. Soon after her election, Augustine was appointed parliamentary secretary to Prime Minister Jean Chrétien, a position, Augustine argued, that ensured she saw the prime minister every day. It's a position, she once told me in an interview, that made her more powerful than some cabinet ministers who did not have the ear of the prime minister on a daily basis and who often asked her to remind the prime minister of some issue or other on their behalf.

Madame Augustine, as she told me the prime minister liked to fondly call her, initially enjoyed a high profile in federal politics. When Parliament was sitting, she would walk into the House at the prime minister's side. And whenever the prime minister got up to speak, the spotlight fell on her, too. She sat directly behind the prime minister, right in view of the television cameras, a position that meant she always had to look attentive, she said, adding as a joke that she could never spend her time in Parliament signing letters and writing postcards to constituents or reading the newspapers, as did the MPs out of the range of the cameras.

Augustine obviously enjoyed the attention. According to a report in the community newspaper, *Pride,* in December 1995, Augustine told a Christmas brunch hosted by the African-Canadian Entrepreneurs that she found her position "enjoyable and challenging." To quote the report:

> She explained to members of the Association that she cannot ask questions in the House of Parliament and is unable to

> move private members' bills. She described her position as being somewhat of a "No-man's Land" where you can enjoy "the privileges and pitfalls of both worlds: cabinet minister and backbencher." She tried to dispel the notion that the post is a training ground for prospective cabinet ministers, while conceding that the knowledge and experience she has gained is useful if appointed to a ministerial position.

Augustine has good antennae in the black community. In her time as a parliamentary secretary, she gave countless speeches across the country. She knew what Blacks expected from elected politicians, and their government. It was instructive that she chose to define her role to this association in terms of what she could not do, rather than what she could. It was almost as if she was signalling to her listeners, and the wider community, to temper their expectations. Then, she moved on to something she could do: bring the message from the government to her constituents. She argued the government line that the last Quebec referendum taught *us* the lesson *that we cannot take Canada for granted.* She also said, according to the newspaper, that the government wanted to ensure that stability was guaranteed and that the needs of all Canadians were met. She added that the government was also aware that small and medium-sized businesses were critical to the economic well-being of Canada. Somehow, the reporter must have missed Augustine's conclusion about what all this means for the daily existence of black people like the ones she was addressing. Either that or Madame Augustine, knowing the dangers of surviving in a no man's land, could not speak for the prime minister in this respect and chose not to.

But the question remains whether Augustine and other elected black politicians are not mere window-dressing—mere political optics, eternally destined to exist in No-man's Land. Augustine genuinely believed that she wasn't, that she would make a difference in caucus and in sensitizing her colleagues to issues facing the Blacks, minorities, immigrants, women and other groups, whom she always had a passion to serve.

But at the same time, many in these communities felt that once she was captured by Ottawa and the political establishment, she was no longer a voice for them. This issue came to the fore with the first budget brought down by the new government. It slashed funding to women's, minority and immigrant groups, and imposed a head tax of $975 on all new immigrants arriving in the country. Many people pointed out that in her activist days Augustine would have been livid with any other government or party that attacked what she claimed to be part of her extended constituency. But on these issues, Augustine offered no public criticism.

"At this point, like most people who are concerned about social programs, I feel the pit-of-my-stomach conflict that we have to do more," she told *The Toronto Star* in an interview soon after the budget. "And we have to make sure individuals are not caught in the situation where whatever supports have been offered to them are lost." On the head tax, Augustine said she felt no pressure to take a stand. "Not one group within the black community in Toronto has made any formal representation to me as an MP on this issue."

* * *

Sitting with Augustine in caucus is another black MP, the third black male to ever win a seat in the Canadian House of Commons. Ovid Jackson was born in Guyana, immigrated to England and then settled in Owen Sound, Ontario. He was the longest-serving mayor in the city before he quit and entered national politics. Remarkably, nobody attacked Jackson for not speaking up on black, minority or immigrant issues. And just as important, Jackson likes it this way, that he does not have to worry too much about whether he is representing black ideology and aspirations. He just wants to be a parliamentarian. No extra baggage as a defender of the race.

Jackson makes no bones that, although he is black, he does not feel compelled to be a spokesperson for Blacks in Canada. Although he admires Augustine and the role she has taken on, Jackson makes it quite clear to me in an interview in his parliamentary office that he sees his job in Ottawa as very different from what Augustine sets herself. In days gone by, Jackson might have been considered as a good ol' CTTR (credit to the race) for his election. Not these days; not if Jackson has his way. There won't be much of a double burden of being black for him.

For a long time, it was always the perception that it is more difficult to be a black politician than a politician from the mainstream. Jackson disagrees. "Not in my case." His actual words, quoted below, tellingly betray how he sees himself in the debate on the place for Blacks, and black politicians, in Canada.

"As you know, I represent Bruce Grey and earned my stripes the hard way. It took me four nomination meetings to get here, and they were always brutal and in the rural areas. I got here by working very hard and building up a reputation over 19 years in municipal politics." In Jackson's world, hard work and perseverance, even against great odds, are everything. While he might not have said it specifically, Jackson had obviously been taking a shot at Augustine for the easy way she arrived on Parliament Hill, as a darling of the party and as the anointed Black. After all, Augustine did not earn her stripes in the trenches of municipal or provincial politics. She was lifted up when the prime minister reached down into the black community and designated her a star candidate. Jackson had no such luck. Petty jealousies can also work against a common interest.

And another perception of being a black politician is that every black person across the country identifies with the elected official. The belief is that Blacks everywhere in Canada would now be turning to someone like an Ovid Jackson to raise specific issues primarily of interest to the black community. Again, Jackson says that he makes sure Blacks see him differently.

"I would say I get those requests, but my first [answer] is that I am a man first, a Canadian second and a black person third," Jackson explains. "I have never felt I wanted to take any particular cause. I believe that Canada has the resources, both people and natural resources. The Canadian people elected me to try to make the best circumstances and give them the best conditions based on efficient government—a government that cares, a government that is Canadian, representing the broad ethnic base and the diversity we have grown accustomed to."

And what does he tell people who approach him and say, Ovid you are a brother, I want to talk to you about black issues?

"The role of a parliamentarian is to represent his riding; then you have the regional requests. You have to take all those into consideration. I haven't chosen any small grouping to become involved with. I never have all my political career. And I am not going to start now. What I can say to you is that I represent everybody equally, whether it is the disabled or the Blacks or the Natives. I have a few Natives in my riding as well. So my job first of all is to do a lot of stuff for my riding, but my being here and being able to deliver is a good example that black people can attain these heights. You notice that I don't run and jump and try to get into the headlines. I just do my job."

This leads to an important question that goes to the very heart of whether Blacks should approach black politicians for help, especially Blacks who come from outside a particular politician's riding.

"I think it's a balance," Jackson says. "In a lot of cases, I think the groups are misdirected. They have a different approach than I have; they have a different understanding than I have; they never have these dialogues with me. They just assemble in these little groups, and they have been trying to do that for quite a number of years. But nobody asks my advice. Usually, I am in a corner here by myself and you guys go off to whoever you want to talk to and nobody comes to see me or ask my advice. All I do is listen."

And why does this happen to him? I ask. "I don't come from a large urban centre," he says. Once again, the obvious inference is that his other black caucus member, even though she is a political rookie, comes from the major urban centre of Toronto and therefore automatically gets the accolades. Still, Jackson says that he would consider any request from black groups in Toronto asking him to intervene on their behalf or to help them. But then again, he says, it wouldn't matter whether the group were black or Korean.

"As a parliamentarian, lots of times I have to be in judgement on things. This political job is a difficult one and you burn bridges behind you because you go after something that you really believe in. You have to choose your fights. My intuition is that when you run off in all kinds of directions, you don't position yourself [well] to do anything."

Ultimately, as Jackson sees it, a politician must work hardest for the people who can actually vote for him or her. If most of the voters are white, then a black politician should work for them first. Of course, on the surface this sounds logical, but for me it runs up against a wall when we ask black politicians why they seek political office in the first place.

Is it simply for personal aggrandizement or is it to help make a difference in the daily lives of Blacks across the country?

"That's part of it; all politics are local. But notwithstanding that, I am not abandoning anybody or any cause. I hope that just by my example people would know they can do whatever they want. In my lifetime I have done most of the things I wanted to do. I think that any black person who wants to put his mind the right way probably could. It's not easy. I ran four times federally and you guys [Blacks from urban centres] never came and said [here is some help]. All of a sudden, Jackson turns up in Ottawa, but I should have been here four terms ago.

"Right now I am working for Canada. I am perplexed that young black males, for example, would run around and say there are no role models when there always have been, and I am not the only one. There is [former MP and lieutenant governor of Ontario] Lincoln Alexander, and you can look throughout history for contributions by black people.... I don't know why they get tribal and get into these little groups and then they say there are no role models and that kind of stuff. I think in a lot of cases we fail as a group because we have different orientations to the way things really are."

But as far as Jackson is concerned, even though he considers himself a role model—perhaps a questionable one with this thinking—Blacks should not be seeking him out just because he is black. "You ask me about a group coming from Toronto [to lobby him]. Well, the first thing they should do is to go to their elected member of Parliament. Their MP could gather momentum by getting alliances with other MPs, do your work through caucus and develop a head of steam. That's the way the thing is done."

So does this mean that Blacks from across the country should not come running to the likes of him and Jean Augustine, simply because they want to identify with them as black parliamentarians and might be distrustful of Whites? I ask.

"Jean will probably tell you the exact opposite to what I am telling you because I got a different orientation. Personally, I think in a lot of cases when things fail [it is] that people are not using the right approaches. I usually make things happen. I don't get into skirmishes unless I have to."

It is more than a difference in orientation that separates Jackson and

Augustine. It is the classic argument of how black politicians see themselves: as pursuing a wider agenda for all Blacks—so that, for example, in America, black congressmen would form a black caucus to deal with black issues from all across the nation—or whether a black politician should quietly slip into the party or caucus, pretend to be the same as any white politician, and become black only during such times as Black History Month when the party and government need someone to fly their colours. These two politicians, sitting in the same caucus and party, illustrate the extreme of the problems facing black politicians. Why can a Jackson get away with virtually no criticism for doing nothing for Blacks, while an Augustine is held to a higher standard? The answer rests with the expectations of a community, expectations that are generally created and sown in the community by the parties. Expectations that are the result of the parties exploiting the black electorate and then ignoring them between trips to the polls. And for this we can blame the usually baseless promises political parties make to curry the support of Blacks and minorities. Often, the political parties cannot meet the expectations they kindled in the black community.

Jackson speaks freely and rejects the idea of his representing a race because that was never his claim. As he says, he was never part of the black community, and he ran for office in a constituency where there are virtually no Blacks besides the members of his family. And in the surrounding areas, there were no Blacks who travelled long distances to work on his behalf, to donate time and money, in the hope that his election would be seen as an elevation of their community.

Jean Augustine's case was different. The Liberal Party ran her as a black candidate—a star candidate, the party called her. So that she would be on the ticket, party leader Jean Chrétien resorted to a controversial move of appointing her as his candidate, so that she did not have to be nominated. To protest Chrétien's intervention, the executive of the riding revolted and sat on their hands during the campaign. This left Augustine even more dependent on the black workers parachuted into her riding to knock on doors. But the leadership of the Liberal Party felt that getting Augustine on the ticket was worth the disruption. The message and symbolism were too important to pass up. For appointments like Augustine's were the party's meagre attempts at some form of employment equity or affirmative action, especially in the urban centres. It actively encouraged—even set aside nominations—for women and minorities. Its message to these designated groups was that there is a place for them under the Liberal umbrella. These star candidates would shine once they got to the national capital.

Everything fitted in nicely with the optics of satisfying the expectations of Blacks and anointing Augustine, and not, say, a Jackson, as some messianic leader. Augustine willingly accepted her role as a superstar black candidate. She genuinely believed she got this billing because she had worked hard and long, which she had, in the black and immigrant communities. Most of her workers were black. All of them must have pointed out to her at various points that they were supporting Jean Augustine and not necessarily the party. The fact that she was running as a Liberal—the chosen party of most Blacks—provided a natural tie-in. Blacks did not have to worry about switching their traditional political alliance to support her.

In my conversations with Augustine, I never had any doubt that she saw her election as part of the march onward and upward for Blacks in Toronto and in Canada generally. I remember having a brief talk with Augustine in the dying days of the campaign. I had gone to her campaign office and had brought with me a mutual friend from Montreal and a visitor from Barbados who was in Toronto for a martial arts tournament. The visitor was born in St. Lucia and was quickly into the conversation; he and Augustine exchanged stories about friends they knew in St. Lucia and Grenada, where Augustine was born. The visitor thought it such a great achievement that a Caribbean immigrant could even aspire to hold an elected office in Canada. Augustine told him that is the type of country she hoped to help build, one in which all peoples—particularly black immigrants like us—can take pride in this country. She would be a voice for the black community and for all others seeking social justice and opportunity and pride of place in this country. The three of us made our political donations, wished her well and left so that Augustine could return to her door-to-door campaigning.

On another occasion, I attended a brunch given by a women's group from the Toronto area to celebrate Augustine's election and her appointment as parliamentary secretary to the prime minister. None of these women lived in Augustine's riding, yet every one of them felt Augustine represented her. More than that, several of them regaled the brunch with stories about their friendships with Augustine, of the bonds they had developed as young Caribbean immigrant women, of how they were now looking forward to Augustine's work on behalf of the young generation of Blacks in Canada. "Remember the youths," said the host of the brunch, Monica Caliste, an old friend of Augustine's. "It is the youths that we have to do something for."

Augustine didn't disagree. Perhaps it was our political naivety that made us expect, or want to believe, that her election would make a difference for all Blacks, women and immigrants—because there would now be a different voice, a different perspective in the caucus and government. While that afternoon was a celebration of great Caribbean food and drink, the swapping of immigrant tales, the handing out of bouquets, it was also sowing the seeds of disappointment, because no single politician could have delivered on the expectations in that room. And the ground that these seeds were sowed in was first ploughed by the political parties. They planted corn while the black community expected strong, independent oak trees.

But is it realistic to expect a single black person to reshape an institution like a political party? Could Blacks be setting up their MPs and other elected officials to fail by putting unreasonable demands on them? History shows this is usually the case. And Augustine is an example of how this can happen. It started with the realization that of a voting population of 60,000 in her riding of Lakeshore-Etobicoke, only 700 are black. To whom, then, does Augustine owe her allegiance? Members of the black community claim her as their own, even though they cannot vote for her.

Jackson would suggest that Augustine owes her allegiance to those who elected her, for ultimately all politics are local. Other politicians would argue that she was born black, came into the party as a black person and was sought by the party to add some colour to its ticket, so she owes it to this constituency to speak for its interests.

It is an argument that obviously frustrates Augustine, at times making her seem at a loss for words to accurately explain her thinking. "I can't live my life because somebody somewhere thinks this is what I should do," she says, adding that she cannot allow herself to get up every morning and start checking in with various community groups to tell her what to say and when. "I have to take what I [am], as a black woman with my life experiences, with the equity issues." From her track record, people should know by now how she will react and perform when she sits at a table with other politicians.

The point that Augustine and I are discussing in her office on Parliament Hill is whether she has to approach politics differently from her white colleagues. Do other white women in the party have to concern themselves with primary issues beyond those that affect their constituencies? And is it realistic to put such a heavy burden on the shoulders of a rookie MP who is trying to find her way around the corridors of power? I suggest that the party has set up a situation in which Augustine is bound to be the loser, unless she turns out to be some kind of a miracle person, with superhuman strengths and constitution. Otherwise, how can she effectively become the MP for all black Canadians? What is going to happen to the dreams and aspirations of Blacks when political reality strikes? And then what will become of Jean Augustine, the superstar black candidate?

"Well, I don't know," she replies. "I think reality has always struck. There have been people who have not been happy with me all the time. They have been people who said to me you shouldn't be principal of that school, you shouldn't be doing this over here, you should be doing that over there. What I am saying to you is that I know what the issues are and I have defined them according to my world and the experiences.... The only thing I can do is to be me and take that me, which is Jean Augustine, a black woman with this kind of experience, mother, with this and that [experience], and bring that to where I am. I can't deal with each and every person, because that is almost schizophrenic, if you have to begin to say, well, there are so many people who don't approve of me and so many people who do approve. I can't deal with that and the community. I am not taking on the mantle of responsibility for the entire world. I'm not doing that."

Still, there is the question of Blacks from as far away as Nova Scotia and British Columbia, people not in her riding, who call her sister and send letters of invitation to attend their functions, letters professing how much

Jean Augustine as a black woman means to them, and letters and petitions asking Jean Augustine, the politician, to intervene on their behalf.

"I will continue to do the affirming things with them," Augustine says. "If someone is coming to Ottawa and I can ensure they have a seat in the House and it doesn't matter which part of the country [they are from], I'll continue to do that. But the only way I can affirm all my black brothers and sisters across the country is to perform the best possible way that I can—not playing somebody else's agenda."

Is this just another example of that double burden of being black in Canada? "It [is] and it certainly will [be] if the expectation is that I am going to be [a spokesperson for Blacks on every issue]. What I am trying to say to you is that for my own mental health, for my own performance level, for my own self-determination, that I have to do what I am comfortable with, not what the expectation is out there for me." And for this, she can thank her party and the cynical power brokers.

Indeed, being female, and a member of the women's movement, might add a third burden on her shoulder—a crippling load that even an Ovid Jackson would not have. "I think that women are highlighted and spotlighted. The fact that I am the first black woman in the history of the Parliament does make for some spotlighting. Ovid is the third black man. I also come to this job with a profile in the community, the women's community, the black community, the black women's community, the immigrant women's community. The fact people are looking to me stems from that interest and does create a certain amount of expectation. I am determined to carry the black agenda forward. What is the black agenda? All the equity issues, to ensure that race and colour and creed and nationality and all those things are not in the way of people's opportunity to access, and also not only access [but] promotion of opportunities in the workplace and other avenues in people's lives. I've had to deal with that in my life and I'm here to help the system ensure it doesn't happen to this generation or the next. The fact that more people will be looking to me, will be coming to me, I can't depart from what I've said. I see that as the answer."

Looking at Jean Augustine as we talk, I keep wondering if she has not allowed herself to be boxed in. Too many hands appear to be reaching out to her. Cynical politics would say that politicians are always looking for trade-offs: if they make one group "mad," they hope to more than compensate by making another happy. This might work in the wider society, of which Blacks are only one of many groups and candidates to be traded off. For Jean Augustine and the black community, there are no real trade-offs unless the political parties are to bend and to absorb the aspirations and raised hopes of this specific community. And as Jean Augustine and I talk in her office, even though it is less than a year after her election and appointment as the black shadow for the prime minister on the parliamentary channel, we both started to come to the realization that some dreams must die, but that they would also die hard. Hard for the community and hard for Jean Augustine. So I ask her how she is bearing up under the heavy workload of answering so many letters and invitations from Blacks across the country, the load of knowing so much is on the shoulders of a rookie politician, the burden of being black.

"The workload is manageable. When you get umpteen invitations, there are times you would want to give some priority to some things. But I've always worked long hours; people who know me know my capacity for getting the task done. Right now the workload is manageable. I am greatly appreciative when I meet people who say, You have my support, you have my prayers and just hold it there, girl. That's affirming. But people who have expectations ... it's so great to play the ballgame from the armchair. All of us can sit in the armchair and say how you should kick the ball and where it should go and who should catch it."

* * *

As a member of the provincial legislature of British Columbia, Rosemary Brown's task might have been even more difficult than Augustine's. Noticeably, when the provincial NDP came to power in 1973, neither of the two black MPPs in the caucus was included in cabinet. It was quite noticeable that a woman like Brown, with a national profile as was seen from her run for the leadership of the federal party, could be overlooked for some rather nondescript colleagues, all of whom self-destructed in a mere three years in such a dramatic fashion that the NDP not only became a one-term party but was banished to the opposition benches for 15 years.

But some of the harshest criticism for black politicians who get caught in the mainstream political parties and fail to speak up on community issues comes from Zanana Akande. She was the first black woman elected in the Ontario Legislature and the first black woman to hold a ministerial position in Canada. After a mere four years in politics, Akande resigned in frustration, arguing that she could accomplish more as a school principal and social advocate than by working within the political system. Here are some of Ms. Akande's observations from our interview.

"It's tough being a Black who carries some of the agenda. If, in fact, we speak in our own voice—a phrase I've come to use, speaking in our own voice—rather than the political double-talk that they will teach you. There are courses and consultants that teach you to do that thing so that you can get by. I think it's tough and it's unfortunate, because as we use that double-talk we skirt the issues. We don't come at them head on. That doesn't mean we don't see them. It just means that eventually we find that that language does not serve our purpose. It is not designed to serve our purpose. It is designed for other people in other situations. The fact that we imitate it may make us seem like good politicians. But can you be a good politician if you have forgotten your goal, if you have given up your agenda, if you have discarded your program? And there are those who say, 'Well, you don't have to say everything you think,' but then who does? When you go to the committee meeting and you do the dance around the issue, it allows others to dance around the issue, and the issue is never addressed."

I reminded Akande of a controversial statement Jean Augustine had made the night of her election, when she suggested that she doesn't always have to be reminding people that she is a black woman. Jackson also seems to share the view that colour doesn't always have to be mentioned, if it even has to be mentioned at all.

"You don't have to do it in all situations, because it doesn't require that. It depends on the context and the situation. I don't. But I can remember that there have been occasions in the House where Caucasian members have referred to their background in order to give particular credibility to an issue they were addressing ... to give some kind of support. I suppose in those kinds of situations you will do that and I don't see any reason why you wouldn't do it. I think that it's not necessary to say it every five minutes, if you speak in your own voice. If what I say sounds almost as if I'm avoiding the topic, if it's an issue related to race, there is a need to remind people that I speak from some acquired knowledge related to the fact that I am of that group, yeah, I would do that. I do that even when they talk about educators. If I'm making the point [I'd say] as an educator, I know something about this."

Akande also said that the cultures of the political parties, regardless of their social leanings, make it difficult for the traditional outsider to change them. And the cultures of these parties have for a long time excluded minorities and Blacks. "There is a kind of camaraderie, a closeness about the cabinet process which means that you support each other and you discuss at cabinet what should be done, but if you want support on *your* issues, you shut your mouth on *mine.* I haven't got time for that. There was too much to be done and I like to have the freedom of my expression. You know, people say it's wonderful to be a role model. Well, we have to stop being enamoured by positions and recognize that power sometimes comes from being able and willing to deal with an issue as it is, by still being able to reach out to those community groups and being able to come back and say in caucus, this isn't happening. I could not do that in cabinet. I could not do that. You cannot because you owe a certain loyalty to cabinet [colleagues]; he's not biting at your elbows, so why are you biting at his or hers, and that whole way of playing the game is something I am not thrilled about."

Where, then, is the trade-off for the politician who is black and who wants to raise black consciousness, but might be constrained by other matters and practicalities? Akande says that when she was a provincial minister, she found a way to handle these seemingly competing interests. "One of the things I had to do was to let my scheduling person know that there are a group of people out there [that do not] have access to the minister. An organization of only a hundred people, not a large organization—for this reason they don't have access to the minister because they are not large enough. So what happens is that they are excluded. I would try to go to small meetings. Our community has a way of being very suspect of people who assume a leadership role because we have been burnt before. We have a way of believing that they are going to be divorced, they are going to be separated from them and this person is going to go on to garnish their own career and to make the best of it. So you have to be certain that they see you, that they know what you are saying ... that they hear you directly and they can see you so they can give you that information, or they will be very suspicious of you. I am aware of that. I show up at meetings that are relatively small and my staff would say, Why would you go? and I would say, It's a group of people that needs to know what I'm thinking, and besides, I need to know what they are thinking because I am directed in many ways by that information, and that would be small black groups and other groups."

Akande says she did not buy into the notion that the black politicians have to somehow make a choice between representing issues of the constituency that elected them and carrying the black agenda.

"I think when I fight for issues of equity, these are issues that affect every Canadian, and if I don't, I couldn't continue to be a Canadian. I know that my riding represents many people. It's interesting: when you talk about equity, they fit themselves into that. A large part of my riding is Jewish, many people from various countries, other people that are immigrants ... some Blacks, some Anglo-Saxons. I can't believe that any of those Canadians would not be interested in issues such as equity. When you hear Canada described, that [equity] is what you hear in the description. So when I strike out on issues that ensure that all people—black people, white people, all people—have equal opportunities, I am not doing something in opposition to my riding. I am doing something well within their expectations as Canadians.

"If there are issues that specifically relate to my community or my riding, I deal with them. When Doctors Hospital has an issue, they phone me. When some of the schools and trustees are concerned about some of the things in the area, I'm there. When the representative from [the municipal] council says there is something that has to deal with this specific area, I'm right there. I'm asking the questions in the House. I'm asking the ministers what about this, or I'm bringing them information. I do not avoid those issues because those issues are important and that's why I am there. So when someone phones me and says I don't live in your riding, I don't work in your riding, but I'm a black person from anywhere in Ontario and I have this issue, I'm also there. Because if the issue is real and it contributes to the betterment of this society, who am I to say that it's irrelevant? Of course it is relevant."

The grinding effect of the culture of the mainstream political parties shows up in other ways as well, in the notion of cabinet solidarity, which extends beyond the buddy system Akande spoke about, or that Augustine and Jackson deferred to. It can also be reflected in the roles foisted on Blacks when they become spokespeople for the mainstream party. One example of this is what happened to Alvin Curling when he became an opposition critic for the Liberal Party in the Ontario Legislature. Curling was once a minister in the Liberal government and had managed to hold on to his seat when many of his colleagues were routed in the 1991 election. The opposition system works on the principle that virtually nothing proposed by the government is ever right, far less perfect. A critic of any minister or ministry is always finding fault.

Curling's position as opposition critic raised some eyebrows in the black community when he opposed a government bill on employment equity, a piece of legislation Blacks and other minorities had pushed several governments to enact, including the one in which Curling served. The question for many Blacks was whether Curling should be opposing this bill, even if he felt it was as flawed as he claimed. Should he accept that a first, even if imperfect, step toward employment equity is better than nothing at all, that it provides something to build on?

Curling chose to condemn the bill. But Curling's actions also raised some other issues, such as why the Liberal Party would use a black member to condemn this bill. Is this tantamount to putting a white argument in a black mouth so as to give the criticisms added legitimacy? For many Blacks, Curling's argument that "this is how the game of politics is played" was not good enough. The argument seemed even more hollow when the next government wiped out employment equity the first day on the job for them, in one act wiping out all the meagre gains for which Blacks had spent decades fighting. Should Curling have been sensitive to this reality and put his foot down, arguing in caucus that there are some principles he would not violate? For even as he played the game according to rules set by others, as he spoke the language Akande warned against, Curling must have recalled how frustrating it was for him when he first entered politics. He knew that without the backing and support of a specific community, his stint in politics might have been very short. Indeed, my first question to Curling when we chatted in his legislative office is whether he encountered racism in the halls of power.

"It's a good question," he answers. "You know, because first you have to define what racism is. I think [U.S. civil-rights leader] Dick Gregory said of his book, when his mother asked him why he called his book *Nigger*, he said, 'Mom, every time they say Nigger, they're advertising my book.' I say that because if I expected someone to call me nigger, that kind of racism ain't going to be there. I ain't going to see it. Nobody ain't going to say that. But you know, what happens is that you are in a meeting, for instance, and you put an idea forward. You get a funny little look on the face of your colleagues and other people and you're wondering if you missed the point. So you say it again and they still haven't gotten it. So you rest your case. Nobody has commented on that. Then about five different speakers will speak and say the same thing and you'll say, 'There must be an echo in the room, I just said that.' And then the chair of the group says, 'Oh, that's an excellent point that you made over there, Tony.' And you say to yourself, 'My golly, I thought I had made the same comment.'

"You sort of put in your mind—didn't he hear me properly? When it happens quite a few times, you know there is a rejection of your thought. So then you have to ask, why did that person reject my thought? That's what racism does: it makes you start to re-examine yourself in a negative way; maybe I wasn't smelling right, maybe something was on my mouth and they saw it or something of the sort, maybe my grammar was wrong. By the time you are finished with yourself, you come to the conclusion they didn't want to listen to you, they don't think your views as an individual are any good.

"Yes, I have had those kinds of racism. I've had my voice mimicked in the House, mimicked by a member of the opposition when I was a minister, about my accent. That's racism to mimic the way I speak because they feel I am different. I look different to the so-called traditional Ontarian parliamentarian because of my colour, so therefore [I am] a free sport to laugh at, to mimic. [This incident happened when, in asking Curling about his policy, David Reville mimicked a Jamaican accent by saying, "Soon cum, mahn, soon cum," and laughed.] When people ask me if racism had been directed to me, I'd say yup."

Political parties and caucuses, especially those that want to appear diversified and representative of all groups in society, like to give off the image of inclusiveness and openness. I wanted to find out from Alvin Curling if, unlike Zanana Akande and Rosemary Brown in British Columbia, he found these institutions free of racism.

"Quite often you do that [make a point and it is ignored] and you wonder, you ask yourself the questions, you examine every other presence you have and then you realize it must be something else. I wouldn't want to feel now after the long experience that there is some sort of racism that is there. The frightening thing is that they don't know, either. I've had discussions about resolving racism not through all these programs we are putting in, but within proper trade with countries like Trinidad, Barbados and African countries because we then come to respect the individuals at the different levels. They perceive most of those countries where Blacks are coming from—when I say 'they,' I'm talking about members of my caucus or members of the white communities—these countries are Third World countries who need help. So it's a matter of what can we do to help them and not a matter of exchange of trade and ideas. Yes, I feel it is there."

And did things change when he became more than just another caucus member, but was elevated to cabinet with supposedly all the clout and prominence that came with his position as minister of housing?

"As a minister, I remember once I was in [the Ministry of] Housing and one of the deputy ministers was doing a briefing, dealing with the Ontario Land Corporation. I am going to be completely candid with you. I had heard about this Ontario Land Corporation, how massive it was. I didn't have a full dollar figure in my head of how massive this was. It was really a massive inventory of the government and it was my second day of briefing. I remember the bureaucrat throwing the book down after finishing his presentation and showing me the billions of dollars of inventory of land the government has. His question was, 'Do we sell or not, minister?' I was kind of taken aback. Is the minister that powerful that he could maybe sell off a billion dollars of land, just say yes or no? I internalized it a bit while I hear him repeat, 'Do we, minister?' I realized just by the tone of the voice that what he is doing is either trying to humiliate me or something like that. I said to him, 'Are you finished?' He said, 'Yes.' I said, 'Next.'

"Some of these things are so difficult to assess. Why is the individual doing that? Is he doing it because I am new and it's a new government or because I'm black? But having years of experience in this country and the experience as an administrator, I can say I can't find any other reason. I think I am quite capable of deciphering when tough decisions have to be made and who should make them and the process that's to be done. The bureaucrat knows the process; why is he asking me when he knew all along that even if I made the decision that he couldn't sell it anyhow?

"Other little events [occur], of course, when you go up to the North and all that. I remember once I went to a meeting. I arrived with my staff, who said to a white female staff of the other group, 'Are we ready for the minister?' The person answered, 'The minister isn't here.' And she said, 'The minister is here.' She said, 'No,' and after the exchange my staffer said, 'This is the minister.' The person was completely embarrassed, the look on her face was saying why would I not believe that he could be the minister?"

By the time Curling started to run into problems in his ministry—criticisms that he always appeared ill-prepared and unbriefed when he came to address issues with which, as a minister, he should have been more than familiar—talk began circulating around the black community that the brother was being set up to fail. There were the stories of how difficult it was for Curling, the first black cabinet member in Ontario, to get the support of bureaucracy and even of his party.

"I would say that the bureaucrats were extremely good. They worked hard. They were not partisan. They were suspicious of this new Liberal government that came in. But, if you look, and are trying to make an assessment of [everyone], all the ministers of the day were very hard working. Everyone was pretty new to the job. People got parliamentary assistants in the tough portfolios; if you look at the stars in the cabinet, the Ian Scotts, the Conways, the [Jim] Bradleys, people who were around, the Nixons, who are old boys in this thing, who feel quite at home in Parliament—all of them had parliamentary assistants. Housing, which is one of the most controversial portfolios, because we were putting in rent controls and all of that, I didn't have a parliamentary assistant and I was off the street. A new individual, no parliamentary experience, no ministerial experience."

The situation didn't get any better for Curling when he found himself caught in a scandal caused by Patty Starr, a fundraiser for a Jewish organization, who made overly generous political donations to individual cabinet members and to the Liberal Party. Indeed, some Blacks were quietly elated when the scandal humbled Curling. Many felt that on becoming a minister, he had deserted the community and was no longer accessible. He appeared more inclined to hang out with the moneyed class, people like Patty Starr who could wine and dine him, provide thousands of dollars for his election campaign, so that he didn't need the meagre proceeds from community raffles any more. With this money, he didn't need people like myself and all the Blacks from across the province and possibly even one or two from the United States who had joined together in what he affectionately called his "rag-tag" team to help storm Babylon, to help get him elected. Many felt that he had not only slipped the bonds of being just a poor black politician, but that he was developing a swagger as well.

"Politics is a blood sport, it's a survival sport," Curling explains. "I think that it's not a matter of winning sometime a seat that is important. I see this the same way with employment equity. It's nice to open the door and let the person in, but many times you never let them upstairs. Yes, I was in cabinet for five years, two portfolios. The Patty Star situation would come to anybody. Once you're dealing with people making decisions and people associate themselves with you, people would posture about the interest they have and don't have. It is important that the party supports you when the tough times come. Yeah, I feel a bit disappointed after the kind of support that I was getting [from the party]. I didn't in any way feel I couldn't weather that storm and had to resign."

Curling feels that black politicians, as was the case with Akande, are considered by the powers that be in the political parties as expendable. They can be dismissed easily because the parties feel there will be few or no repercussions. What is the black community going to do if one of its representatives is forced to swallow political hemlock? The political leader can make decisions that are unpopular in the black community because they can afford to live with the consequences. "He knows that having me in cabinet and having me on the team and caucus as a black individual, as with Zanana, enforces and enhances the kind of philosophy that they so-called project. If the support is not out there, they can play with that kind of stuff. If he pulls back and there is a backlash, he would fight. Not because it is right or wrong, but because of the support. Now the black community—they are dispensable."

Curling recalls bitterly the meeting at which his premier asked him to step down. This was making Curling not only the first black cabinet minister in the province, but also the first Black to resign from any Canadian cabinet—and under a cloud. Once again the double burden of being black: you rise as an individual—as the likes of Ovid Jackson no doubt believe—but fall as a race. The premier wasn't just asking Curling to leave cabinet, but was silencing the entire black voice in his caucus.

"We had a very good talk. He asked me the usual stuff, said that he's going to ask me to step down because the pressure that was coming to bear was too great and I'd be too much focused on. I said fine. I told him I come from a lifestyle of survival. Each day I don't have to remind myself I'm black and that I'd be subjected to many things and that we are the underdog. That's a normal thing. I said to him I understand what he's doing. I said that being a captain of a team, you feel you have to do some scores and it may distract [to have me around]. I gave him a way out. I said I'm sure it might distract from some of the issues you'd like to do. But again, if he chooses that I should step down, I'll obey. But I told him emphatically that there was one thing he can't choose: that I should step down in my riding, that [my leaving politics was up to] the people who have elected me with a solid mandate. And I told him outright, it is his loss and Ontario's loss not having me as minister. But if you choose as the captain for me to step down, I'll step down."

Curling did step down, or had the podium ripped away from under his feet. This added one more chapter to the experience of Blacks trying to change, or even influence, the mainstream through politics. One thing appeared to be common from all these experiences: regardless of the stripes of the party, it will use the black candidate only to further its cause. Blacks seeking change through the established political system might want to keep one other example in mind. Ultimately, Curling was cleared of any wrongdoing in the scandal. But by then the damage had been done to his career. Fortunately, that was not the last we would hear from Curling, and neither would it be the last time the party would understand the importance of having a black face in caucus, especially one willing to do its dirty work.

In the fall of 1995, a new Tory government in Ontario arrogantly introduced a massive omnibus bill, seeking to amend about 43 pieces of legislation in one fell swoop. The government also wanted to pass this bill to essentially dismantle most of the province's social safety net with a minimum of debate. For days the opposition parties tried to get the government to relent from its timetable, but to no avail. The opposition seemed to be out of tactics to stall the progress of the bill, which was scheduled to be passed within a day. Then, the bill came up for a procedural vote. The opposition refused to vote on the bill, breaking the rules of the Ontario Legislature that MPPs at their seats must vote yea, nay or abstain when their names are called. The Speaker of the House was forced to take action to remove the protestors. He called the name of the first Liberal opposition member, who was duly escorted from the House when he refused to vote. Then he called on Alvin Curling, who by now was beginning to get mixed messages as to whether the prearranged protest had been called off, because the original plan was for every member not to leave the House gently. However, Curling stuck to the script. He refused to vote and to leave. The sergeant-at-arms approached to remove Curling, but the members of the opposition blocked his path. So began a 19-hour sit-in by Curling. To end the protest, the Tories agreed to compromise and send the omnibus bill to committee meetings. Curling left the House and was suspended for a few days until he issued an apology.

Although Curling basked in the praise from the black community—even the famed defence lawyer, Johnnie Cochran, who was in town for a speech, praised Curling's protest at a meeting with black community leaders—some troubling questions remain. Would anyone but Curling, a black man who, by staging a sit-in, evoked images of a Rosa Parks and the U.S. civil-rights era of the 1950s to 1970s, get away with such a protest? For after all, the first MPP who had a chance to be the political guinea pig walked away without a struggle. The second question is whether the opposition parties were willing to sacrifice Curling. Suppose the protest hadn't worked. Would Curling have found himself, as he described, black and therefore dispensable? The doubts linger in Curling's mind.

One thing that is clear from these experiences is that we are helpful to the mainstream only when we are expedient and not when we want, or demand, change. Sometimes, the game is just too tough for us and that is why so many Blacks often choose to sit out the charades.

And at the federal level, it didn't take long for the farce involving Jean Augustine and Ovid Jackson and the ruling Liberal Party to play itself out. At the halfway point of his mandate, Prime Minister Jean Chrétien decided to shake up his cabinet. He also made drastic changes to his so-called B team—all the parliamentary secretaries described previously even by the prime minister as "ministers in waiting."

The farce was played out with some irony: in discarding all the parliamentary secretaries, Chrétien dropped Augustine, his star black candidate and dispatched her to the powerless back benches of his government. This means that, to use even Augustine's words, she was no longer in this no man's land, but neither had she moved on to bigger things. The star candidate for the black community had flamed out—and in only two years. Chrétien was smart in picking Augustine's successor; he chose Dr. Rey Pagtakhan, a Filipino rookie politician.

Chrétien could now play the same game with the Filipino community that he did with the black. And if Blacks criticize his handling of Augustine, he can always argue that a Filipino has as much right to be window-dressing for the prime minister and the party, has as much right to be seen walking to and from Parliament, has as much right to be sitting in the view of the parliamentary television cameras so as to provide the same multicultural optics as Augustine ... has the same opportunity, essentially, to be the water carrier for the party and prime minister but held away from real power, from doing anything to galvanize the ambitions and aspirations of his community.

But there was a final irony to the shake-up of parliamentary secretaries. Chrétien reached into the back benches and elevated none other than Ovid Jackson to parliamentary secretary for the Treasury Board, joining the B team of ministers in waiting. This is the same Jackson who does not necessarily see himself as representing a black community, a Jackson who feels that he does not have to be concerned about the agenda of urban Blacks. It will be interesting to see how the prime minister and the Liberal Party will present Augustine and Jackson to the black community in the next election. Could this party dare to ask Blacks to put their hopes, aspirations and trust in Augustine? Will it try to dress up Jackson as the black representative that he claims he doesn't want to be? As is quite likely, the party might simply find another, and perhaps as equally dispensable, black person to be its star candidate in the community. For if the Liberal Party doesn't, undoubtedly the other parties will be eagerly looking for a superstar black candidate of their own. Such is the story for Blacks in Canadian politics.

All of which leads to a rather indelicate question for Canadians: is it possible to contemplate the day when this country will elect a black premier or prime minister? Pioneers like Rosemary Brown and Howard McCurdy tried to get Blacks to dream the seemingly impossible by running for the leadership of a federal party. Other politicians have tried to break in through other mainstream parties only to find themselves marginalized, willingly or otherwise. They can rise only so far and no further, with the zenith of their political career usually their election-night celebration. Ironically, their election seldom serves as a springboard for greater personal and community achievement.

It is unlikely that many young Blacks will join the political process until, and unless, the black community believes that the political process can work for them. However, the United States appears to be coming to terms with the idea of electing a black president or vice-president. In the run-up to the 1996 presidential election, the main question in political circles was whether General Colin Powell would either run for the Republican nomination or accept the second spot on the party's ticket. Until Powell declined to enter the race, polls showed that many Americans felt he would make a good president, and many felt he could run and win. Powell might have his chance yet.

Although Canadians will argue that the United States is much more racist and much less tolerant—and maybe it is—at least a black youth can dream of becoming president. In Canada, the greatest test of whether integration can work is whether we can even begin to dream at all.

CHAPTER 7

MEDIA TURKEY SHOOT

What do we think of when we think of poverty? Images of African children with bloated bellies?

The Toronto Star
November 20, 1994

For well over a year, the talk in black communities was about the call by the leader of the Nation of Islam (NOI) for one million men to march on Washington. The call was aimed mainly at the black population in the United States, but it also resonated in Toronto, Montreal, Halifax, Vancouver, Edmonton, Ottawa, Windsor—in every Canadian urban centre where the NOI's presence is growing.

The summons from Minister Louis Farrakhan was for black men to stand up in the fall of 1995 and be counted. It was time for black men to start taking care of their families, for them to beat their breasts and recognize that too often black males have shirked responsibilities to family and community. The call was for the making of a new black man, a more positive and caring partner for the black female, a self-confident man who was mentally liberated by becoming drug and alcohol free. An entreaty to bury all the ugly and vile stereotypes.

As so often happens, a call like this usually has unintentional repercussions and implications. In this case, the call provided the opportunity for many in the black community to switch the spotlight on the news media, turning the tables on those who usually descend on the black community looking mainly for bad news. This episode was instructive in revealing the wide gulf in perception and even the distrust between the black community on one hand and the news media on the other. It provided a striking example of how the mass media in Canada cover (or don't cover) black people and culture. When the examination was finished, nobody could doubt how disconnected the Canadian mainstream media is from a sizeable segment of the Canadian population—a segment that many people in the black community believe the media appear quite happy to ignore when there is only good news. Everyone knows that this situation is undesirable: for Blacks, who do not like how they are depicted, and for the mainstream media, who ignore discussion of urban issues. Why is this the case, and isn't society as a whole paying a big price?

Minister Farrakhan's invocation to resurrect a new man unsullied by the usual unflattering black caricatures was heard loudest among black male youths in Canada. It is in this group that the call found its most fertile ground. Plans were made to attend this gathering, even though it was happening far away. For the youths, the location of the march didn't matter; the message did. It spoke to them of the alienation they experience in Canadian society. They could testify to the disaffection that was as strong for them as for African-Americans south of the border.

Nobody in the black community could have missed the discussion and the planning for this day of atonement. Not if they were involved with or knew members of black clubs at universities and community colleges. Not if they visited black barbershops and hair-styling salons, or bought groceries at West Indian and black stores. Not if they went to black restaurants, read the community newspapers, played dominoes, poker, cricket or soccer in black clubs, and attended their churches.

An active Million Man March Committee had sprung up in Toronto. Members met in the office of a prominent lawyer, gathering together many of the outspoken activists in the black community. Members of the fledgling group of Nation of Islam converts and NOI officials from the United States were also involved. Community newspapers carried advertisements by entrepreneurs who saw the possibility of making a quick buck by organizing bus tours to Washington to coincide with the march.

And the community newspapers also provided regular updates on the planning for the Million Man March committee in the United States and the intention of its Canadian contingent. In Canada, the jungle drums were beating loudly. It was hard for anyone in touch with the black community to miss the planning.

In the Canadian mainstream media, the event was virtually ignored all year long. A week or two before the march, perhaps catching on late to the grassroots rumblings, the newspapers began running the usual critical pieces, most of them lifted straight from U.S. publications. Few bothered looking for a Canadian angle to these stories. There were the discussions about Minister Farrakhan's anti-Semitic remarks and of a power struggle between the Nation of Islam and the black churches. Predictably, the media focused mainly on whether the march was a power grab by Minister Farrakhan for the control of black minds.

The big question for the mainstream media was, how dare this anti-Semite even pretend to be another Martin Luther King Jr.? To call for a march, just like King did two decades earlier, was simply too laughable to be taken seriously, or for reporters and researchers to spend time monitoring. Nobody took a look at the reasons for the call; nobody saw or heard of any connection between the march in Washington and what was happening in urban centres in Canada. Nobody noticed that some of the people heading across the border had themselves condemned Minister Farrakhan's anti-Jewish statements. As was the case, the last-minute coverage was predictable, part of an us-versus-them approach. Obviously, the news media were operating under the assumption that not only were their readers and viewers white, but that they also had nothing in common with Blacks. Planning for the march wasn't a part of their society. They didn't care about it, didn't need to be informed, didn't think it worthy of their ongoing attention. Therefore, the news media needed only to inform Whites of what Blacks were doing. But this news was only important if it fitted in with the Whites' perception of their world; that is, only if the news alerted them to any threats to their way of life posed by Blacks who tend to show up in mainstream news mainly as dangerous stereotypes. Otherwise, they never bothered informing Blacks about what was happening in their community. Instead of building bridges among communities, the news media are often responsible for widening the gulf. The

Million Man March proved this to be the case.

Two days before the march, I received a call from a producer at the CBC Radio's national syndication department. She was blunt with me: we don't know what to make of this march in Washington. Should we ignore it because of the many people, including some Blacks, saying it is only an exercise in demagoguery by Farrakhan, or is there something newsworthy to this gathering?

I was prepared for her. Just hours before she called, I had turned down an offer by some young black men of a seat in the car they had rented to make the trip. This was just one of the many carloads and busloads that were heading for Washington from across Canada.

I told the producer that to ignore the Million Man March would be to disregard one of the biggest events of the year.

The producer decided to trust my instincts. Would I be willing to give a series of short interviews on CBC radio stations across the nation the morning of the march? Essentially, I was to explain what the march was about, who the Nation of Islam are, and why this religious group and the call for atonement by its leader would appeal to Canadian Blacks. How many stations would carry the interviews? I asked for obvious reasons: the more numerous the stations, the bigger my paycheque. She could not tell. Technically, she would offer the opportunity for interviews to scores of stations on the network. But, ultimately, the individual producers of the morning shows had the final say. Later in the day, she got back to me with the news that three members of the CBC network were interested in the interviews—stations in Toronto, Thunder Bay and Edmonton. All others declined. What about Montreal? I asked. Are they going to be doing anything about the march? She didn't know, she said. Later in the day, I got a call from the interfaith television network, Vision TV, also asking if I would appear the day of the march on one of its programs.

The morning of the march, I got up early to tune in to the television coverage. Even the American networks seemed to be caught off guard by the hundreds of thousands of people who, even at that early hour, were already gathering in the dark. As I waited for my first phone call from CBC's "Metro Morning" in Toronto, I watched the crowd swell. And I watched as the major television networks scrambled to get reporters, cameras and crews to the site. Canadian networks, who were even more unprepared, started carrying the feeds of the American stations. So much for logistical planning in their newsrooms, I thought. This is not the same kind of planning that would happen automatically if the call for this march and the issuer of this call had been taken seriously in the first place. This would not have happened if people of importance and influence, such as news directors and producers, understood what was happening in the community; if they understood that Minister Farrakhan had struck a chord when he spoke about the poor condition of a black person's life in North America; if they knew that almost on a monthly basis the various NOI groups in Canada organize caravans of bus trips for black youths heading to some mosque or convention in the United States to hear Minister Farrakhan speak.

It would have been different if the news directors, producers, reporters and researchers understood the different hats the Nation of Islam wears in the black community. For at times it is as an activist group, an advocate of black pride, a mouthpiece for grassroots issues, a redeemer for the imprisoned, a disciplinarian and yes—ultimately—a religious force, but just for a very small number of Blacks. But few media planners and influential people understood that the NOI is much more than religion and that many NOI supporters aren't Muslims.

I completed the first CBC radio interview and, while waiting for Thunder Bay to call, the phone rang. It was from CBC Radio in Montreal, one of the programs that had turned down the interviews. This march is bigger than anybody thought, the caller said. Would I know if there are any people from Montreal who might be attending? Tongue in cheek, I reminded him that I was in Toronto, hundreds of kilometres away. It was a bit bizarre that he would be calling me about a Montreal angle to a developing story, I said. Yes, the caller atoned, he knew that, but it was too late to send a reporter out to scour the streets of Montreal, and the station didn't have a list of any community leaders to call. If at this late hour I knew anyone who might help him out, it would be greatly appreciated. Fortunately, my sister-in-law, Rose, who lives in Montreal, was spending some time with us. I woke her. She rattled off the top of her head some names and numbers of people who might be attending the march or might know of others who were. She also pointed him to various community publications and suggested where he could get hold of members of the Nation of Islam in Montreal. I suspect that some poor souls in Montreal were awakened by a frantic CBC researcher telling them how important they were—at least for one day. I also wonder what quality of analysis listeners in Montreal heard about the march. For, plainly, that radio station had done no planning or research, even with a year's notice. Obviously, it did not have its finger on the pulse of the black population in Montreal.

By now the crowd was mammoth. The radio stations were gradually waking up to the event and working it into their newscasts, but usually with little analysis or content. I did my interviews with Thunder Bay and Edmonton. Then, not wanting to miss Minister Farrakhan's speech, I drove downtown to the studio of Vision TV and did the interview. On my return home, the talk-radio shows around Toronto were abuzz over the Million Man March. But it was easy to tell they were winging it. They were falling back on the usual hackneyed questions: Will this march cause bigger problems between Blacks and Whites? What would happen if a million white men were to stage their own march? What do these black people want, anyway? Despite the improvising, it was obvious many of them were relying on notes from earlier programs when they trashed affirmative action in the United States and employment equity in Canada. Or when they discussed the white outrage over the verdict of the O.J. Simpson murder case a few months earlier. The usual suspects, the red-neck, anti-immigrant, anti-minority, right-wing callers, were on the air. But there was a noticeable difference. Several black males called in. They sounded proud and responded to the talk-show hosts who tended to give them short shrift. Black women were also calling, most of them to support the march, thereby pouring cold water on efforts by the hosts to divide Blacks along the lines of gender. There was a noticeable difference to the colour and complexion of the talk-radio shows.

For this moment, the black community was under the collective national microscope—and it wasn't because a black man had shot a policeman; wasn't because Blacks were killing Blacks; wasn't because Blacks were shooting the most baskets or hitting balls out of baseball parks; wasn't because some intrepid reporter had discovered a black mother cheating on welfare or a Somalian refugee ripping off the system and sending the money back home. It wasn't because of any of those negative stereotypes that are the basic ingredients of news about Blacks in Canada.

By the time I got home, there was a long list of radio and television stations asking me to return calls or to simply turn up and come on their show. Among them were CBC Radio in Winnipeg, where there is a sizeable black population, and two CBC-TV *Newsworld* talk shows as well as the provincial TV network, TVOntario. I declined their offers. A researcher for one CBC *Newsworld* program got hold of me half an hour before the program was to start. "Can you make a dash down to the station?" she asked.

"It would take me at least half an hour to drive into the city," I explained. "And an hour ago I was downtown at Vision TV. If I knew, we could have ..."

"Well, then we can do it by phone," she interrupted.

"But I thought we were talking about television," I said, laughing at the seeming folly of discussing a story like this on television by *phone*.

"I know," she said, as I heard a phone ringing in the background. "Wait a minute, there goes my other phone. Can you hold? I'll see if that is someone else returning my call." It was—a black lawyer whose office was near enough to the studio that he could drop everything and make it over to CBC Television in time for the start of the show.

The other programs and radio stations I simply turned down. I felt they were practising shoddy journalism. This haphazardness in the coverage of the Million Man March is the likely outcome when the news media are made up of people who live and operate outside the minority communities. There is no awareness of what is happening beyond their workplaces and usual watering holes. So, when news breaks in these *other* communities, the reporters and producers usually have no contacts. They practise Rolodex journalism, referring to a few names that might be filed away on source cards, hoping someone on the list might be an expert on the topic at hand. Or they simply hope to have a black voice, any black voice, if they can't get a black face—even on television.

If this had been a march organized by a dissident wing of any mainstream group—far less, a respected one—the newsrooms would have done much more preparatory work. There would have been what is known in the business as "scene setters," reports and analysis in advance of the event on radio and television stations, newspapers and magazines—that would have prepared us. There would have been panel discussions.

The radio and television stations would have developed a long list of credible people to talk about the issues. Reporters and producers would have turned the black community upside-down looking for Canadian angles.

* * *

I am one of a small number of Canadian Blacks to make a living working in mainstream journalism. Since my arrival in Canada in 1979, I have maintained links with community publications and established media outlets. I have now worked in every medium—newspapers (both general and business), magazines (both general and business), radio and television. I have worked in front of cameras and radio microphones and behind the scenes writing scripts for announcers. In addition, I teach journalism at a university and community college and write books, both fiction and nonfiction. I think I understand how the Canadian media work.

After almost two decades in this field, I do not believe I have ever been fully accepted into mainstream journalism. The primary reason is that I am a poor, black immigrant, while most Canadian journalists are white and middle class at the least. But that is another matter.

However, because of my experience in the mainstream media, I am often invited by black groups to explain why the media treat Blacks with such disdain. Supposedly, my hosts tend to think I can see the issues from both sides and help them come to some understanding of what is happening around them. As a journalist, I can explain how the media work and think; as a black man, they hope I have some special understanding and affinity for what is troubling them. I like attending these sessions, but I sometimes wonder how much I help. For it is often difficult telling even Blacks the truth about the media, to get them to develop realistic expectations, to get them to realize that the media are primarily business outlets that do not normally see Blacks as making money for them. Try telling Blacks that the media do not see them as having the rich and affluent lifestyles that advertisers portray. Blacks can, however, be sold as threats to the accepted lifestyles. This is a truth that Blacks usually find hard to accept. They reject this explanation, even though many of them live the reality of not seeing themselves depicted as fully human in the media.

One recent example illustrates this. I was invited to join a panel discussion by a Malton Black Business Development Association, a group of blacks to the northwest of Toronto. Its members provide role models and counselling to black youths. One woman in the audience told of an experience that really hurt her, and from her retelling of the story she was gaining great empathy from the listeners. They instantly identified with what she was talking about and they understood her frustration.

The woman recounted how her son had worked his way through the Canadian school system and into university without once running into trouble with the law. He had gone to university in Ottawa, to study to become an actor. He got somewhat of a small break when *Chatelaine*, the top women's magazine in Canada, mentioned a play or movie—I can't remember which—in which he was involved. Feeling pleased with her son's achievement at being recognized by *Chatelaine*, the woman went to work beaming all over. She began telling everyone that her son was in the magazine. Then a white colleague asked what her son had done to be imprisoned. She was devastated. For obviously, she explained, in the mind of her colleague a black youth can only make the news when he does something bad. This perception is fuelled by the media—as stories such as the one about her son are such a rarity—so that her colleague did not even understand the racism in her statement. Why do the news media continue to maintain these stereotypes? she asked. Others wondered, what can Blacks do to get the media to recognize their responsibility to reflect black people positively as well as negatively? A positive image would help readers and viewers to see Blacks as well-rounded humans, faults and all, and not just as undesirables and misfits.

My explanation didn't appear to help much. I suggested that one reason for the negative stereotypes is that the news media often do not see Blacks and other minorities as part of their audience. As was the case with the Million Man March, they do not plan for minorities. Most of the programming is for the friends and family of the people that produce the programs. And these planners and producers are traditionally white. When they deal with Blacks and minorities, it is not from a position of explaining one of them to the wider group. It is to explain a group that is either exotic, threatening or something in between—but definitely not part of the wider circles of friends and families. So that if this woman were to ask *Chatelaine* for a profile of its typical readers, the stuff magazines prepare for their salespeople to target advertisers, she would see that she is not expected to be a reader.

One possible solution is to get more Blacks into the newsrooms and into the programming departments. Not only must they get into positions of influence, but Blacks and other minorities must be allowed to do their jobs.

Unfortunately, the outlook for having more Blacks in the media doesn't look good. A recent study by John Miller, who was then the chair of the School of Journalism at Ryerson Polytechnic University in Toronto, shows that newspaper owners and editors do not rank the question of minority representation in their newsroom as a priority. This study, commissioned by the Canadian Daily Newspapers Association, finds that the editors and owners feel they have bigger problems in such areas as pagination, declining advertising and decreasing government subsidies of postal rates. Another study by Miller and a journalism student found that Blacks appear in the news stories only when they are in conflict with the law and other institutions, or when they excel at sports.

> When you read the largest newspapers in five of Canada's most cosmopolitan cities, it's easy to form the following impression of visible minorities: Half are either athletes or entertainers; if they're in the news otherwise, they're probably in trouble of some sort. And few make any contribution to business or have noteworthy lifestyles.

The study was done in cities that have the largest concentrations of Aboriginals and visible minorities in Canada, ranging from 26.8 percent of the population in Toronto to 12.8 percent in Montreal. According to the 1991 Canadian census, visible minorities and Aboriginals make up 13.2 percent of the Canadian population.

These findings are also reflected in the composition of newsrooms at radio and television stations. And it might be getting worse. Budget cuts to public broadcasting are forcing some of the older black faces and voices into retirement, with few young Blacks to replace them. Indeed, a 1995 magazine article, published by the Ryerson School of Journalism, summed up the situation all too well, describing Canadian newsrooms as too old and too white. A look inside the news operation—a view that is not often available to Blacks—would illustrate how the presence of just one reporter or researcher with a different view from the mainstream could make a difference.

* * *

In one of the conference rooms just a short walk away from the newsroom, reporters, editors and good friends meet to say goodbye to two members of the family. CBC National Radio is losing two of its most venerable faces and public voices. After two decades of service, announcer Dwight Whylie and general editor Keeble McFarlane are retiring—if somewhat prematurely—from the network.

To most observers there might be nothing too significant in the leaving of another two senior workers at a network struggling to remain viable, a network shedding employees all around as it faces deep budget cuts imposed by its sole provider of funds, the federal government. All around, these are hard times in the public sector and elsewhere. Two resignations from a Crown corporation in the first week of 1996—a year that starts out promising to be one of the worst for cut-backs at the federal, provincial and municipal levels across the country—could safely be considered as no more than par for the course.

For this public broadcaster there are bigger problems than just losing another two stalwarts. The mandate around the newsroom is doing more with less and in such a way that the listener will not notice any changes. Yes, something will be lost from not hearing the Caribbean cadence and nuances of a Dwight Whylie reading the news and weather on national radio. And Keeble McFarlane will be missed for his thoroughness in the newsroom, for keeping a watch for all those stray peccadilloes of grammar, pronunciation and on-air misuses of ethnic and other stereotypes. For he is one of the CBC's tireless language watchdogs. But to listeners, Keeble's departure will go largely unnoticed. Such is the lot of an editor working behind the scenes who only occasionally ventures out into the limelight as a reporter.

Listeners will probably not miss the behind-the-scenes discussions of a Dwight Whylie or a Keeble McFarlane. They would not have heard, in the

daily course of planning and producing news cover
certain stories to be given more prominence and wei
on at all. They would not know the contribution
senior announcer or editor like these two can have in a
they can affect the long-term planning of news coverage and help esta-
lish the emphasis and weight reporters should place on a given event.

Think of the junior writer and editor putting the final touches on a story. Now, it is time to pass it on to someone else. Suddenly, a line or perception in the copy that might have appeared innocuous to the junior news gatherer becomes questionable in the hands of a veteran. The writer or editor sees the copy the way a Dwight Whylie or a Keeble McFarlane might, and a whole world of hidden meaning emerges before it gets on air and enrages segments of the wider society.

As Keeble and Dwight look around the room at this event, they see many very junior reporters and editors, many of them just out of university and learning the craft as news "busybodies"—called editorial assistants. Others have spent countless hours working with Keeble and Dwight, watching carefully, for Keeble and Dwight have been a team for several years, preparing the short newscasts that are heard at the beginning of each hour. And the hourlies, unglamorous as they are with emphasis strictly on breaking news, are the closest to a training ground in the newsroom.

The listeners in the remotest corners of the country and the border states would not know how the presence of senior news gatherers and presenters like these have an impact on what is heard on the radio, and just as important, what is *not* heard. For even if they wouldn't want to acknowledge it, news people of the status and calibre of these two retirees are not just reporters, editors and announcers. Often they are also the cultural eyes and sounding boards for the communities of which they are members. Too often, they are the conscience of the establishment, the little voices that always seem to be asking "what if" and "suppose." They, too, have a double burden for being black.

For many following the careers of these two journalists, especially members of the black community starting the fledgling Canadian Association of Black Journalists, their departure from active news gathering at the CBC signals more. It is an indication of how little has changed for minorities, specifically Blacks, in the newsrooms across this ntry. And, perhaps even more chilling, the departures portend how any small gains that have been made in the past two decades to change the complexion and sensitivity of newsrooms in Canada can be wiped out with the stroke of a pen or with a resignation. Indeed, when in 1989 I left *The Globe and Mail*, 100 percent of the black editorial staff went with me. This was also the case when I left *The Financial Post* four years later. As of the time of this writing, nothing has changed at these two publications that both claim to be national newspapers, reflecting the Canadian business world to itself and others.

With Dwight Whylie and Keeble McFarlane leaving, the entire complement of the on-staff black representation in the CBC National Radio newsroom is going through the door. The colour of 50 or so staff on the CBC National Radio employees' list in Toronto is much the same as before Dwight and Keeble arrived in the newsroom. And that is two decades ago—before the federal government and the CBC launched drives to recruit more Blacks and minorities. That was before the now well-entrenched notion that a national network should be represented by all minority groups in Canada. When Keeble and Dwight, two immigrants from Jamaica, broke the colour bar and joined CBC Radio, the network was predominantly white and male. Back then, the joke was that CBC represented the men's sauna in the YMCA. Twenty years later, they are leaving. More women have made it onto the employment list, but the unblemished colour of the network is still white.

As Keeble reminisces, he says one of the criticisms he has always heard in his two decades at the radio network is that certain groups always seem to get their stories on the radio. Why is this so when other groups always seem to be ignored? Or when they do make an appearance, someone invariably calls up to protest that the network has it all wrong, or there is a bias. Once again, the coverage of the Million Man March springs to mind.

It is not that journalists in the hurly-burly of putting together a newscast deliberately set out to favour one group, he suggests. Rather, the journalists make judgement calls about what is loosely considered the public agenda. The success of some groups in getting their stories out is really a test of how well they manipulate the public agenda.

Perhaps Keeble is right, or maybe he is being generous to his colleagues. Or in keeping with the spirit of the event—with the table laid out with the patties, the dips and vegetables—he is trying to shore up the spirits of those left behind, former colleagues who, in Keeble's words, "now have to do much more with less." As Keeble and Dwight look around the room, they must recognize that the "much less" doesn't apply to financial resources alone. It also applies to human resources, to a newsroom not fully reflecting the ethnic spectrum of Canada. It is a newsroom with limited exposure to and understanding of what should be the full public agenda. And if they carry their thoughts to the logical conclusion, these retirees can make quite a strong case from their experience alone for having an array of different colours, voices and sensitivities in the newsroom. This way every group would have its say in defining this elusive public agenda. Every group would have a voice and a good chance to be heard. One group would not automatically appear to have both the first and last word on any issue, the supposedly inalienable right to decide what is an issue of concern to the public. No one group would have an almost exclusive authority to frame the moral or ethical question for public discussion.

In this light, obviously the retirement of the only two black employees of the CBC's national radio network on the same day is a backward step for the corporation. For how can anyone say that the newsroom is representative of modern-day Canada? How can it be representative without Aboriginals and Asians or any other group that remains outside the mainstream? Unfortunately, examples of this insensitivity resulting from this exclusion are too readily apparent in most Canadian media. A look at stories published by the two major newspapers in Toronto on November 20, 1994, provides a good case study.

* * *

The quote at the start of this chapter is a good indication of what can happen when newspapers fail in their sensitivity to minority groups. Worse, it is an example of what can happen when the ugly stereotypes of places and groups associated with them are allowed to continue unchallenged in general usage by the media. In this case, the caption ran underneath a picture depicting child poverty in Canada. The accompanying story was about how thousands of young Canadians are going to bed with empty bellies every night. But as everyone knows, child poverty and hunger have their own connotations. They are not associated with Canada but with Africa, at least in the mind of the writer of the photo caption. In a few sentences the writer condemns all Africans to hunger and poverty, but also succeeds in demonstrating how deep-seated stereotypes can be.

For the writer of this front-page story, child poverty and black people and Africa all go hand in hand. Think of one and you automatically get the other. This is an example of what Blacks have been screaming about for decades, when we claim that the media simply reduce us to grotesque stereotypes and stick figures. In this story about child poverty in Canada, the writer could find no other way to shock readers than falling back on the image of hungry black children. Yes, the newspaper was implying, we are so conditioned that if we think of child poverty, we automatically envision a big-bellied child somewhere in Africa—not where the Whites live, mind you, but in some poverty-stricken village. Everyone knows of those images: the fly-infested environment; babies with runny noses, eyes and ears; children with horrendous sores all over the body; mothers staring into blank horizon, seeing only death approaching; or the white hand of assistance reaching across the ocean.

We see the images nightly on television, as missionaries and desperate-sounding aid workers beg and cajole for a few dollars to dig a well, to irrigate a plot of land and to save the next generation of black youths in Africa. Yes, the media teach us, child poverty has its beginning and ending in Africa. Or in the Caribbean in places like Haiti and the Dominican Republic—places all in the popular thought where Canadian tourists often have to face the indignity of children begging for food or alms. That is why in the mind of the writer at *The Toronto Star* it would be so shocking to think that some children in a white society like Canada go to bed without a crumb of bread in their stomachs. That revelation was tantamount to showing how much this Canada—this rich country—has degenerated. Indeed, often the letters from readers published on the editorial pages reinforce this notion. It is the same stereotype, Blacks argue, that many Canadians in power and authority see when a Black applies for a job, speaks out in the classroom, or applies for welfare or housing allowances. It is the same conditioning that governs how Blacks are treated in the wider society.

At the time, if the writer wanted a fresh image of starving children, he or she might have turned to the international news wires or even *The Toronto Star* itself for examples. There would have been many more recent examples that were not black. The same time the *Star* was preparing this exposé, there were no images on television or on the front page of newspapers of starving children in Africa, the Caribbean or even North America. The story was coming a long time after the Rwandan death camps of that year had disappeared from the news. The United Nations' efforts to fight starvation in Somalia were over, with many Canadians and Americans having sober second thoughts about what went wrong for their men and women on that mission. But those were second thoughts—"post mortems," as they say in newsrooms when assessing the previous day's news—of the mission. International reporters had moved on to the next hot spot.

At the time the article was published, international attention was focused on what was happening in the former Yugoslavia. In Bosnia, the civil war was raging with renewed vigour as winter was beginning to set in. Serbs, Muslims and Croats were slaughtering one another. The media images were of death and hunger: of little children being shot down in sniper's alley in Sarajevo, or the Serbs starving men, women and children in several towns across Bosnia, of refugees and displaced people huddling around broken pipes for water, of the United Nations using Canadian planes to fly in tonnes of food and medicine for the poor and starving, including children.

Or there was the devastation in parts of Russia. Anyone could have come up with pictures of thousands of children in the columns of refugees streaming out of Grozny in Chechnya, a result of the instability and slaughter caused by that province's war of independence from Russia. Instead, the writer reached back into the collective memory and drew out a stereotype, perhaps arguing that every reader would identify with the plight of a starving African child.

The Toronto Sun gets into the discussion through its front-page headline in big bold letters—**A 'TURKEY SHOOT'** it screamed, flagging an inside story on an investigation of the Canadian military in Somalia. This story should act as a constant reminder of the effects of negative stereotyping and what can happen from the degrading of a specific group of people. For as this story shows, the selfless Canadian peacekeepers who had gone to Somalia to save from starvation the next generation of African ingrates had really gone on a hunting mission. According to the newspaper, members of the Airborne Regiment had prepared traps to entice Somalians "to steal" so that the Canadians could then shoot at them, the same way they would hungry wild animals. Then they took pictures of their quarry, pictures of the hunter and hunted, of supremacist white Canadian soldiers and a murdered Somalian.

The story was based on an interview with Canadian trooper Kyle Brown, a member of the regiment that went to Somalia on a famine-relief mission sponsored by the United Nations. Brown was sentenced to five years in prison by a court martial for his part in the torture and killing of a Somalian youth, Shidane Arone. The Somalian had been taken into custody by the soldiers for allegedly stealing. According to the *Sun*, Brown said that on March 4, 1993, one of the Somalian looters was killed and another wounded in what he could only describe as a "turkey shoot." He said: "There was a volley of gunfire followed by yells and screams. Then I heard a Canadian shout, 'I got one.' A second volley was fired. There were more screams and someone else yelled, 'Hey, I got one too.'" A few days later, Arone fell into the custody of the soldiers.

Brown's confession, newsworthy though it was on this day, was not the first report that Canadian soldiers were "hunting" in Somalia. Only a week earlier, the Canadian media had published and televised shocking pictures of some of these soldiers "posing" in photographs. With them was a battered and bloodied Arone, his hands and legs bound in the pictures. Not only had they illegally beaten this so-called thief, but for mementos of some of the most macabre scenes, the soldiers actually pulled out their cameras and took pictures. The most graphic shots showed the pools of blood, the young and bloodied man stretched out, with a soldier holding a wooden rod across his face.

Nobody seeing these pictures could mistake them for what they were originally intended: trophies of big-game hunting. Otherwise, why would these soldiers take such damning evidence? Why would they pose with a human being reduced to pulp and blood and why were they laughing? Indeed, to whom did they intend to show the pictures when they got back to Canada? Obviously, in their minds, this could be no different from the time the Canadian hunters and missionaries used to return from Africa with their pictures. When the explorers invited family and friends over to their homes for slide presentations from the exotic lands. Or when, in true colonial style, the civilizers gave lectures in their churches, military halls and museums. When the idle rich reeled out the pictures that were the evidence of successful hunts of the big game.

Only three years before the so-called turkey shoot, members of the Toronto black community were arguing that this kind of treatment was a natural outflow from negative stereotyping. A case in point happened when some militant youths protested a 1991 art exhibition at the venerable Royal Ontario Museum. The exhibition was called *Into the Heart of Africa*. It purported to tell from the missionaries' perspective what happened when they invaded African societies at the turn of the century. The exhibits were some of the loot the missionaries brought back home to Canada. The black community argued the exhibition was dehumanizing and degrading to Blacks and that it could have an adverse effect on how different minority groups view one another. The protest was so boisterous and controversial, it was heard across North America, causing the ROM to call off a planned tour of several North American cities of the exhibition.

For many white Canadians, the issue at the heart of the protest was freedom of expression. In their case, it was their freedom to say whatever they liked about the other guy, even if there was no avenue for an adequate response, even if what they said hurt and was demeaning. Blacks saw it differently. The issue was about what rights a group of people have in deciding how they should be depicted.

Supporters of the exhibition claimed that it was a body of art and that it was clearly not historically correct. The exhibits were objects brought back to Canada by missionaries who went to the "dark continent" to take Christianity to the wretched there, and along the way to save them from themselves by fighting child poverty, teaching them how to wash clothes in streams and also pacifying some elements who were so violent. Anyone seeing these exhibits would know that the thinking of the missionaries was no longer acceptable, supporters said. That was from the past, not-so-enlightened an era as this, but from a time when Blacks were considered to be less than human, and heathens to boot. And because they were heathens, any ill-treatment was acceptable. Today, such treatment would not be countenanced. So no harm could be done by exposing Canadians to these images from backward times. History, they argued, should not be whitewashed or blacked out. It should be treated as folklore or tales that would hardly influence anyone with a modicum of enlightenment today. But is life this simple and is it true that old perceptions never die? The turkey shoot in Somalia suggests not.

Envision this: the first scene on entering the ROM for the *Into the Heart of Africa* exhibition was of a white man. His foot is on a prostrate black man. He is about to pierce the man's heart with a spear. The picture of the conqueror astride his game. For all we know, the poor black man might have been caught stealing from the missionary compound. Harmless pictures, you say, brought back by the missionaries in the last century. Just history.

Let's jump ahead to the pictures splattered in blood across the pages of newspapers across North America in 1994. Pictures of the Canadian Airborne peacekeepers with their trophy after the turkey hunt in Somalia. Pictures of the foreigner symbolically piercing the heart of Arone, as his blood gushes out and forms pools at his bound feet, symbolically out of the heart of Africans. What has changed?

But there was still more in the day's newspapers. On the inside page of *The Toronto Sun* was a column that fitted well into the package of opinions and news in vogue that day. "Are we into real change in immigration?" asks Douglas Fisher, writing from Ottawa, where he has been a fixture, and somewhat intellectually calcified on minority issues for decades. "Or will the majority of entrants continue to be of the so-called family class *and from Asia*?" (my italics)

This is not just another question from a sleepy old columnist. Rather, it is a telling explanation of why mainstream Canadians would have a turkey shoot in Somalia; why thoughts of pot-bellied black children keep running through their heads. For many of the old guard still believe that Canada should be lily white. And Fisher is honest enough to put into print what so many white Canadians have been thinking. They are concerned that Canada has become too multicultural, that too many immigrants are coming to this country from non-European countries.

The basis for Fisher's column was a recent announcement by the Canadian government that it was cutting back on the number of immigrants annually allowed into the country. It had also decided, perhaps most importantly, to shift the criteria for selection to attract more immigrants from Europe. In essence, the Liberal government was repudiating the Just Society ambitions of its own party in the 1960s and 1970s, when it adopted a more humane and fair immigration policy, when it had asserted that Europeans should not have an automatic right of entry into Canada over the vast majority of humanity unfortunate enough to live elsewhere in the world.

The new policy—coincidentally announced by an immigrant and for a parliamentary caucus with the largest number of immigrants—is aimed at tilting the balance in favour of the cleaner, nicer, non-criminal Canadians who happen to be all of European stock—the kind of stock some columnists and right-wing politicians mean when they speak in code of Canada choosing "the right type of immigrant." Or would it?

Fisher is not yet ready to concede it would and that was the reason for his posting this intriguing question about what is seen as a proliferation of non-European immigrants. This also gives him the opportunity—the news peg—to profile a group called the Immigration Association of Canada. This is a collection of former federal employees, apparent malcontents who had resigned as far back as the 1960s to protest the tilt in Canadian policy toward a more open-door immigration process. This is a group that, as Fisher notes in his column, "has been marginalized by the conventional wisdom and tagged as racist and reactionary—a throwback to a vanished time of the Empire and white superiority."

Now, Fisher claims, the group has been vindicated. Its dire warnings of the havoc that was in store for Canadian cities "from reckless immigration and immigration programs" have been proven right. The federal government is finally listening to groups like the Immigration Association of Canada. And it is ready to act. Or, at least, it says it will take corrective action. But until the policies have been carried out, nobody can be sure.

As Fisher posits, "Proof of real change will be a quick rebuilding of a system in Europe to seek and screen "independent" applicants: As for the family program, so much used by immigrants from Asia, it may be somewhat curbed but sheer numbers already here mean that henceforth, as now, the bulk of our immigrants will be from Asia, and increasingly of Chinese stock."

Fisher's is not a lone voice with this point of view. Around the same time one of Fisher's former colleagues, Peter Brimlow, had published a controversial book callled *An Alien Nation* in the United States suggesting that North American countries were debasing their culture through non-European immigration. Brimlow, an English expatriate, had developed some of his thoughts while working as a journalist and columnist in Toronto before moving on to better things in the United States. Obviously, there are like-minded writers left behind.

These points of view were not the only ones in vogue at this time. Others were arguing the exact opposite. However, on this day, none of them had a ready-made pulpit for their views. And this is part of the inequity of how the media view minorities and certain groups, of how they help to entrench the social and intellectual segregation.

The inequity of this situation is that Fisher obviously shares the views of the group he is profiling. And because he has a national newspaper column, he is able to write a soft, laudatory profile on the group, a portrait that is obviously intended to showcase the work of the group's members and to elicit wider support for them. Totally immune to the notion of objectivity or to putting distance between himself and the people he is writing about, Fisher even publishes the group's mailing address. I could only wonder what kind of column would have run in this space if a minority writer had access to this prime spot. Or if instead of profiling a group he admired, Fisher were writing of a so-called pressure group he obviously detests. Would it be different if he had given over the use of his column to an opinion and view on life that wasn't in keeping with his Eurocentric vision of Canada? What would have been the tone and tenure of the column if it had been written by an Asian, or as Fisher put it, someone of Chinese stock?

* * *

But let's go back to the questions black audiences like to ask about the media: Do they always have to be so stereotypical? Don't the media recognize they have a role to play by helping to develop harmonious relations in society, and by not fuelling misapprehension among groups? Of course they have this responsibility, and the media can change and be different. A case in point is the coverage of sports. With the exception of hockey, all professional Canadian sports teams are primarily black. This is true of the Toronto Blue Jays and Montreal Expos, the Toronto Raptors and the Vancouver Grizzlies, and just about any of the Canadian Football League teams. Yet, there is very little negative stereotyping about these athletes. Managers like Cito Gaston of the Blue Jays, or Toronto Raptors' front-office manager Isiah Thomas, are seldom referred to by their race. They are presented as wholesome role models, the kind of people who have glowing commentaries and columns written about them. Often these columns in the back of the newspapers are in stark contrast to the negative perception of Blacks in the front sections of the newspapers. And TV and radio talk-show hosts who are known for bashing minorities and immigrants are quite deferential when dealing with these heroes. The same is true for the players on the field and court. No reporter has written that *black* slugger Joe Carter hit the winning home run to help Toronto clinch its second consecutive World Series title under *black* manager Cito Gaston. So when the media want to present wholesome Blacks—boys and girls next door, heroes who won't frighten little white boys and girls when they ask for autographs or when they scream and cheer for them from stands at the game—they have no difficulty. They can find wholesome Blacks when they want to.

However, they are not always consistent, not even in entertainment. For example, when was the last time anyone saw on Canadian television a Canadian black actor in a drama, sitcom or documentary? This is quite striking when compared to American television, for there isn't a lack of black talent in Canada. There is, however, a very noticeable difference in the approach to minorities and the arts in Canada. For example, many African-American comedians cut their teeth on national television—some of it in Canadian homes—on *Saturday Night Live* and other variety entertainment shows. Specialty channels like HBO and others provide additional outlets for new black talent. In Canada, there is a blackout of homegrown black talent. While I write, the two most successful Canadian comedies are *The Royal Canadian Air Farce* and *This Hour Has 22 Minutes*. I have yet to see a Black or any other minority in these shows, unless a white regular impersonates a minority, so unlike

America, where at least the black talent is showcased.

The poor representation of Blacks in the media will change when society starts to see Blacks differently. It will change when Blacks are seen as capable of creating all kinds of news, so that they might be businesspeople, academics, politicians—all the usual people that are considered to have a positive effect on society in general. In my years in mainstream journalism, I have yet to meet a black public relations officer for a Canadian company. And although it is usual for good reporters to be approached by companies offering public-relations jobs, I do not know of any black reporters in the mainstream media who have ever had such an approach. I have often asked myself why U.S. companies can have spokespeople who are of all colours and races. But not in Canada. Obviously, when selecting public-relations people, companies all over the world look for the people who would bring prestige to the company. They want people who fit with the desired public perception for the company. Needless to say, seldom do Canadian companies see Blacks and other minorities as fitting this picture—not even retired athletes.

I have my own test for when Blacks can claim they have arrived in the Canadian mainstream. It is when any of the top-ranking companies in Canada call a press conference to make a major announcement. Representatives of all the media attend, and nobody really notices that several of the reporters, producers and researchers are black. On the podium announcing the reason for the press conference is a public relations officer who is black. Sitting at the table ready to answer questions is the company's chief executive officer, who—you got it—is also black. Can you imagine the impact these images would have on young people who see them on television? If these scenes become commonplace, we might even reach a point where a proud mother can go to work all gushing with news. She might talk endlessly about the publicity her son or daughter is getting in the media. Not once will anyone interrupt her to ask why her son or daughter is in prison. I just wonder how long it will take into the next millennium for this to happen.

CHAPTER 8

BLACK AND BLUE

At its heart, the colour of Canadian justice is blue. At least that is the case in Etobicoke Courtroom 208 Metropolitan Toronto on December 7, 1994. This is the day the state begins bringing to justice one Clinton Junior Gayle for the murder of a Toronto policeman, Todd Baylis, and the attempted murder of his partner, P.C. Michael Leone. This is the trial that would be the catharsis for an entire nation, especially for those who feel this country is too soft when it comes to questions of law and order, when it comes to dealing firmly with perennial whiners and misfits, such as members of the black community.

In this case, colour means everything. Gayle is a black man accused of killing a white policeman. After the shooting, the media and talk shows did not try to disguise the racism in their commentary. Neither did anyone appear to pretend that Gayle would, at the very least, be considered innocent until proven guilty in the court. From the moment the story of the killing broke, media reports and talk-show hosts dispensed with the routine use of the word "alleged" when describing a murderer named Gayle. Such a formality might have been misconstrued as a weakness, a sop to the black community, an encouragement to others harbouring such bad intentions. In this case, the general population doesn't worry too much about a miscarriage of justice or about ensuring that Gayle gets a fair trial. Rather, it's about retribution. In this case, in the eyes of many, Clinton Junior Gayle represents all black men in this country, and dealing with him appropriately is the right way to send a stern message to all those whiners, to all those who do not respect Canadian institutions, to all those living outside the Canadian mainstream who should be brought to heel.

Gayle's case had ramifications for many, including a nondescript immigration adjudicator, Ivan Rashid, who ordered Gayle released from jail while waiting for deportation. Rashid, his identity made public before an almost incensed Canadian citizenry, had to atone publicly for a "bad" decision.

Gayle was held up as this brutal and brutish thug who gunned down an officer of the law, robbing the community of a fine young man, and Baylis' girl-friend of a future husband and father of her children. All of which was true. But the condemnation went further than just a battle of good and evil: race and skin colour made a difference. Soon broad swipes were being taken at any breathing black person.

That Gayle is black and from the Caribbean, specifically Jamaica, gave added colour to the incident and eventually made it an international issue. But the harshest effects were felt on the streets of Toronto, especially in neighbourhoods with a strong black presence. In one fell swoop, Blacks were painted as gangsters, irresponsible louts who had little respect for life. Furthermore, here was an example of what happens when Canada throws open its doors to the dredges of the world, people with no respect for institutions, for law and order, the result of an immigration policy too lax and ill-suited for this country.

There were some factors that gave legitimacy for these virulent attacks on Gayle—but not on all other Blacks. Gayle had been in trouble many times with the law, running up 13 convictions, including possession of firearms, and had been ordered deported to Jamaica. At the time he fired the bullets that killed Baylis and wounded Leone, Gayle was under a 10-year ban prohibiting him from possessing firearms. Along the way, his deportation papers got lost. Some critics jumped on this as an example of how the immigration process and the justice system had broken down, how the two federal departments were conspiring to let loose on society heinous criminals, most of them black, and notably, Jamaican or West Indian. The Metro Toronto Police Association, supposedly also representing the black members of the force, took the argument one step further. It followed up its virulent anti-Black rhetoric with action: a lawsuit for $100 million, in the names of the slain, against the federal government. Somebody has to pay for the killing of one of its members, and the police association was not willing to settle only for the price that society would demand of Gayle in a criminal trial.

For months preceding the shooting of Todd Baylis, there was much talk about justice and Blacks in Canada. Several months earlier, the mainstream media had a special story to tell. It was about young black men in Nova Scotia who set up a white prostitution ring across the country. As the story was told, innocent young girls from Halifax were finding themselves in Montreal, Toronto, Vancouver and any big city or town in between, in the inescapable clutches of black pimps. This was not just another prostitute and pimp story. Nobody in the media worked to find out if any of these supposedly innocent white women were runaways, attracted to the big city, and finding themselves having to get by the same way many others have always had to survive in the streets of Los Angeles, New York or Toronto. Also noticeable was that nobody seemed too concerned about whether any of these innocent young women on the hustle were black. But the colour of the pimps was of the utmost importance. Here is how the issue was reported in *The Globe and Mail* on April 24th, 1993:

> When Joan is out on the baseball mound, the ball spinning toward her, she likes to imagine she's about to swing her bat at the head of a black pimp. She knows she shouldn't harbour such anger towards other people, but she just can't help it. Joan is mad as hell at the men she blames for destroying her daughter's life.
>
> Hillary, her eldest child, is one of hundreds of hookers who got their start in the Halifax area in recent years. Today many of these girls, most of them over 13 but some as young as 10, populate big-city "strolls," the streets and byways walked by prostitutes across Canada and as far afield as New York, California and Europe.
>
> Most of these young prostitutes, virtually all of them white, work for a loosely organized community of Nova Scotia Black men.

The writing could hardly be more graphic or coloured. With so much talk of this white slave ring, life became a lot tougher for young black men in the Preston area of Halifax. The police came frequently knocking, often with the national media in tow. Some of the youths saw the inside of jails. Others just had to put up with police harassment. Some men from the Preston area were arrested across the country, charged and convicted. Of course, the convictions were duly recorded as if to ease the fears of the wider community that the black menace was finally under control.

The concern about Blacks and justice took on an even greater dimension across the country in the summer of 1994. In Toronto, three black men entered an eating establishment named Just Desserts in a trendy part of the city. While robbing the restaurant and its patrons, a patron was killed by a shotgun blast. The city, and indeed parts of the country, reacted viscerally. The murdered woman, Georgina "Vivi" Leimonis, became a representative of all the ills black men can inflict on white women. Just as with the hype over the so-called white prostitution ring, the colour of the perpetrators seemed to be the most important aspect of this robbery and murder. The police also acted as though colour were the only thing that mattered; they issued out-of-focus photographs to the media with instructions that citizens call the police if they saw any of the men. The pictures were splashed on the television screens and on the front pages of newspapers, along with instructions for people to clip them out and keep the pictures handy in their car for easy reference. But the pictures were so murky, the only thing clear about the suspects was the colour of their skin. Immediately, every black man became a suspect. As was the case in Halifax, the mainstream dismissed this concern. Much emphasis was placed on the loss of innocence in the city. Who would not shed a tear for a young woman cut down in her prime, a woman who wore her intended wedding gown as a burial shroud?

Similar claims about the city being robbed of its innocence had been made only two years earlier when a crowd of primarily black youth "rioted" on Yonge Street. This so-called riot coincided with the destruction and pillage in Los Angeles that came to be known as the Rodney King riots, the spark occurring when an all-white jury acquitted some Los Angeles police officers for brutally beating a black man. The fact that Rodney King's beating was captured on video was dismissed by the jury. Blacks across North America rose up against this affront, and the hard feelings boiled over in Toronto, too, where there had been many recent flashpoints over police shootings of Blacks. This would not be the first or last time that parallels would be drawn between the treatment of Blacks in Canada and the United States. As the Yonge Street disturbances proved—as did smaller but similar incidents in Halifax and other Canadian centres—few people in the black community see any differences in the way the police and justice systems treat Blacks on either side of the border.

Eventually, the ranting quietened down. Many people, in sombre reflection, examined why society felt so threatened over this one killing at Just Desserts. It was pointed out that the only difference in this case was that three black men were accused of killing a white woman. After all, murders and heists at restaurants are quite routine in major Canadian cities. Most people argued that it was the "randomness" of the shooting that frightened them. "You mean to say that you can't even go into a restaurant to eat a piece of cake without getting shot?" some asked. But two points were undefeatable in this argument. For a long time, these types of killings had been happening in the black community. Many young men and women had been slaughtered at illegal house parties and after-hours clubs. Some of the killings hardly merited mention in the newspapers and certainly not an outpouring of sympathy. The national media paid no attention when anyone was brought to trial, or when the murdered persons were buried. It seemed that as long as Blacks were killing Blacks, the city was still safe. Also, there was no doubt the security of feeling that as long as Blacks killed Blacks in black areas, then the wider community didn't have to worry. If a white person walked through a predominantly black area of Toronto like Jane and Finch, Lawrence Heights or the Peanut in North York, then they deserved what they got.

People reacted to the Just Desserts killing as though it were anything but random. They made it appear as though the entire city had become lawless—black youths with ski masks were running rampant throughout the city, and anyone, especially Whites, could be slaughtered. What they were, in fact, arguing is that because the killing had spilled over into a middle-class and largely white area, the mainstream was sitting up and taking notice. And they wanted this supposedly random violence stamped out.

Gayle's shooting of Constable Todd Baylis in the garage of an apartment building in a mixed neighbourhood was another example of this violence, spilling over into other areas, affecting the wrong people. It would become the lightning rod for feelings in the mainstream.

The morning the news came that someone had shot a cop, I was in the newsroom of the CBC writing news scripts for *World Report*, the first major newscast heard right across the country every morning. As I read the news flashes on the wires, I knew this shooting was serious, and I hoped that I would not have to write that a *black* man had killed a policeman. (Many black people have admitted feeling the same way when they hear the first reports of a shooting, murder or robbery. How they hope a black person is not involved and how they release a collective sigh of relief when they find out the criminal is white. Talk about collective guilt; or is it collective responsibility? Either one, many Blacks respond this way to news because they know that if the criminal is black, innocent Blacks can expect to be scrutinized on the subway and on buses, in convenience stores, and at work and at play.)

At the time we began to write the scripts, we knew only that two cops and the alleged gunman were in hospital. One of the policemen was in critical condition. A short while later, CBC police reporter Raj Ahluwalia arrived in the newsroom to prepare a report. He confirmed that the worst had happened, although the news was not official. "Looks like the cop is dead. They are holding off making the announcement until they have informed his family." The first edition of the newscast to the Maritimes told of the shooting and critical wounding of a cop in Toronto. Shortly thereafter, I would read the confirmation of the death on my computer screen, and would amend the newscast. Listeners in Manitoba, Alberta and British Columbia and in U.S. border states were to hear on their first major newscast about the murder of a cop on the beat. Eventually, the news of the shooting would be broadcast around the world on the various CBC national and international programs.

In the following week, listeners, including many in the Caribbean, would hear similar reports on the discussion about the violence and lawlessness, of the failure of the judicial and immigration systems. And they would hear the explanation that all of these things were responsible for the death of one of Metro's finest at the hands at one of Canada's most undesirable. Most of the media unquestioningly bought into the statements of the Metro police, and their reports resorted to caricature, depicting Gayle as lawless, a drug dealer, fatherless, a street hustler and someone who should have been kicked out of the country long ago. *The Toronto Sun* took to running billboards across the city under the caption, "We'll be there." Underneath the statement was a picture of three men with the word DEPORTED stamped across their faces. Many in the black community felt that these billboards had a direct connection with the death of Toronto policeman Baylis. And it was hard not to make this connection after a series of articles and columns linked the crime with deportation.

"Almost every day now, we could present another case of someone who should have been deported, and wasn't; or was deported, but came back; or was ordered deported, but was then released to disappear into the streets," wrote *Sun* columnist Christie Blatchford.

"This is how dreadfully routine such cases have become, this in the 20 days since Clinton Junior Gayle, a Jamaican immigrant whose deportation order was never executed, was arrested in the slaying of Metro Toronto Police Const. Todd Baylis and the wounding of his partner, Const. Mike Leone.

"Today's poster boy fits all three categories, with the added little fillips that a) he apparently enjoys posing with a gun in his hand and b) that on one of the last occasions his presence was officially noted, he was driving Clinton Gayle's car."

And to bring home her point, she later added: "If it is safe to say that the Gayle case has opened eyes and lips both ... and provided Canadians with a window into the shambles that is their federal immigration department, it is also a sure thing that this is just the tip of the proverbial iceberg."[3]

Who says hysteria doesn't sell?

The general outcry in reaction to this death would come from across the country and would be heard across the nation. Police officers poured into Toronto from all corners of the world, including Jamaica, to form the largest contingent of foreign police officers to attend a funeral in Canada. (That some of the policemen came from Jamaica was important to the media because Gayle is Jamaican. But more important, Gayle's biological father is a superintendent in the Jamaica Police Force and on hearing of the shooting is reported to have roundly condemned his son. Apparently, that was the first time Gayle's father had heard of his whereabouts in years.) And the funeral was huge. Local television stations carried it live.

---

[3] *The Toronto Sun*, July 6, 1994.

The streets of north Metro Toronto were closed off for hours as police officers paraded and paid their last respects. Photojournalists snapped pictures as members of 12 Division of the Metro Toronto Police Force, colleagues of the slain officer, served as pallbearers. The coffin was draped in the Canadian flag. And once again, every Black in the city felt those eyes on us. We were all Clinton Gayles, cop killers and murderers.

Now, in this courtroom, society was seeking to start the long process of handing out justice for someone cut down in the line of duty, by someone who ought not to have been in the country. But does the fact that the man who shot Baylis grew up in Canada, learned to become a criminal in Canada and knew nobody in the country of his birth matter to this discussion? It certainly did enter the debate in the Caribbean, where the argument was intense and became an international issue. But Gayle was Jamaican and was being rejected physically and psychologically from the country in which he had lived almost continuously for 20 years.

This case of *Regina v. Clinton Junior Gayle* was to be a test of the will of this country. Can a black person ever fully become a Canadian citizen? At what point do you stop being a Jamaican, Barbadian, Trinidadian, Ghanaian or Nigerian and become a full-fledged citizen of this country, to be accepted, faults and all, as a product of this society? This preliminary hearing was the start of the process of sending a clear, unmistakable message. Someone was going to sing the blues for this killing. Real Canadians were going to take back their country. And they were going to impose some common sense on how real Canadians run this country's judiciary, police and immigration systems.

* * *

The setting for this hearing could not be more conspicuous. The provincial courts in Etobicoke are situated in one of the most decayed and ugly areas of Metropolitan Toronto, a fitting symbol of the decay of the economic strength and open-mindedness of a society once affluent enough to accept the poorest from around the globe. This area shows all the scars of an economic recession that lasted too long; the manufacturing base laid bare as the country adjusts to free trade with the United States and

Mexico; the decay that leaves people mean-spirited and looking for someone, anyone, to blame for the economic uncertainty. At this juncture, the finger is pointed at immigrants, especially those from the Caribbean. And for many critics of the immigration policy, Clinton Gayle is what this country gets for being too soft.

But at the heart of this courthouse on this day is Courtroom 208, squeezed into the northwest corner of the building. At the main entrance, people attending this hearing undergo a preliminary search by court officers using metal detectors. Several people huddle in the cold, having a smoke.

Once past the security desk, a visitor takes a long walk into the bowels of the building, makes a right turn past the notices about changes in the Young Offenders court, then a sharp left. Right at the end of the corridor is room 208. The doors are painted light blue. Outside the courtroom is a Jamaican woman in a red blouse arguing with her son who is about 18 years old, dressed in baggy pants with Walkman headphones and a baseball cap.

"I told you that I was too busy the last time," the boy says, raising his voice and walking away.

"Wait there," says the woman. "Don't think me 'fraid to give you one big lick to yuh face right here this morning for talking to me like that. You shoulda think 'bout being too busy before this happen."

The very angry young man flops into one of the chairs forming a row against the wall. The woman sits behind him. I doubt if she would risk hitting him. Chances are that on a morning like this, the last thing she would want to do is to publicly scold her son, and at a court of law. But with no father around, what can she do? It must be tough being both mother and father to a boy like this. I think of the man whose preliminary trial is starting in Courtroom 208. Gayle is the product of a home without a father. I wonder if Gayle's mother, Meryl Powell, will be on hand to witness the trial.

Inside the first set of doors is another court officer with another metal detector. He is dressed in blue. After the second security check-point is another set of doors. Same colour—blue. The cramped courtroom is painted a light powder blue. But the 10 high-back benches, the railing and the raised table for the judge are a darker blue. And just about every major player in this room is wearing—you guessed it—blue. The Crown attorney, Paul W. Culver, who happens to be the top prosecutor for Metro Toronto and the proud son of a police officer, is in a blue suit. So is the defence lawyer, Michael McLachlan, and his fellow defence lawyer, John Fitzmaurice. The uniformed police milling around, the court officers, the court recorder and even the reporters and journalists are all wearing blue. Todd Baylis' family are wearing blue ribbons on their lapels.

The spectators are unevenly divided. Three of the four rows behind the Crown attorney are filled by the Baylis family, their supporters and members of the police force. The other side, presumably the area for Gayle, is empty except for this reporter. Somehow I am reminded of a church wedding, with representatives of the bride and groom having to sit on the appropriate sides. Obviously, the lack of support is not lost on Gayle's lawyer. "Members of [Baylis'] family are all here," McLachlan would tell me during one of the breaks in the hearing. "My guy has only his mother and she isn't here. She has to work. But she will come for the main trial."

At 9:15 a.m. comes a knock at the side door. Someone pushes it open from the outside and in shuffles the accused trailed by a male and female court officer. The defendant, too, is wearing blue: a dark blue T-shirt with a V-neck and dark blue blazer. His jeans are faded blue.

This is the first time I have seen Clinton Gayle. Immediately, I am struck by the muscular build of his upper body and neck. He looks strong and powerful, as though he works out with weights. He wears his hair like most young Blacks on the street: low cut at the sides, high cut at the top, a small pony-tail. The haircut is stylishly hip but not new. It does not show the fresh razor marks or the shine that would indicate he had rushed over to the barber for a special touch-up for such an important appearance. I had seen only pictures—mainly mug shots—of Gayle in the newspapers, and I was expecting a tall, slim man, something close to my own stereotype of the street gangster, who lives by his wits, making a dollar selling drugs. This is the image I had drawn from the descriptions I had heard on radio and television and had read in the newspaper.

Gayle reminds me of a former roommate of mine when I was at university in Jamaica. I am startled by the resemblance. My roommate was from Antigua, and as far as I know, Philmore James is probably leading a respectable, law-abiding life in Antigua or somewhere in the Caribbean, where he might even be a medical doctor or a biologist. Their features are strikingly similar, or so it looks to me as I view Gayle from the side.

McLachlan goes over to the prisoner's box, a glass-panelled affair on a wood casing. They talk briefly in whispers. The accused sits in the box, his chin inches from his chest, his eyes focused ahead. It appears as though a mask has taken over his features. Gayle shows no emotion, and will show none, for the entire hearing. He looks as though he is listening to some deep reggae beat in his head, as though he has blocked out the world. Occasionally, he scratches his nose or rubs his eyes. But the mask on his face remains unchanged. As though he has resigned himself to the inevitable: a black man facing a justice system in which all but two of the players—lawyers, police, judge, witnesses, spectator, the presence of the deceased—in Courtroom 208 are white. The other Blacks in this court are myself and a very officious court clerk, who would later admonish me and some others for chewing gum in the court. And yes, I am wearing blue jeans and the court clerk a skirt that is dark blue.

The scene is set for what, from all appearances, should be a routine day in court. The Crown simply has to prove there is enough evidence to hold Gayle over for trial.

But there are aspects of the proceedings that are very much not routine. It is unusual for anyone attending a case in the Etobicoke courtroom to go through two separate security check-points. A quick survey of all the other courtrooms reveals that only 208 has a second security point. A brief chat with some of the security people confirms that they were told to take no chances. Perhaps the court authorities feel a Jamaican posse would be riding in to spring Gayle. Or that some crazy person, not prepared to rely on the slow work of the state, might take matters into his own hands. Whatever the reasons, the authorities are taking no chances.

When Gayle is not in court, he is held in isolation and in handcuffs. His lawyer protests this treatment, arguing that although Gayle is being held in protective custody, he should not be in isolation and should be allowed to mix with the general prison population. In a concession to McLachlan, the court eventually agrees to take the handcuffs off Gayle during his confinement. But they keep him in leg irons.

Even in the black community, Gayle is much more than just some criminal who gunned down a policeman. For many of us in the Caribbean community, he is one of us, the immigrant who got stuck on the wrong side of the tracks. There but for the grace of God go I. That is why his resemblance to my former roommate springs to mind and haunts me. And not only does he resemble Philmore, but he also reminds me of a young man, an immigrant from Barbados, who is a photographer in Toronto. For me, Gayle is just like any typical young man I might meet in the barbershops or West Indian stores, or see hanging out on basketball courts or in front of some popular entertainment spot. Come to think of it, the haircut and Gayle's stocky build remind me of some of those black rappers I see in videos on TV. Or maybe, here again, I am the victim of television stereotyping. His haircut is the same style, "the Gumbie," that my 11-year-old son Michello demands whenever he visits the barber. In many respects, Gayle's life is so typical of a West Indian immigrant. Still, he is more than just a West Indian immigrant gone bad.

It was a nightmare come true when Clinton Gayle pulled the trigger and killed Todd Baylis that summer night. So many social workers in the black community had predicted that it would take an event like this for the wider society to take notice of the hurt and pain in the Canadian black community. As I watch Clinton Gayle, my mind flashes back two summers earlier. I was researching an article for *Toronto Life* magazine on the sour mood in the black community. I wanted to write a piece that touched on the anger among Blacks, especially the alienation of black youth. At the time, the community was being brutally whipped by the recession. Manufacturing in Ontario, the industrial heartland of Canada, was suffering badly. And by and large, black males in Ontario tend to work in manufacturing. They find their jobs making furniture, cars and buses. But their industry was being brutalized by the recession and free trade. Lay-offs were an everyday occurrence. Economists and politicians were not holding out hope for better days.

But there was another reason for the anger in the black community. There was a feeling that the political winds were blowing against the black community in Toronto, and it was felt most in the conflict with the law. In the previous 16 years, the police had been shooting or killing Blacks at just under the rate of one a year, accounting for some

12 shootings. In all those incidents, only one policeman was convicted. But the victory for the black community was snatched away when the judge, at the end of the trial, gave Constable Carl Sokolowski an absolute discharge. The humiliation from being tried for shooting Jonathan Howell on November 9, 1991, was punishment enough, the judge said, with a straight face.

There was also the Marcellus François case in Montreal, where the police shot a black man in his car, claiming that he looked like a wanted man. And there were near riots in Halifax over police heavy-handedness, and in Ottawa over police shootings of Blacks.

One other aspect of all these shootings is important. In just about every case, it came down to a question of a judge or jury having to decide whether to accept the word of a white police officer over that of a key black witness. In all cases in which a police shooting caused death, the police's word was accepted and the black testimony rejected. What these cases tell us is that members of the black community are slow learners. After decades, we haven't learned not to start fights with Metro police officers with small knives, big knives, guns, folded fists, swords or even the nozzle of a garden hose that a policeman can claim he mistook for a weapon. When these things happen, the police always get the right to plead self-defence and usually that is all a jury or judge needs to hear.

Two reports published in 1994 are unequivocal about the treatment of Blacks by the mainstream. The first is a report on how the RCMP spied on Canadian Blacks, particularly in Halifax, during the 1960s and 1970s. The files show the RCMP feared Blacks, especially some activists in Nova Scotia who were members of the Black Panthers in the United States and who might want to incite violence. So the RCMP kept files on them, tapped their phones, tampered with their mail, ransacked and torched some of their houses. "Some files from that period contained racial stereotypes and portrayed members of the black community in a derogatory manner," RCMP commissioner Philip Murray admitted when the reports were discovered by a reporter under the Access to Information Act. Black women were portrayed as "prolific child bearers" and black men as "layabouts, thieves and drunks."

The files also reveal how the RCMP spied on Caribbean and African politicians who were in Canada for legitimate business reasons, but who happened to meet with the activists or to visit Halifax. The reason for spying on the Caribbean officials was solely because they were black.

Many Blacks paid dearly for what was in these files. According to newspaper reports, the personal price was stalled careers, gutted job prospects and fouled-up credit ratings. "I don't think that we as black people or as Canadians generally should say this is the end of it," said Rocky Jones, one of the men who was spied upon at the time the existence of these reports was revealed. "We must go the step forward to have a redress of grievance, to deal with what were the effects of what happened and how we are going to deal with that."[4]

Jones' demands went unheeded. The wider society cleansed its hands of the issue through a written apology from the RCMP commissioner. The Canadian solicitor general of the day, Herb Gray, said that apology was good enough for him and put an end to the matter. He refused to launch a review of past RCMP activities, arguing that news of these dirty tricks was old hat from a past era.

But was it? Later that year, the Metropolitan Toronto Police force grudgingly acknowledged it had compiled a secret list of suspected black trouble-makers. This was two decades after the RCMP and other police forces were supposed to have stopped their dirty tricks. On the list were the names of several leading members of the Toronto community, some of them having committed no greater sin than criticizing the police. Around this time, Blacks began paying closer attention to what is known in police circles as the "black crime squad"—a group of primarily black police whose job is to check up on other Blacks, a group whose methods are said by some defence lawyers to be even more brutal than those of the rest of the force.

For many in the Toronto black community, confirmation of the secret list was no surprise. There were always tell-tale signs—such as comments in the press and by police officials about the black leadership—that such a list existed. More obvious questions are whether there are other files and what is the cost of these lists to individuals. So far, there are no answers. Only the doubts and the need to be eternally vigilant continue. The price of a shared heritage.

---

[4] *The Gazette* (Montreal), July 21, 1994.

* * *

For the *Toronto Life* article, I met with a group of black youths and social workers in Etobicoke, a short distance from the building that houses Courtroom 208. It was a summer day, with young Blacks lazing around in the courtyard of the housing project, one of those areas marked by government assistance and seem to be occupied largely by people of the same colour. The housing policy seems quite deliberate, as if the intention is to classify people by colour and not by income or housing needs, so that these projects become as multicultural as Canada. The result is the ghetto, a breeding ground for crime like the more infamous projects in the United States, and a killing ground like the apartment building where Gayle shot Baylis, a complex well known for drug dealing and violent crime.

In no time, with my tape recorder running, the group in Etobicoke was pouring out its collective heart. One of the social workers was Angela McCormack, widely recognized in Canada for her work with black youth. She has been profiled in such national magazines as *Chatelaine*, and she is generally considered to be one of the leading black spokespeople. Angela waited patiently while the youths talked of the discrimination they face daily. One talked about problems in the school. Another about problems in the home. Others about problems adapting to the new environment that is so different from what they knew in Jamaica, of parents working too hard and too long to be around when the youths need them, about the indignity of going into a convenience store to buy a greeting card and having the owner suspiciously watch every move, about problems most teenagers have and a bit more.

Angela responded to a question about when the wider society would become aware of the time bomb ticking away in the black community, when the violence plaguing our community and our children would stop. She made this startling prediction: "I don't think it is getting better. In fact, I've predicted we are going to have quite a few killings more and I think, as I told a couple of police officers a year ago, until a black person goes out there and kills a couple of white people, a couple of police officers, [that is what it will take] before they really take hold of what really is going on with our youth. Our youths are very angry; they have a lot of reason to be angry, and until people start taking the time to give them respect, love and direction, it's going to just get worse. You see it in the courts every day. You go into the jails and it's there."

Clinton Gayle was the partial fulfilment of that prediction. So was the Just Desserts shooting. The federal government reacted to the killing of Todd Baylis by starting a crackdown on all immigrants and refugees—an ongoing and far-reaching one that seems unable to satisfy the mean-spirited mainstream in this country.

* * *

Clinton Gayle arrived in Canada with his mother at the age of eight. He could have become a Canadian citizen at age 11, but his mother did not exercise this privilege. By the time Gayle thought seriously of becoming a citizen, it was already too late. He had had his first run-ins with the law. This is important, because a character clean of criminal activity is a prerequisite for citizenship, along with three continuous years of residency as a landed immigrant. It is also important because, whereas a landed immigrant can be deported to his or her native country, this is not the case for citizens. A citizen might be deported if it is proved that he or she lied to get citizenship or committed a deportable offence before becoming Canadian. But once the landed immigrant becomes a citizen, nothing he or she can do from that point on can result in deportation. Gayle continued to run up his criminal record, and ultimately the Canadian authorities decided that—despite the many years he had spent in Canada, despite his becoming a criminal in this country and despite his having no real ties with Jamaica—he should be sent back where he came from. Some time after his final deportation hearing, Gayle dropped out of sight.

Following the shooting of Baylis, the federal government decided to go after illegal immigrants, primarily Jamaicans. In a short while, scores of illegal immigrants were rounded up and and sent packing, with the largest number headed for Jamaica. Next on the list was Trinidad. Yet, that was not enough. Some bright people in the immigration department decided to start fingerprinting Jamaican entertainers upon entering this country simply because 10 percent of them tend to become illegal immigrants. It would seem that the numbers hardly deserved going to so much trouble, for only about 300 Jamaican entertainers come to Canada annually, and they must be screened for a Canadian visa in Jamaica. Following an outcry by the Jamaican and black communities, this policy was dropped. But the message behind it was unmistakable.

The shooting ultimately caused a diplomatic rift between the Canadian and Jamaican governments, forcing the Jamaican government to develop a policy on expatriation that could affect all of us from the Caribbean who still harbour thoughts of going back home some day, if only in retirement. The policy was enunciated by Jamaican prime minister P.J. Patterson at a speech he gave in Toronto, when he argued quite forcefully that wealthy countries like Canada cannot solve their social problems by dumping them on poor countries like those in the Caribbean: "We must take care that we address the cause and not merely the symptoms. Pointing a finger in the wrong direction may only serve to exacerbate social tension or allow racism to rear its ugly head. No country can hope to dispose of its social problems by dumping them at the doorsteps of its neighbours. We have to work together in creating the proper human environment."

This speech came at a time when Canada and the United Sates were sending scores of hardened criminals back to the Caribbean. Most of them had learned and practised their life of crime in North America. But to return criminals-gone-bad was an easy solution—to inflict them on poor countries that are even less capable than Canada or the United States to deal with them. Caribbean countries had become alarmed at this attempt to off-load these criminals, simply because they had Caribbean nationality. And in his address, Patterson spoke on behalf of the Caribbean community to say that this approach is no solution.

But Clinton Gayle was still more than an alleged murderer. He was the monster, the bogyman called up when witnesses representing the police appeared before a parliamentary committee in Ottawa to discuss proposed changes to the Immigration Act. "I ask simply this: that if the next victim of one of these individuals was your son or daughter, could you go to your spouse and say, 'I did enough to prevent this situation from happening again'?" asked Constable Susan Cieslik, the first officer on the scene of the Baylis killing. Breaking into tears as she recalled the events of that night, Cieslik said, "We must protect both the police officer and the citizens from dangerous criminals who are not Canadian citizens."

How could the committee not be moved, especially when it was pointed out that the witness comes from a family that takes it as an honour to be a police officer, who had a father and brother who were also police officers, and who had become so frustrated with the shackles civilian authorities were placing on the police that she was quitting the Toronto force?

And Gayle is a bogyman of another type. Even Federal Justice Minister Alan Rock dredged up the image of Gayle and his illegal handgun in a sales pitch for proposed legislation banning some types of firearms. In radio interviews and elsewhere during public meetings, Rock explained that his legislation would force owners to register their weapons and that when they die the guns would have to be handed over to the state. The legislation would also force owners to report when the weapons are stolen, so that if a gun was used to commit a crime and the weapon was later traced to the owner, that registered owner would not be in trouble with the law. And here, he explained, the aim of the legislation is to stop occurrences such as when the gun that shot the Toronto policeman was, in fact, stolen from a home in Etobicoke—an incident that happened in the minister's own riding. Yes, Rock explained, he understood the pains and concerns of the powerful gun lobby, which borrowed tactics from the National Rifle Association in the United States, in that it portrayed Rock's legislation as an attack on fundamental freedoms. Faced with thousands of gun owners and supporters packing halls where he was meeting with them, what could Rock offer as a foil? Who could be the bogyman that he could pull from the hat to frighten off the anti-gun lobby? Clinton Gayle had unwittingly become an arrow in the justice minister's quiver for the war on handguns.

CHAPTER 9

SOMEBODY'S SON

Well, this thing's bigger than you son. In a certain sense, every Negro in America's on trial out there today.

Richard Wright
Native Son (1940)

As Clinton Gayle sits in the courtroom, still and emotionless, another image keeps running through my mind—that of the character Bigger Thomas in Richard Wright's famous novel, *Native Son.* It is a story of a Black who becomes a social misfit and criminally violent as the result of relentless and stultifying racism. That story was written decades ago and was set in Chicago, a cold northern city. I could not help but think about what must have gone through Wright's mind when he created this character. Wright was using the raw materials that he saw around him. He was also trying to analyze the conditions—social, political, financial and environmental—that would create someone as violent as Bigger Thomas, the conditions imposed by a dominant culture that would cause a member of a minority group to commit a crime, willingly or unwillingly, against a white woman and his black girlfriend as well.

In *Native Son,* the lawyer representing Bigger Thomas went on to make the trial a case against the state and the power structures of the day. Several decades later, and in an Etobicoke courtroom, I feel Wright would have more material to help develop his character, Bigger Thomas. Also, I feel that with the seemingly overwhelming evidence against Gayle, the public mood against him, that his lawyer also has no choice but to also put on trial the Canadian system, a system that took a young impressional boy and turned him into a cop killer. Indeed, Gayle is a Bigger Thomas.

I had first tried to visit Gayle a few months before this court appearance. I was contacted by a Toronto film producer who wanted to make a television movie on the shooting of Todd Baylis. I was asked to do the research on Gayle and I had approached his lawyer, Michael McLachlan, requesting that he ask Gayle if he would co-operate. In the initial contact, I spoke briefly on the phone with McLachlan and we agreed to meet for dinner. I went to McLachlan's office and we drove to a Thai restaurant where we chatted for a couple of hours. McLachlan's wife, Jane Farnan, who is also a lawyer, joined us. She had represented Gayle on a firearms case. "It was a dog of a case," McLachlan acknowledged. Gayle was convicted. Some of the Toronto newspapers had taken to painting the picture of Gayle as a hardened criminal who often changed lawyers because he could not get along with them.

In fact, McLachlan said that Gayle was a good client. For example, when he was arrested he refused to make any statements to the police. "As least, he learned enough from me to keep his mouth shut," McLachlan said. It was a very friendly meeting. We enjoyed the Thai food, all the while both McLachlan and I were feeling out each other. "What do you know about this case?" McLachlan asked. "Do you have any contacts in the community who might be witnesses?"

Unfortunately for Gayle's case, I had none. McLachlan went on to detail one serious problem for the defence: a lack of witnesses. The only witnesses were two young children who claimed to have seen the shooting from the balcony of a nearby apartment building. Their statement corroborated what Gayle had told McLachlan. Gayle's story was that he was walking along, heading for the basement garage of the apartment, when he was set upon by the police. They sprayed him with pepper and, blinded, he started to run. The police started shooting and Gayle fired back, using his left hand to fire across his body as he ran.

The children's statement backed up this account, McLachlan said. But there were two problems with the evidence for the defence. One, the prosecution felt that the mother of the children had set them up to tell this story. And McLachlan feared that under cross-examination, in a court and all, the prosecution might discredit the children as witnesses. The other problem was more crucial. The forensic studies, including the powder burns, show that Baylis was shot from about six inches away. "Now, if you are the prosecutor, you will turn to me," McLachlan said to me rather dramatically, "and ask, How is that consistent with the idea of your man running away, Mr. Defence Lawyer?" McLachlan admitted he was stumped for an answer.

However, there were some answers. The shooting of Baylis was inconsistent with Gayle's earlier behaviour. Although he was convicted of carrying a gun, he had never been convicted for use of a firearm. In fact, McLachlan explained, Gayle carried the gun for protection. Once, some guys had beaten him up and he had decided to arm himself from then on. We talked about Gayle's life in Toronto, of his mother, a typical, hard-working immigrant from the Caribbean, trying to keep a low profile despite all the publicity around this case. The last thing she wanted was the notoriety associated with having a son accused of murdering a policeman.

"When this happened, you must understand," McLachlan explained, "she had just made a step up in life. She had bought a town house and she is a member of her church and has her job at the hospital. Also, because her last name is Powell, nobody would automatically associate her with Gayle. So she wants to live a quiet life and to look after her younger son who has some problems."

However, he explained, she has gone to see Gayle in jail and continues to support him.

In terms of strategy, McLachlan said that he would try to prove that Toronto police are not properly trained to deal with members of minority groups. As members of the dominant group, they are prone to expect trouble when they approach a black man. This attitude in and of itself creates the environment for trouble. So that on the night in question, the way these policemen approached Gayle would have forced him to defend himself, especially if he knew he had committed no crime, especially if the police are known for beating up on Blacks in the area.

The latter was going to be a crucial point. McLachlan said that his investigation showed that Todd Baylis and his partner, Michael Leone, had manhandled other Blacks in the area. Some of the cases had been brought to court and he believed internal police investigations had been launched against at least one of the officers. He planned to raise this issue in cross-examination, but he expected the Crown to object to his using this evidence in court. The Crown would argue that the evidence was not relevant. If he succeeded, this could be his trump card, his way to re-enact a Bigger Thomas-versus-the-state strategy.

As for a movie, McLachlan at first appeared enthusiastic. He would suggest to his client that he co-operate, especially since the producer had already received approval from the Baylis family for co-operation. We talked about possible scenarios and endings of the movie, of the parallels in the lives of Gayle and Baylis. "Do you know that just before that shooting that Clinton was hoping to become a policeman? He was planning to go back to Jamaica and see if he could join the force there." Of course, this would mean refusing to disclose his criminal record in Canada and hoping his father pulled some strings. McLachlan said that Gayle's father appeared ready to do this, but then came the shooting and Gayle's father disowned him.

By the end of the evening, we agreed that McLachlan would ask Gayle to co-operate. "Of course, you realize that at this point in his life, a movie is the last thing on my client's mind," McLachlan said. The following week, McLachlan reported that Gayle had declined. He wasn't interested. I really felt it was McLachlan backing out, perhaps a ploy to have some editorial control. This became more evident when McLachlan said he was willing to meet with the producer. That meeting in the lawyer's office did not go well. McLachlan was adamant Gayle would not co-operate. The producer was unyielding; a story would be made with or without Gayle's co-operation, and Gayle stood to lose a lot by not participating.

I suggested that I would still like to meet Gayle. But McLachlan said that with only two weekly visits permitted, he didn't want to use them up that way. "The last thing on my client's mind is making a movie," McLachlan repeated. "He is in the general population of the prison; he's getting his physiotherapy and that's all we want right now." However, McLachlan promised to ask Gayle to reconsider his position.

The next week, word came back through the producer that McLachlan reported that Gayle would not change his mind. However, McLachlan wanted me to call. When I did, McLachlan said he would like me to meet Gayle and that he thought it would be a good idea if Gayle read my novel, *No Man in the House,* a typical Caribbean story of a young boy growing up without a father. I promised to drop off a copy of the book, which I did, and that McLachlan agreed to make arrangements for me to visit Gayle. But it was in court that I saw him for the first time.

* * *

At 9:23 a.m., the black court clerk pushes open a back door and shouts: "All rise, this court is in session." Clinton Gayle, like everyone else, rises and watches as Judge Amy Bonkalo, in a black gown, takes her place underneath the provincial Coat of Arms. The lawyers introduce themselves and the court is ready for the arraignment. The only black woman in the court rises with a sheaf of papers in her hand. Michael McLachlan, looking very serious, arms folded across his chest, walks across the room and positions himself in front of the prisoner standing in his box. He looks as if he is physically trying to shield Gayle. Speaking slowly and clearly, the clerk reads: "Clinton Junior Gayle, you are charged ..." She appears to pause after each phrase, as if waiting for a look in Gayle's eyes that he understands. "Charge one ... first degree murder; charge two ... attempted murder; charge three ... having an unlawful weapon; charge four ..." By the time she finishes, nine charges. Then she advises Gayle that on "charges three and four" he has a choice: trial by judge and jury; trial by judge alone.

"How do you elect for charges three and four?" she asks.

"Judge and jury," McLachlan shouts and quickly walks back to his post. Gayle sits. There is no plea of guilty or "the one hundred percent absolutely not guilty" theatrics I had seen on American television in the O.J. Simpson case. The only other formality is that the judge again warns of the publication ban on evidence to be heard in the court.

A court trial is really a series of small legal battles all going to result in one final win. It is like chess, when moves and counter-moves are planned way in advance. But it is also a game of steel nerves, similar to poker. In Gayle's case, it's clear that the overall win would be a "not guilty" verdict some time down the road, or if he is lucky, for Madam Bonkalo to rule at the end of this preliminary hearing that there is not enough evidence to order a trial. Going into the preliminary hearing, I sense that Gayle's lawyers are not optimistic of getting the latter. Even before this preliminary hearing started, McLachlan had already told me about the possibility of this case going all the way to the Supreme Court of Canada.

So both the defence and Crown attorneys engage in the first skirmish. Gayle's lawyer asks for all potential witnesses to be excluded from the hearing. His aim is to clear the room of all police witnesses. "My client takes exception to police officers listening to other officers and amending their evidence," he says.

Paul Culver objects. He wants the police witnesses in court, especially those officers who had worked on the case and had helped compile the "mass of material" that will be the evidence against Gayle.

But score the opening victory to the defence. The court orders the police officers out of the room, all of them except the lead detective, Sergeant Jim Crowley, who is sitting at the lawyers' table with Culver. It might be a victory, but Gayle seems unconcerned. His demeanour does not change. He sits staring ahead, blinking rapidly.

Culver calls his first witness, a Dr. David Chaisson. He is a top pathologist with the Coroner's office in Ontario and a professor at the University of Toronto, a consultant to several hospitals, including Hospital for Sick Children. He says he is an expert in the business and that he has working experience in Boston, where he handled at least "100 homicides with more than 50 percent of them gunshot wounds."

The defence says it will not challenge his qualifications and expertise. Dr. Chaisson starts to give his evidence, the summary of which is that he examined Baylis after the officer was declared dead at Sunnybrook Hospital. He found a wound "3.5 centimetres from the right ear." He knew it was a gunshot wound because of the gun-powder stippling, which indicates that the gun was fired at close range—between 24 and 36 inches from the target. The bullet moved through the head in "a right-to-left, front-to-back direction, with little up-and-down movement." The bullet was recovered from the skull. Chaisson says that, based on what he saw, it was unlikely doctors could have saved Baylis and that the constable was probably unconscious immediately after the impact.

The evidence is detailed and gruesome. The language is precise and medical. Most of it is too technical for non-professionals. Much evidence is given about bruises on Baylis' body, which indicated that he was in a fight any time between "one minute and 48 hours" before death. This evidence will later prove important to the testimony of Baylis' partner, Michael Leone.

McLachlan begins his cross-examination, but from the point of view of a layman in the body of the court, he appears unable to shake the pathologist from his evidence. And on the score card of minor battles, he loses one when Culver objects that McLachlan is not "using the exact words of the witness" but is paraphrasing the doctor's statements too loosely. The judge agrees. With that, the court is ready for its first recess at 11:24.

On resumption, a fourth black person enters the court. He is Philip Mascoll, a police-beat reporter for *The Toronto Star.* He sits with the other reporters and I again take my position at the back of the courtroom. Mascoll signals me to join him. When I do, he says, "The police fellows are wondering who you are."

"What do you mean?" I ask.

"What do you mean, what I mean?"

The message is clear. I am not acting like the other reporters: going to the prosecution and talking to the Crown and the senior detectives. So, I guess it was strange for all of them to see this lone black man in the back taking notes. I continue to sit beside Mascoll.

"The guy looks just like his dad, you know, man," Mascoll says in his Jamaican accent. We look at Gayle. His demeanour is unchanged. He stares ahead, seemingly at nothing.

"I remember him when he was a little boy, but I don't think he even knows me now," Mascoll says. He tells me he knows Gayle's father, the police superintendent in Hanover, Jamaica. This is the same father who from news reports denounced the son he had not seen for most of the younger man's life. "But his father wasn't much of a father." Mascoll says the obvious.

The case continues. The next witness is Finn Nielson, an expert on firearms. He departs from the apparent dress code by wearing a grey suit that matches his short-clipped beard and thinning hair. He, too, is very methodical in his evidence. Obviously, Nielson has learned much about the ways of the court from the 600 or so cases at which he says he has testified. So that when he asks to consult his notes to refresh his memory, it is the voice of someone who knows exactly how to phrase his words.

Nielson describes the semi-automatic P-38, the gun that killed Baylis. It was manufactured in Germany for use during the Second World War and was "probably brought back to Canada by a returning officer." (Irony of ironies, I think: even the gun in this case is an illegal immigrant.)

Nielson begins to demonstrate how a similar gun works, paying attention to how easily it jams. After every second shot, it jams. The gun recovered at the Baylis shooting was jammed. Nielson produces an ugly-looking gun from a brown leather bag and begins handling it, pausing to reassure the court that the gun's magazine is empty, and that he is not using the weapon found at the crime scene. But even then, he appears to be treating the gun with caution, giving it the respect and care that he, an expert, possibly insists upon when dealing with such potential for destruction. For the first time Gayle appears to be paying attention, his head is cocked slightly in a position from which he can get a better view of the gun, as if he is mentally taking lessons on how to prevent a P-38 from jamming. Nielson's evidence is that the gunpowder removed from around the wound showed that the gun was discharged "three to six inches from Constable Baylis' head." He also explains that he has examined the guns issued to Baylis and Leone that evening. "Baylis' gun had not been fired since it was cleaned last." Leone's gun had been fired.

Nielson is still on the stand when the court adjourns for lunch. At this time, I notice some police officers beckoning to Ted Baylis, the father of the dead policeman and himself a detective, to join them. He is introduced to a tall, beefy man in a beige jacket. They are standing across from me.

"This is Myron Thompson, the Reform Party member of Parliament," one of the policemen says by way of introducing Ted Baylis and the man in the beige jacket. "He is the Reform Party critic for justice and immigration in the House of Commons."

"I'm here to see how justice is done," Thompson says.

More proof this is not just another trial. Members of Parliament are busy. Few of them take the time off to attend murder trials. Even fewer of them bother with preliminary trials, even in their own riding or in Ottawa. But not Myron Thompson, MP from Alberta, the critic for a party with many self-described rednecks. The message from the Reform Party in sending him to this trial is clear.

Outside the courtroom, I have a brief conversation with Thompson. He repeats, "I'm here to see justice in action." I ask if he has gone to other trials: No. It is only recently that he decided to see first-hand what is happening in the courts. As the Reform Party critic for justice and immigration, he is also checking up on immigration and customs in Toronto, so he decided to visit Toronto at this time.

"Why start with Toronto?" I ask.

"Toronto is the biggest centre in the country."

"Have you checked on any courts or immigration centres in Alberta?"

"No. I haven't."

"Will you be making a report to your caucus?"

"Yes, I will."

Later, I ask Michael McLachlan if Thompson met with him. He had not. "I guess he is here to learn about gun control," the lawyer says. He is referring to the opposition by members of the Reform Party to the proposed legislation banning the ownership of many types of guns, including handguns like the P-38, the one cited by the justice minister as a case for gun registration.

Obviously, everyone is cashing in on this trial. If Thompson needed a stage to start his investigation of the immigration and police systems, he could have found one in his backyard—the case of David Anthony Lawes, a former Jamaican policeman who was handed a life sentence for murdering a Calgary policeman. There are some similarities between the cases against Gayle and Lawes. Both are from Jamaica. Lawes was in Canada illegally, having arrived in the country in 1992 on a visitor's permit and overstayed his welcome. He shot Constable Rob Vanderweil during a routine traffic check and left him to bleed to death.

But there was one significant difference. The Calgary police did not crank up their public-relations machine to the same extent as their

Toronto counterparts did following the shooting of Baylis. Neither did the media get as hysterical, never pointing to the Vanderweil murder as an indictment of a decrepit immigration policy. Because the Calgary case did not get the national attention of the Baylis case, and Myron Thompson had to look beyond Calgary for a case with enough of a national profile to use for his campaign.

* * *

What is happening in Courtroom 208 is of interest not only to the Reform Party but to the wider community as well. This is the situation among Blacks. Stepping out of the courthouse into a sandwich shop across the road, Mascoll and I begin debating the implication and impact of shootings like the one that killed Baylis.

I have argued that the black community as a whole has a responsibility. Mascoll was adamant that fellow Blacks should not feel they have to apologize for some "thug" like Gayle. "I've heard people on the radio talk shows apologizing. What are they apologizing for? I see black people at the Leimonis funeral and I have to ask, why are they there unless they know the family or something?"

In a way, Mascoll and I were playing out face to face a debate we had carried on in the *Star*. It started when I wrote a column after the Just Desserts shooting, arguing that members of the black community must speak up about the uncontrolled and escalating violence in the community. I was concerned that the quality of life for black people was suffering because of the escalating violence in the clubs and watering holes where Blacks like to hang out. My concern was that Blacks ought to speak out, use moral suasion, so that black youths would no longer think it hip or cool to be walking around with loaded pistols.

In writing this column I was thinking of statements by some leading African-Americans, particularly from the Reverend Jesse Jackson, about how African-Americans must take care of problems in their community. I also recalled Minister Louis Farrakhan, of the Nation of Islam, exhorting Blacks to put aside violence and to stop being their own worst enemy by killing themselves.

That column drew fire from just about every quarter. One of the most blistering attacks came from Arnold Minors, the only black representative on the Metro Toronto Board of Trade. Minors referred to the gist of my column in an address to the Black Business and Professional Association. He could not understand why anyone would talk about communal guilt on these matters. At the end of his speech, Minors was given a standing ovation. Mascoll also felt I had gone too far. In his column he also argued against any notion of community responsibility.

Now, here we are having the argument all over again. "I have a responsibility for my children, my nephews and nieces and the responsibility of people I know," he tells me in the sandwich shop.

"Well, where do you draw the line in terms of community responsibility?" I ask.

We decide to agree to draw the line at different points. I do not change his mind; neither does he sway me. I still believe a minority community must act differently from the wider community. If Mascoll had been thinking, he would have seen, just an hour earlier, that we in the black community are treated differently, are more noticeable. Otherwise, why would the police ask him who this black guy was sitting in the back of the courtroom taking notes?

Back in the courtroom, everything is going along just fine for the prosecution. The testimony by P.C. Michael Leone, the only witness and participant in the shooting, is the final icing on the cake. Gayle is ordered to the next round of the process to bring him to justice.

* * *

Prisons are intimidating places. They strike fear into the heart of even the visitor. The Toronto West Detention Centre is such a place. It is in an industrial area of Etobicoke, a short distance from the Lester B. Pearson International Airport, the country's largest international airport, and seemingly a century away from civilization. A woman at the last restaurant on the street leading to the prison points out the building through a window. It is the mammoth brown building at the end of a winding road, a building with a light that can be seen almost a mile away. She acts as though this information is best kept a secret.

This prison is intended to make life uncomfortable, even for the visitor. After going through two sets of doors, a visitor talks into a speaker to two men sitting behind smoked glass. It is almost impossible to hear the men over the small speaker imbedded in the wall. But with effort, the procedures for a visit are completed. Name of the prisoner? a guard barks. Clinton Gayle. The worker checks a list of names on sheets of paper. Identification? he demands. The visitor fishes into his pocket, brings out an Ontario driver's licence. A sign on the wall says that other accepted forms of identification are passports, Canadian citizenship cards, Canadian social insurance cards. The man motions for the visitor to hold the licence, picture up, against the glass. Eventually, a cylinder under the glass grinds open and a sheet comes out. At the bottom of a list, under the prisoner category, is the name Clinton Gayle with a number next to it. The visitor must write his name, relationship to the prisoner (given as friend), his address and signature.

"Have a seat and wait," one of the men says through the speaker. The lobby of this prison does not invite anyone to sit. There are no chairs, but slabs of tiled concrete. It is as alienating a place as any. Two pay telephones, one at either side of the room, a vending machine for chocolates and candy, another for coffee, a machine for making change from paper money. To one side are some plants, but they look in need of care. Two cameras peer down from opposite sides of the lobby. Signs on the wall spell out in English and French the rules for visits. They start with a note that if a visitor knows of anything that could cause damage or put the prisoner at risk to tell the management. The language is such that it is hard to tell whether this is a request for co-operation or a demand that visitors ignore at their own peril. Below the statement is a list of do's and don'ts—no cameras; no radios; change of clothing once every six weeks; two visits per week; money for fines and cafeteria can be left at the office; rowdy people will be asked to leave.

The lobby is filling up with people, a combination of those coming out at the end of visits and those waiting to gain entry and go through the identification ritual. Those who believe justice is blind and Canada is multicultural can take some comfort in the mix of people in the lobby.

Just about every group of immigrant is represented in this lobby and there is a clump of Native visitors. One group is speaking in a language that sounds like Spanish. Young women with babies and children mill around. Noticeably, they all have the unmistakable look of immigrants, of people not sure about the system. They all appear to be the same class, the underprivileged of this society. And they are all standing huddled in front of the electronically secured door through which they must enter the bowels of the prison.

After a wait of almost 30 minutes, there is a noise over the speaker. Everyone goes silent when there is a noise over the speaker: it is so difficult to hear or to make out what is being said, and so everyone strains to listen. There is also a respectful silence whenever a guard passes by. The group in front of the door reacts to the squawking on the speaker, looking around the lobby expectantly. Then someone shouts, "Visitor for Gayle." Now, I realize the squawking is for me.

Inside, Clinton Gayle is waiting in a room framed by Plexiglas. He sees me right away and signals to me. He is wearing blue jeans and a blue T-shirt. He directs me to the right phone and we begin talking like old friends.

Gayle says he is glad I am visiting him. "You will see that I am not the type of person you have been hearing about. People do not realize that people like me are human, that we have mothers and family. That we are the sons of some people. But I am leaving everything into the hands of God. He will deliver me."

The eagerness of the outburst momentarily throws me off guard. Fumbling for words, I ask if his mother visits him. "Yes, she does. I have the full support of all my family."

"Including your father in Jamaica?"

"Yes, man. Full support." The conversation is off and running, with Gayle in the lead and me trying to catch up. Gayle is like a man with so much on his mind to say. And with ease, he broadens the conversation, making it a discussion on the plight of black men in North America. While waiting in the lobby, I had wondered how he would react to my visit, what we would talk about, how we would skirt around discussing what happened that summer night. For I had promised his lawyer not to talk about the night of the shooting, not unless I wanted to be dragged before the court as a witness. "I'm spending my time reading the Bible and praying. God will take care of everything."

"Are you a Christian?" I ask.

Yes, he says. He was raised a Roman Catholic but he is not a practising Catholic. He recognizes that all Christian denominations, including Catholic, Seventh Day Adventists and Jehovah Witnesses, preach some of the truths but then they deviate. He does his own religious study. He is studying the books of Moses not included in the Bible. This is a gift from his sister. This, he explains, is why he hasn't read my book yet. "But I will get to it. I have time," he jokes.

As he talks, I realize that he is right about the stereotype of him and I tell him. "I thought you were a tall, lanky guy for one thing."

"See, that's what I told you." Then he tells me about how the stereotypes can affect his treatment in prison and in the holding cells when he goes to court. A few people, including guards, call him names and threaten him, but he knows how to handle them. He doesn't pay them any mind. But in his conversation, he repeatedly returns to the perception of him, a false picture, he says, fed by the media and by society's hate for Blacks in general. He tells me of a guard who was giving him a tough time. And he tells me of the story in *The Toronto Sun* that says he is being held in maximum security. Gayle says the point of enlightenment happened for the guard one day after he returned from court and a friend showed the guard the report claiming that Gayle was held in maximum security. "He said, 'I have always believed what I read in the *Sun*. Now, I know different.' From that day that guard has been nicer to me."

Throughout the discussion, I keep thinking this is a very articulate man, capable of acquitting himself well in any debate. "Did you ever try to go to college or university?" I ask.

"No," he says, "and I was good in science and things like that. In general levels, I was always getting in the 70s and 80s [percentage] on my tests." Then he tells me three anecdotes that seem to sum up his life, that indicate why he deviated from going on to higher education and why he ended up a prisoner. When he was attending high school, he says, "I did something that I shouldn't do. We had a test. I gave my answers to three guys in the class during the test. I know I shouldn't do that. The three of them passed the test. I failed. The teacher told me it was because my writing was sloppy. I didn't believe it."

The second incident happened after a female teacher visited Jamaica and returned to tell the class "that Jamaica is the worst place and all the people are bad. I asked her in front the class if she was talking about all Jamaicans or about some people. She said she was talking about Jamaicans. I told her that she shouldn't be saying those things and pointed out some things about her people, how they are liars, thieves and murderers. How they build cities in this country with the blood of other people. She didn't like it and sent me to the principal. I told the principal to ask the class what she had said. After he asked the class, the principal turned to the teacher and right there in front of the class made her apologize." But Gayle says that although he won this victory, he had lost in the larger scheme of things. He was branded as mouthy, especially since he had a reputation for standing up for his rights, for asking to be dealt with as an adult, and for refusing to go the principal's office at the whims of his teachers. Eventually, he was moved out of the class taught by the teacher with whom he had the show-down.

These events helped to shape him, Gayle says. He recognizes that this society has no intention of helping black people. "If two of us go for a job, each one of us have to be stabbing the other in the back. I am not for that." One of the results of this attitude, he says, is the make-up of the prison population. In the Toronto West Detention Centre the population is mostly black. And he says that he continues to cultivate his interest in "his people's culture." While growing up he spent a lot of time in the library reading, and watching such television programs as *National Geographic*, all aimed at getting a better understanding and knowledge of black people.

Does he regret coming to Canada? "No. My mother brought me with her, so I have no regrets about that. But I was planning to go back home to Jamaica."

Through the conversation, he laughs heartily—at himself and at life. "So, you do smile," I say. "When I saw you in court, you looked so serious."

"Yes," he says, setting this up for his third anecdote. At his first court appearance, he was his natural smiling self. The newspapers jumped on that and said he was not showing any remorse and was being too happy-go-lucky. So he decided to be serious in court. Then the newspapers said he was too serious, showing "no ... no ..."—here he snaps his fingers trying unsuccessfully to recall the right word. "So you see, you can't win in this system. It's like when I was growing up and my mother gave me a glass of orange juice for breakfast. If I drank half, she would ask why I didn't finish it. When I drank it all, she would ask why I didn't save some for another time. You can't win." And he laughs.

The conversation is free-wheeling and lively. As Gayle talks he waves his right hand in the air. It's the same hand that took the bullet the night of "the incident," as he calls it. The nails on his thumbs and little fingers have grown long. "So how is the hand?" I ask. "It is fine." He rolls up his sleeve and shows me the scar from the bullet, bumpy keloid scars so typical of the healing process in black people.

Quickly we move on to another subject and this is the closest he comes to talking about "the incident." Gayle says he is surprised by the lies presented as evidence in the preliminary trial. He sounds resigned to being committed to stand trial and at this point I caution him to take care not to stray into discussing the incident. Gayle says that from the evidence presented, he is even more confident of the outcome. "A lot of people are going to be surprised about what will happen in this trial. The case they are presenting, I could win defending myself. A lot of people are going to be surprised. And *they* will have a lot of explaining to do about this case. They will have to explain a lot of things they've been doing."

Time has flown by so quickly, I haven't noticed. "They are calling my name," Gayle says. "I have to go." The visit is over. I promise to come back and see him again. He smiles and invokes God's blessing. We hang up the phones, he smiles broadly and walks through the door a warden is holding open for him. Outside, many of the people I had left in the lobby are still waiting expectantly for their chance to enter the prison.

* * *

By the time I returned to the prison for a second visit, a lot had already happened. As was expected, Gayle was bound over at the preliminary trial for a full trial. His lawyer had failed to get the court to allow McLachlan to question Leone on his past history. The decision was under appeal.

There were other notable developments. Out of the blue came the news that several officers at 12 Division had been suspended with pay while the police conducted an internal investigation. The officers were accused of planting evidence on people they arrested. There was a question of drugs disappearing. As a result, the police had withdrawn as many as 200 drug charges laid by these officers. Lawyers for some convicted clients were busy seeking a review or appeal of their cases in light of this development. All of these developments were important to the Gayle case in a big way. First, it was reported that the police had quietly dropped the drug charges against him. Could this be the bombshell Gayle was promising?

For my second visit, I arrive at the jail around two o'clock. This time I know what to expect. I have my identification ready and join the long line that extends almost through the outside door. At the last moment, a tall, lanky man pushes into line ahead of me. After about 20 minutes, I get to the window and sign in to see Clinton Gayle. The guard makes a mark beside Gayle's name and asks me to take a seat.

About half an hour later, the announcement comes: "Visitor for Gayle." I move to the door, but ahead of me is a young black woman. The guard says to me: "There are two of you to see him. She was here first." The woman disappears inside. I sit down and wait, and wait, and wait.

Eventually the man who had cut into the line in front of me sidles up to me. His name is Trevor, he says, and he hates having to come to this place. Trevor says that he is a Jamaican and that he had come to the jail "for instructions" from a friend on what to do with a car.

Apparently the friend is about to be deported to Jamaica. He has been caught once before for living illegally in Canada, was granted bail, and never showed up for the hearing. Now, Trevor says, there is no doubt where this guy is headed even though he is married to a white woman and has a baby by her. Which leaves the problem of the car.

Trevor says that he had sold the car to this friend as a means of helping him to get a job and make something of his life. But he had not changed the registration of the ownership or the licence plates of the car. So the friend was driving the car when it broke down at a stop-light, and he left the car at the intersection and disappeared. The car was towed to a police pound, where it had been held for about five weeks, at a cost of five dollars a day. The police had traced the car to Trevor from the ownership and he was on the hook for the towing and storage fees. Two weeks after the car broke down, the friend was captured by the police, given a 10-day sentence for some offence and was about to be sent back to Jamaica. Now, Trevor wants instructions from him on what to do about the car. "If I have to pay the charges of keeping the car, I might as well take it back myself. The cost for storing the car is as much as he paid me for it in the first place."

This is not the first time Trevor has had dealings with someone in this prison. There was once a "big, big man," he says, who was a friend and who was having family problems. So he decided to find a place for himself. "Him making good, good money, about $19 an hour, at a butcher shop. But him ask me to lend him $1,000 to help him move out and get an apartment of his own. This is money my wife and I planned for a vacation."

After receiving the money, the "big, big man" disappeared and for weeks on end Trevor could not find him. One day, Trevor's wife got a collect call from the Don West jail. "My wife never accept collect calls from anyone. I asked who it is? She tell me it's my friend. Him in prison for a year." Trevor stopped to think for a moment.

"What about the loan?" I asked.

"It dead. When him back on the streets, I have to write that off. My wife ain't please at all. That was the vacation money."

Needless to say, his wife isn't pleased either over the sale of the car. So to settle things, Trevor arrived at the prison early this Sunday morning to get his instructions. Except that visiting hours are not in the morning, and since the prison is a long way from his home, he decided to hang around until visiting time. Which means, Trevor laments, that he won't get any sleep. He has to be at work for 7:30 that night and he will be working 14 hours straight. "Good money at $9 an hour on Sunday." The job is cleaning moulds with chemicals at a factory. When that job is finished, he heads for his regular work making furniture, which begins at 7:30 and runs to 4:30. "No sleep," he said.

"Then you should be careful with the tools. Don't fall asleep and get hurt," I tell him.

"Visitor for Bennett," the voice says over the speaker.

Trevor jumps to his feet and in seconds disappears behind the door into the prison. I continue to sit and wait. About half an hour later, Trevor comes out. His face looks just as angry. He runs out, jumps into his car and pulls out of the parking lot. I guess he wanted to catch a few winks before work.

I wait for almost another hour. Finally, I approach the window to ask if something is wrong.

"Who you are here for?" the guard asks.

"Gayle."

"Oh, it's you. You didn't hear us calling for you about an hour ago?"

"No. I was sitting right there," I say, pointing to where I was sitting, indicating it was right in the guard's view.

"We were calling you. We wanted to tell you that Gayle has had his two visitors for the week. You can't visit."

"But I was sitting there in front of you all this time," I remonstrate.

"Sorry, we were calling for you all the time. We even had someone go out in the lobby and call for you."

There's nothing I can do. I may be willing to accept that I didn't hear the call over the speaker, but there is no way that a guard could have come into the lobby and I didn't see him. Others around me would have seen him and alerted me.

"A fresh week starts tomorrow," the guard says. "You can come back tomorrow."

* * *

By the time defence counsel Philip Campbell rises to give his final address on the first day back at work in the new year of 1996, the case of *Regina v. Clinton Junior Gayle* has been reduced to its most common denominator. Which of two contradictory stories would a jury of 12 of Gayle's so-called peers believe: That of a police officer or the word of a confessed drug dealer who was carrying an unregistered gun, an extra clip of bullets and was under a deportation order to Jamaica when he killed Baylis and shot Leone? Would they believe a white policeman or a black killer?

Despite the mountain of evidence and witnesses that appeared in Courtroom 6-1 of the Ontario Court of Justice in Toronto, the case has come down to deciding which of the only two witnesses to the shooting is credible and should be believed. Should it be Gayle, pleading that he shot Baylis in self-defence, and therefore should be acquitted of the first degree and attempted murder charges? Or Leone, who says Gayle executed his partner Baylis and would have killed Leone if Gayle's semi-automatic pistol had not jammed.

As Campbell, a young, bulky man under his flowing black robe with a close-trimmed beard, began to present his case for acquittal, he might be tempted to believe that his is a lost cause. A look around the courtroom would tell him that most of the audience has made up their minds. They support the police. His only hope would be that the 12-member jury, none of them black, might hold off making up their minds.

The audience in the body of the courtroom is predominantly white. In an unusual move, four rows of seats to the left of the court—the side, coincidentally, where the jury and prosecution sit—are marked "Reserved." These seats are quickly filled up by members of the Baylis and Leone families and their friends. Members of the Police Association are there, in uniform and in civilian dress.

In the middle row of seats are members of the news media. Symbolically, most of them sit in a way so that they are positioned right behind the prosecution, right next to the reserved seats. This position seems only fitting. The news reporters appear to have already made up their minds about the case. Their body language, including the close proximity to the police, betrays their true feelings. An observer would not have to wait long to notice that the reporters somehow tend to spend time talking with police officers and Crown attorneys. It also wouldn't take an observer longer to notice that none of the reporters talks to the defence lawyers.

Only a few people sit on the left side of the court. They are all black. This is the section behind the defence lawyers and, obviously, is Gayle's side. For the next two days, as the defence and prosecution sum up their cases, the Blacks and the Whites take their places.

It is hard to think that this seating arrangement is merely coincidental. Yet, there is nothing to suggest it is forced, either. Just the way people naturally gravitate to one side or the other. Undoubtedly, this is exhibit number one against those arguing that justice, and, just as important, the appearance of justice, is blind and that Toronto—indeed Canada—is not segregated. Indeed, in light of the hard feelings and racism this trial has generated—the realization that it has been transformed from just a case of a thug killing a policeman into a trial of Blacks and immigrants—it is hard to escape the message in the arrangements and preferences in this courtroom.

Perhaps in sensing this alignment, Campbell begins his summary by dealing straight up with the issue of stereotyping. This is a continuation of the strategy by the defence not to minimize the role racial stereotypes play in the Canadian society and in this case. The defence's first move in this direction was to announce at the outset of the case that their client is no saint. They agreed that Gayle was a drug dealer and that he had $3,000 worth of cocaine on him the night of the shooting. He also had a pager, a tool of his trade, a loaded illegal gun and extra bullets. And they acknowledged that Gayle did kill Baylis, but accidentally and in self-defence. However, they did manage to keep away from the jury the list of Gayle's 13 convictions. But to do that they also had to abandon efforts to get the appeal court to throw out the restriction at the preliminary trial as to how much they can delve into Michael Leone's history.

The defence might have been hoping for something else. At the time of the trial, North America was abuzz over the treatment of Blacks by the police. This was in the wake of the acquittal of O.J. Simpson in Los Angeles for the murder of his ex-wife and his wife's male friend. That case had turned on what is known as the race card: whether the lead detective in the case was a racist and would fabricate evidence and lie against a Black in court to gain a conviction. And by extension, do Blacks in North America—including the many in Toronto who claim so—have a case when they say that Blacks are policed differently and that police officers can lie with impunity in the courts. Indeed, during this trial, none other than Johnnie Cochran, the lead lawyer for O.J. Simpson, had visited Toronto, to much media attention, on a speaking engagement. In his addresses, including a pep talk to black activists at a luncheon, Cochran argued that policing issues for Blacks are the same around the world. They are the same in South Africa, London, New York, Los Angeles and

Toronto. And these issues require the same solution: exposure, and for Blacks the world over to see the commonality of their struggle against the police. "I say to white people, when you advance the right of African-Americans or African-Canadians, you advance the rights of everyone," he said, adding that the same cops who abuse the rights of Blacks and get away with it do the same thing to the white people they don't like.

Gayle, certainly, is no O.J. Simpson, but his case, too, had become a watershed for a black community. So, would a jury in Toronto, mindful of the police-black community relationship in North America, do the right thing as the O.J. Simpson jury did? It was a gamble by the defence, a risky strategy that included putting Gayle on the stand to contradict in his own words the statements by Leone and to call the policeman a liar. In its most base form, the case had eventually come down to whom the jury should believe: a black drug dealer facing deportation or a white police officer?

This question was more than just academic, for both the prosecution and the defence in their own way had argued that the police officer had not always told the truth on the stand. Campbell and the defence argued that Leone openly lied and concocted evidence and events to explain away why he and his partner were harassing a black man in an underground garage—an incident that turned deadly when the black man tried to run away and the police shot at him, forcing the man to fear for his life and to fire back. And, by the way, the defence said, we know that our man has several major flaws, that he was involved in illegal activity the day of the shooting by dealing in crack and carrying a loaded unregistered gun, but he had no reason to lie on the stand.

The prosecution had argued that the differences in Leone's testimony—where his statements and omissions on the witness stand appeared at odds with earlier statements he had given to fellow officers—were simply inconsistencies brought on by the passing of time, by Leone giving statements within hours of the shooting and while obviously under stress. The prosecution also had suggested that some police officers who attributed statements to Leone—which he later denied—were poor note takers. With respect to Gayle, the prosecution argued that Gayle lied on the witness stand, and that his 13 previous convictions, drug dealing and fear of being deported meant he was not an ideal witness.

There are two different stories of what happened that night. Gayle said that he was walking in the basement of the apartment building, minding his own business, when he saw the pants of two police officers on the stairs above him. The officers were looking for something because they were using their flashlights. Gayle, knowing he was hot with drugs and a loaded gun, and that he had an outstanding deportation order, tried to slink away because the last thing he wanted was a confrontation with the police. He had the keys to a locked door and decided to make an exit through it. The police saw him and went after him, cornering him against a locked door. One of them said, "We have him." A fight ensued. Gayle lost his shirt and a vest. Leone pulled out his pepper spray and hit Gayle in the eyes, blinding him so that he could barely see. The pepper spray caused him to get an adrenaline dump, instead of forcing him to his knees as expected. Gayle exploded, threw off Baylis and tried to run. Leone, frustrated that he was getting away from the fight and suspecting that Gayle had a gun, drew his gun and fired. The shot missed, but Gayle, his eyes shut and stinging and now concerned for his life, turned and fired at the blur he saw lunging at him. He ran and heard a shot and felt the wound in his back. So he turned and fired again. Finally, he was shot in the leg and collapsed. Later, he found out that the blur was Baylis who took a shot to his temple; Gayle had also shot Leone before Leone finally felled him. In all, Gayle says he fired three shots and that he was hit in the back first, when fleeing, and then in the leg when he turned around to defend himself.

Leone's story is that he and Baylis were doing a normal walk-through at an apartment complex to indicate a police presence. When they drove in, they saw what they thought was a drug deal going down, but the people scattered. Using their flashlights, they decided to walk through the apartment basement to look for discarded drugs. Baylis entered the basement and saw a man and asked, "What's up?" The man punched Baylis with such force that he fell back on Leone. A foot-race started down a flight of stairs and finally they caught Gayle trying to unlock a door that would have led to his escape. They tried to arrest him for assaulting Baylis. A fight ensued with Gayle getting the better of them. Leone used his pepper spray but either missed Gayle, because he was moving, or hit him on the head. The spray had little effect on Gayle. He threw Baylis to the ground and pulled his gun. He shot at a diving Leone, hit him in the shoulder and narrowly avoided severing his vertebra. Then he pointed the gun at Baylis and shot him execution style in the temple. Baylis did not even get a chance to draw his gun. Noticing that Leone was not dead, Gayle spent the next nine and a half seconds trying to get his gun to unjam so he could finish Leone off. At this point Leone—who had never fired his gun except on a shooting range—emptied his gun, hitting Gayle in the leg first. As Gayle fell, his body twisted and he took another shot in the back. Leone was saved only because Gayle's gun jammed after the second shot.

Now, in their summaries, Campbell and chief prosecutor Culver acknowledge that while their star witnesses might disagree, the lawyers agree on one thing: that Gayle, a black drug dealer under deportation, is entitled to a fair trial.

* * *

A break during the summation of the case by the Crown prosecutor leads Paul Walters, head of the Metro Toronto Police Association, to look for a cup of coffee. This is my chance to talk to him, for the two of us to informally talk about how times have changed since Gayle shot Baylis and Leone. During that time, Walters, a tall, beefy man with a gentle smile and voice, has taken over from a strident president of the association, who was one of the key people behind the decision to launch the multi-million-dollar lawsuit against the federal government as a result of this shooting and the one at Just Desserts. We talk about how Walters and the appointment of a new police chief, David Boothby, have helped to lower the level of vituperation aimed at the black community. This, I suggest, is good for all society. We cannot live forever with the black community on one hand and the police and the mainstream on the other, shouting across the divide. And, as I tell him, I often wonder how black police officers feel going into meetings of the association with all the investigation aimed at their community.

Indeed, Walters says, there is a need to keep a lid on the heated rhetoric, and he volunteers that several black members of his association have been taking him to task for some of his statements. They did not like that he publicly criticized Arnold Minors. Although Walters claims that he criticized Minors on questions of competence, he notes that the black members of his association felt that the criticisms had racial overtones. Some of the same criticism, he says, had come from a group called the Association of Black Law Enforcers, a group representing black police and prison guards in Canada. Walters says he has entered into dialogue with this group to talk through any differences, perceived or otherwise.

But as we talk, obviously our minds are on what is happening in Courtroom 6-1, where we know a pivotal case to both the police and the black community is riding on the word of an accused black man against a police officer. Walters offers to members of the force in the hallway that he thinks the case is going well. He is happy with the summation and likes the chance of the jury returning with a conviction. Of course, at the back of his mind might be the realization that on the question of a black person's word against the police, in the law courts of Canada, it is usually no contest. The police always win.

History and statistics are on his side. Two high-profile cases have been heard since Gayle was charged. The first was brought by a Jamaican visitor, Audrey Smith, who claimed that she was strip-searched in public and humiliated by police officers thinking she was a crack dealer. The association fought valiantly on behalf of its members. It took three attempts—with Smith having to return to Toronto each time—before the case was heard. Ultimately, the case came down to who to believe. The police officers were exonerated. In the verdict, Smith was chided for bringing on herself whatever humiliation she got. The case so outraged the black community that O.J. Simpson's lawyer, Johnnie Cochran, cited it as an example of police high-handedness in their treatment of Blacks.

The other noteworthy case involved a black news editor at a Toronto television station. He was driving his car late one night when he was pulled over by police and ordered to stretch out on the ground, face down in the so-called take-down posture. Dwight Drummond complained about this treatment, alleging it was racist, and that there was no reason for the police to stop him and to treat him as a threat to public safety. The policemen argued that they had been told by a hooker moments earlier that a car similar to Drummond's might be carrying two armed men. They took no chances, they argued. Once again, the truth of what happened could only be decided by accepting one of two contradictory versions. Once again, the police's version of the events was accepted.

*   *   *

At the end of the second day of deliberations, the jury of nine men and three women opt to believe Leone. Immediately, the celebrations begin in the courtroom. As Philip Mascoll reports in his newspaper, of the more than 200 people packed into the courtroom at the time of the verdict, only two were black—one the mother of an old friend and the other a social worker Gayle has never met.

Six floors below the courtroom, the television cameras start humming and radio stations break into regular programming with bulletins of the conviction for first-degree murder and attempted murder. The word is flashed across the city on police radios. Suddenly, the entrance to the court on the ground floor is a sea of blue. Police officers who have been waiting for the verdict congratulate the prosecution team. Television cameras find members of the family of the slain officer while others mob Leone, who ventures to say that while the verdict will not bring back his dead partner, it exonerates Leone by showing that he did tell the truth on the witness stand. Many officers gladly oblige reporters with a quote as the national, regional and local news media soak up the story.

Except for two reporters, there are no black people anywhere in sight. Even the black policemen usually present in the court during the trial are absent. Perhaps they didn't get word in time that the verdict was coming down and therefore missed the celebration. Somehow, this seems strange because the front of the court and the ground floor are crowded with police officers.

Or maybe even the black members of the police force, some of the same ones who have been at odds with their association, understand what this celebration really means. That this case, placed in the context of a change in immigration laws, the gun-control legislation, the crackdown on deportees and the deep, scathing attacks on the black community in the media, has long ceased to be the case of a bad man killing a policeman. It has always been the case of a black man killing a white man, the black beast killing the virginal lady, just like in *Native Son*, just like in the Just Desserts restaurant. And they, too, must have heard that this killer, like so many Blacks in this country, should not only have remained on his side of the divide separating Blacks and Whites, but that like so many Blacks, he shouldn't even have been in the country in the first place. And perhaps in their hearts, these black officers know that, stripped of their blue uniforms, guns and badges, they would look just like a Clinton Junior Gayle. They are black first, and anything afterwards. Black and possibly immigrant. Black first, and then a cop. Black first, and then a father, brother, uncle, lover, human. Black and therefore a beast in the eyes of those who do not understand that, as police, they work on the other side of the divide.

As they cross the divide to rejoin friends and family on the other side, they know there isn't much to celebrate about this tragedy. For with the conviction of Gayle, despite the claims by the defence council and the prosecution, despite the laborious and painstaking charge to the jury by the judge not to let race or station in life enter into the decision, they know that an entire community has long been charged and is now convicted. And for proof of the gulf separating Blacks and Whites in this society, Blacks and the police, they know that, coincidentally, they only have to pick up one of the daily newspapers, on this very day, to realize that society is bringing to justice, symbolically, much more than a crack dealer who killed a policeman. "Blacks wary of police, study shows" is the headline on a story about the results of a poll on people's attitudes toward Metro Toronto police. Almost 80 percent of Blacks contacted by pollsters from York University said they felt Blacks are treated worse than Whites by the police. Because whenever there is a human tragedy, there is nothing to celebrate, black or white.

CHAPTER 10

CARIBANA DREAMS

I remember my first year in Canada, how four months after arriving in a new country and feeling homesick, I went to the Caribana festival in downtown Toronto and instantly felt at home. There, I found the music, the faces, the people, the accents, the food and the excitement of the Caribbean. Over the years, we would joke that Caribana is the best spiritual tonic for the social and political alienation so many of us feel in Canada, including so many of us born and raised in this country.

One of the great things about this festival is that you never know who you will meet for the first time, or which old friend or acquaintance you will rediscover in the crowd. Perhaps an actor like Lou Gossett Jr. or Billy Dee Williams will show up and mix, excited as little boys at being in such a festival. The parade with its glamorous costumes is secondary to the joyful camaraderie along the parade route. And for the participants, Caribana is not first and foremost about making money, about their festival being reduced to simple balance sheet issues. Caribana is always a renewing of the spirit—more than just dancing, something spiritual.

And over the years, I have noticed how young black and Caribbean people, especially teenagers, blossom during Caribana. So many of our children seem so lost. They do not know who they are, confused by what they are hearing at school and in their home and church, unsure of their place in a white-dominated society.

With Caribana comes a breaking out. Suddenly, these youths appear free, strong and confident. They are proud of discovering their heritage and exult in it by dancing in the streets, just like their elders. Oh, to see the young people liberated! Could this freedom come about through paying an admission fee and sitting passively while watching some pageant? I don't think so; Caribana's spirituality is fed by spontaneous participation, by the celebration of a way of life.

Now, I think of the times I took my children to Caribana: they were so young they felt overwhelmed by the crowd. But, like so many other parents, I was looking forward to their cultural awakening, when they, too, would discover a festival like Caribana and feel it belongs to them, that it is a festival that makes them special Canadians. A festival that, were it not held, would make the task of helping my children and others to find their place in this society—to discover who they are and what sets them apart culturally and spiritually—so much more difficult.

On the Canadian cultural calendar there is simply nothing like Caribana. Nothing so authentically outside the mainstream that makes as big an impact on the cultural landscape of Canada. Nothing is so beneficial to the psyche of black and Caribbean people in this country. Nothing is so capable of causing the colourful political leaders in this community to be so divisive and so viciously attack one another as putting together one of the world's most spectacular and glamorous festivals. Nothing so epitomizes the mountain peaks and deep valleys of being black in Canada. For Caribana has become a symbol of the divergent paths facing Canadians in the area of race relations: the harmony that can arise from different ethnic groups working together with the financial help and encouragement of the wider society, or the discord and economic uncertainty that can result from too much distrust and infighting.

Caribana is a two-week festival of rhythmic Caribbean and African music, of humour and brotherly and sisterly love openly displayed, of dancing on the streets and meeting new friends, of enjoying exotic foods and, for many businesses, hearing cash registers ring. Caribana is all pageantry and glamour, when men, women and children abandon themselves to frolicking, to decking out in elaborately designed costumes and parading on a route in downtown Toronto, with the eyes of the world looking on. It is a musical cacophony of different voices and accents; of faces representing the cultures of the world and, in turn, reflecting back a peaceful multicultural Canada to the rest of humanity.

And it is an outstanding symbol of black and Caribbean pride; for the black nationalist within us, it is an indication of what can be achieved when a minority group sticks together, a blueprint of what can happen elsewhere on the continent when Blacks pull together.

Caribana is put on by a community-based organization named the Caribbean Cultural Committee. No other black organization runs a show with as much economic clout in all of North America. For two weeks every summer, the committee of literally hundreds of volunteers brings hundreds of thousands of people together for the annual Caribana festival in Toronto. The highlight of this gathering is the street parade. For the entire festival, the eyes of Blacks across North America, in the Caribbean and even in Europe and Africa are on Toronto, perhaps the same way the world looks at Brazil and Trinidad and Tobago every February for their carnivals. The Toronto festival is right up there with the top carnivals in the world, one more jewel in the crown for a city that now claims quite proudly to be world class. And it is a jewel that over the years costs the city virtually nothing, that shines despite the contempt exhibited by the various levels of government toward the festival.

Every year, hundreds of thousands of tourists come to the Toronto area for Caribana, providing a lifeline for the region's tourism industry. Most of them plan their visits to coincide with the street parade with its beautiful, costumed bands, for the two days of music and revelry at all-day picnics on an island at the foot of Toronto. CNN carries pictures around the world, as do other members of the international media. Western Union, bus companies, trains, airlines and rental car agencies in the United States and Canada all know when it is Caribana time in Toronto. There is a rush for these services as far south as Miami, and west to Houston and Los Angeles. Licence plates of cars and vans testify to visitors from Michigan, New York, Pennsylvania and Ohio.

This is when, according to the 1990 *Decima Research Report,* 400,000 Americans swarm across the border annually for the festival. Almost all of them are African-Americans, making them the fastest-growing single group of visitors to this country. With this rush, most hotels around town are sold out during the event, with many of them booked solid a year in advance. Restaurants do a rollicking business, as do theatres, the local Blue Jays baseball team and any other game in town.

Caribana ploughs about $250 million into the Toronto-area economy in just two weeks, making it one of the biggest economic windfalls in the country. This is the same kind of economic impact from, say, the Toronto Blue Jays cramming 60 baseball games into two weeks.

But Caribana is much more. There are also very important social and political elements at stake. In North America, this is the place to be for the throbbing celebration of mainly Caribbean and African culture. There is no other gathering for Blacks in North America as big and culturally significant.

In most American states, there is still no official holiday to mark Black and African achievements and heritage. Proponents have not succeeded in getting the birthday of Martin Luther King Jr., for example, proclaimed a holiday in all states. In Ontario, it is different. There is an unofficial weekend to celebrate Caribbean and African culture. Supposedly, this long weekend in August revolves around Lord Simcoe Day, named for the former British governor, but in reality everyone simply calls it Caribana Weekend, a weekend that coincides historically with celebrations marking the emancipation of African slaves in the British Commonwealth, particularly in the Caribbean, back home for most members and organizers of Caribana. So Caribana is also a liberation-day celebration, with just as much significance for the modern-day descendants of those slaves who still feel left out of society's mainstream.

For Caribana is a time when in the context of the celebration this notion of liberation is taken a step further, by often damning with faint praise various Canadian institutions, for challenging the status quo. For dreaming of a time when people from the four corners of the globe can play, dance and live together in harmony for more than just a few days. It is a time when thousands of people gather on the streets, in dance halls and at various masquerade balls to mock the mainstream institutions of this country, and in so doing to make these organizations and their office holders more human, more accessible. When in their costumes, the masqueraders—all those colourful characters in costume—turn the natural order of the world, and of life itself, on its head. So that in a masquerade band, symbolically a pauper can dance with a banker; the political outsider can rub shoulders with the insider. It is a time when skin colour, status in life, political persuasion or the size of a bank account seems not to matter. Caribana is a chance to liberate us—if only for a few days—from the stark reality of being black in Canada.

For these reasons, the people who control the Caribbean Cultural Committee have clout and recognition beyond Toronto. They are recognized across North America for putting on the most successful carnival every year, the most successful exhibit of African culture. The Caribana model is being studied and copied in many cities across North America, centres as far away as Atlanta and San Francisco. And in many respects, the people who run the Caribbean Cultural Committee rightfully have high status among the leadership of Toronto's black community. These are the people who meet government and corporate leaders to talk on behalf of the black community, to allocate budgets and resources obtained from grants and through sponsorship in the community. And in any community where there is power, there is also a struggle to hold onto and exercise this authority. The black community in the Toronto area is no exception. And although it is true there is no other outdoor festival on the continent as big as Caribana, perhaps it is also safe to say that none is more politically divisive, with a future as precarious.

This is the public face of a festival that started three decades ago with the decidedly political and social agenda of displaying and celebrating the contributions of people from the Caribbean to Canada. In 1966, a small group of Caribbean expatriates met in a now-demolished Toronto fire hall to talk about how they could show that Caribbean and black people have pride of place in Canada.

Like Canadians all over the country, they were preparing for the year-long birthday party to mark Canada's centenary in 1967. For this party, the government of the day was encouraging ethnic groups to put on a show of the best of their cultural wares. A Caribbean street festival—based on the African heritage of the slaves that lived in that region—was to be the highlight for these expatriates. And the celebration was to have been a one-time affair.

By underscoring its Caribbean roots, the Caribbean Cultural Committee group was acknowledging that the festival would belong to more than just black or African people. For the modern Caribbean is made up of various ethnic groups mainly from Asia, Europe and Africa that have come together to produce what is now considered a Caribbean culture. At the very least, they would be transferring a celebration from one multicultural community in the Caribbean to a larger one in Canada.

Caribana proved to be much sturdier than even its mothers and fathers thought. Taking on almost a life of its own, and demonstrating a resilient will to survive, it evolved into the multicultural festival that has become much more than a cultural and political expression for its host community. It has become so vitally important to the Canadian economy that, to survive, Caribana faces the circumstance of having to desert its historic and social roots, its very *raison d'être*.

It has flourished to the point where it has become an event that might now be too big for the community that gave birth to this festival—too big for those who nourished this festival during the lonely years when many in Canadian officialdom thought that a street parade by Black and Caribbean people year after year was a bit much, had become a nuisance, really, and should be discouraged, if not banned altogether, or banished from the city streets to some suburban stadium.

As Caribana prepares for its next decade, it seems to be losing sight of its purpose, of its character—so typical of what can happen to Blacks in Canada, the price for selling out to become mainstream. The organizers are struggling, often bickering among themselves and with the wider community to keep control of the festival. And they are fighting, too, with the wider society over a vision for the festival. The organizers want a Caribana that is more than just merriment; more than just having a spectacle of mainly black and Caribbean people putting on a show every year, a show that fills business coffers because of the throngs of visitors to the area, a show that amounts to no more than a demeaning display of sound and dance in the eyes of some black and Caribbean detractors. They want a Caribana that is a spiritual as well as an economic success. However, the organizers have one big problem: they have not yet found a way to tap into the economic benefits of Caribana, so that after almost 30 years the Caribbean Cultural Committee has to constantly negotiate and re-negotiate Caribana's future.

On the other hand, those who do tap into the economic benefits want a pageant that continues to attract visitors to the region. For them, Caribana has proven dependable over the years; it delivers free-spending crowds. Until now, the businesses were more apt to complain to Caribana's officials than to offer financial assistance to improve the festival. Therefore, there has been, and still is, a struggle over the future of Caribana, a struggle that eminently demonstrates what can happen when minority groups, like Blacks, and the wider community do not subscribe to the same dream. It is a struggle that also underlines what can happen when there is no common vision in the black community over something like Caribana, what can happen when community politicians exploit this lack of vision.

Caribana—perhaps more than any other event—underscores the folly of the wider community that keeps black and Caribbean people outside the mainstream. The festival is a strong argument for integration and inclusion, because it demonstrates the absurdity and short-sightedness of the black and Caribbean community that pretends that its culture can exist and flourish, that it can remain pure and untampered, in isolation. Nobody wins through isolation. Caribana, so symbolic of what will happen to the children of black and Caribbean immigrants, will atrophy if it does not take pride of place on the Canadian cultural stage, the same way that young Blacks will find the festival wanting if it does not move beyond re-creating the Caribbean in Canada—if it does not become a Canadian festival with Caribbean and black roots.

Similarly, the organizers cannot continue to produce a meaningful festival without the help of those who have the economic means to support a gathering of such size and influence. And those who benefit the most, financially, from the festival are becoming well aware of the implications for regional businesses if Caribana falls below its potential, if governments and the wider business community do not financially support this festival that means so much to everybody. Caribana will also atrophy in a business sense if Blacks feel the festival is becoming culturally meaningless; that it is amounting to no more than endless debate over levels of government funding; that it has nothing to do with Blacks asserting their presence in the Canadian mosaic.

For many in the host community, when the pageantry and glamour is stripped away, when all the money is counted and divided among the businesses outside the community, Caribana is an economic failure. It is an event that exploits the people who sacrifice the most. And in a very big way, the black and Caribbean community, the people now fighting to maintain control over what they have built into Canada's most glamorous festival, in part have only themselves to blame for not benefiting from what they created and nurtured. The disappointment and uncertainty of what to do with an obvious success like Caribana are part of the reality of being black in Canada—of thanklessly producing a world-class festival. Obviously, this reality has to change for the good of everyone.

How could this have happened and how much is the black and Caribbean community to be blamed? A trip into the politics of those running the festival—into the very heart and rationale for Caribana—will show how Caribana was brought to a crisis point that threatened its very existence. A crisis in which the black community and the wider society equally had a hand.

* * *

Above the din of the conversation and the central heating, the lonely voice drones on. One by one, it calls members of the Caribbean Cultural Committee to the front of the hall, where they receive slips of paper and return to their seats to wait as the man in the white shirt and black pants calls more names.

For anyone listening carefully, the strained voice calling members to vote is symbolic of what has gone wrong over the years. It is a voice that must make do without the help of a microphone. A voice that few seem to take seriously, despite the importance of the issues at hand. For this is another sign of a meeting that does not appear well planned, something that unfortunately has been the hallmark of the Caribbean Cultural Committee for too long. And as has always been the case for too long, too many of us are willing to overlook the obvious inefficiencies, lack of planning and ineptitude, and make excuses. Maybe, we reason, this lack of preparation is to be expected when the executive director resigns in protest a mere two weeks before the meeting—walking off, like all others before him, with the organization's plans in his head. Or, perhaps, the organizers simply can't afford to rent a PA system. Shouting over the noise, the voice gets hoarser by the minute and is in danger of fading altogether.

Symbolically, this is the voice pointing to the way of politics in black communities in North America. For Caribana is the plaything of community politics, a prize for the winners. But it is a trophy badly in need of polishing by those community leaders entrusted with Caribana's care and safekeeping.

At this annual meeting, required by the Ontario Securities Commission, held at 10:00 a.m. on February 11, 1995, at the Bickford Centre in central Toronto, nothing about Caribana's future really seems secure. Even in the black community, some would say this is what can happen when a group so unused to being in authority gets its hands on a modicum of power and influence, with at least the perception of control. And God knows, the people who have organized Caribana have been waiting a long time—a long, long time—for power and control; for the festival to become profitable and independent; for the festival's board to become accountable; for the peace of mind that next year there will be another Caribana festival; for members of the black and Caribbean community to start reaping real benefits from the successful festival they have created. Others simply dismiss this chaos as part of the so-called crab-in-the-barrel syndrome that always seems to afflict minority groups. Within these two contexts, the battle for the control and destiny of Caribana is to be waged.

Nine names are on the ballot for eight places. Eight of the names represent the official slate. For many of us, the outcome of the election seems pretty certain. The only drama is whether the lone outsider can mount a strong enough challenge to displace one of the officially blessed. Others stick around simply to talk about the pageantry of the next Caribana street parade some six months off. For it is the promise of the next Caribana that makes the tedium of this annual meeting endurable; the belief that out of disarray and uncertainty will eventually come a thing of beauty. For no matter how many years and times people have given up on Caribana, it has always managed to get by for just one more year, producing an even bigger festival at a time when even some of its keenest supporters felt it had run out of time, money and reasons for existing.

Several times during the meeting, the fire alarm goes off. It is only a false alarm, and after the second or third time nobody bothers to leave the hall. On one side of the debate is a minority who would immediately fire the existing board but feels thwarted by the rules. They are up against the seeming majority who are committed to keeping the current leadership and to using every rule and regulation to make sure this happens. Hope, patience, stamina and political suasion—these are the main ingredients for surviving this annual meeting. For members of all factions, the buzzword at this meeting is "accountability," a way of asserting and maintaining control of the management of the festival. Accountability is a sword they want to keep hanging over the heads of the current board of directors.

But it is also a sword the directors know how to use to cut down opponents. For anyone to become a candidate in this election, he or she must contend with a rule requiring candidates to be accountable—there is that word again—to the organization. This means the candidate must not only be in good financial standing, as is the case with most volunteer nonprofit groups, but must now meet the new requirement of having served on some committee under the current board. This is a cut of the sword against all those who would simply join the association and throw out the leadership. This is politics fought at its keenest. But more important, it is a short-sighted stroke simply to entrench a few political ideologues, a move that would come back to haunt its supporters and to starve the board of the talent and new blood desperately needed during the crisis for the survival of the festival that is less than a year away.

Outside, it is frigidly cold. There is snow on the ground; it is the dead of winter in Toronto. Elsewhere in the city, several events celebrate black history and culture in the only month of the year devoted to this celebration. Perhaps it is no coincidence that this is the month for the annual meeting of the Caribbean Cultural Committee, arguably the highest-profile black and Caribbean organization in Canada. It is a meeting that shows who really has power in the black and Caribbean community and how this power can be ruthlessly wielded. The black community in the Toronto area is the largest in Canada and quite sizeable by North American standards. How it governs itself is a lesson for black groups elsewhere. How it safeguards the community spirits and aspirations embodied in this festival can be an object lesson for Blacks in cities like Atlanta who are planning their own carnivals. An inspiration to those black groups looking to Toronto to see how the supposed masters do it. And, one hopes, also taking copious notes on how not to end up in a fine mess.

The Caribbean Cultural Committee meeting gets off in fits and starts, with some directors sitting at a table near the front of the hall and trying to explain procedural rules to govern the day's activities. There is also the sense of things not tidied up properly because the meeting has to wrap up some constitutional matters that were left hanging from a previous meeting. It is hard to tell when the previous meeting ends and the day's real business begins.

So, the disorganization is obvious, telling and pitiful. It is disheartening that an organization with so much economic clout does not have the money to hold a streamlined annual meeting, does not have the staff and people to plan a proper meeting with computerized voting lists, with a microphone and speakers.

Despite their ability to generate huge amounts of money for the Canadian economy, Caribana and the Caribbean Cultural Committee are essentially broke. They live a hand-to-mouth existence, merely surviving between festivals. This experience comes as no surprise. It is symbolic of the kind of survival, on the whole, most Blacks have learned to live with and must confront on a daily basis in Canada. Caribana is an extension of the black Canadian psyche and reality.

The struggle on the floor of the meeting, culminating in the election of directors, is about how to break this cycle, how to make Caribana and the Caribbean Cultural Committee financially sound. It is about how to make Caribana an enduring symbol of black pride and empowerment well into the next century. At the heart of the discussion are these questions: Should Caribana become more than a street parade, more than just an annual diversion from the everyday problems of surviving in Canada? How can it become a genuine expression of black culture and at the same time a mechanism for economic growth in the community? Could the black community find a way to offer academic scholarships to youths, employment for community artists and grants to organizations working in the political trenches, the prisons and in other areas of need by tapping the wealth created by the festival? It is this dream of what Caribana could become that causes many people to wait for the man to call their names, to get their pieces of paper and to wait for their chance to vote. For many people don't care two hoots about the annual street parade, but only about how the community can mount a successful parade and then invest the money in the black community. Their vision goes beyond the festival itself.

Judging from the words of the mayor of Toronto, Barbara Hall, and other regional, municipal and provincial politicians, all levels of governments plan to make this festival an even bigger business. "Caribana is the largest tourist attraction in Canada," Hall tells the meeting before members get down to the business of elections. Hall is the first mayor to bother showing up at an annual meeting, although the Caribbean Cultural Committee invited other office holders. In almost three decades, it must be some kind of feat, or conversely a symbol of disrespect, to be visited only once by any of the city fathers and mothers. But Hall, having had only a few months in office, breaks the mould. She promises to work her darnedest to make sure the Caribbean Cultural Committee gets the proper funding and government support to do an even better job. For according to Mayor Hall, Caribana not only stirs the economic pot but also shows the world that in Toronto and Canada different ethnic groups live in harmony. Thousands of people can have fun and dance in the streets—and in Toronto, culture is big business. In the next year, Mayor Hall's commitment to Caribana will be tested on several occasions.

Lennox Farrell's chairperson report, delivered just before the roll-call, outlines ambitious goals for Caribana, a vision more in tune with those who see beyond the immediate festival. "The priority will be the continued enlargement of the presence and prospects for Caribbean culture in Canada generally, and more specifically in this province and region of Metropolitan Toronto. This enlargement will be guaranteed by the Caribbean Cultural Committee's ongoing drive to become self-sufficient. When we achieve this long-desired and attainable goal, the Caribbean Cultural Committee will be able to play a more productive role in assisting our communities to become autonomous. This role is spelled out in the Caribbean Cultural Committee's mission statement adopted in 1992: 'To achieve social development, economic empowerment and unity within and among the Black- and Caribbean-Canadian communities through the industrialization of Caribbean culture.'"

Although he does not say it, Farrell, through these words, is signaling that Caribana has to be more than just a city-wide party. He wants it to be a business and political force as well. But even as he speaks, the genie is already out of the bottle. For the Caribbean Cultural Committee is in no position to keep these promises. Others, who hold the purse strings to Caribana, see the festival as just a party that makes money.

* * *

There is a widespread feeling that Caribana is broke and disorganized because it is a black and immigrant festival, that it is destitute because the governments and businesses want it that way. Why should they worry if Caribana brings in hundreds of millions of dollars into the general economy but provides hardly anything for the black artists, singers, musicians, costume makers, graphic artists, dancers—anything for its main sponsor, the Canadian black and Caribbean community? Caribana, as many critics in the host community see it, is another example of the exploitation of black and immigrant people in Canada. The society squeezes $250 million out of the festival, forcing members of the Black community to face the indignity of having to pay out of their own pockets to put on the festival so that others can reap the financial benefits. Participants must buy the very costumes that attract so many tourists to the city. In return, the society gives back a piddling $300,000 annually in operational grants to the organizing community. Hotels that are booked a year in advance are content to remain parasites, rather than make a donation to the organizers. Area hoteliers have long rejected a suggestion of a small room levy for the Caribbean Cultural Committee to defray its operational costs. Other groups are just as unappreciative.

The organizers had suggested that they would pass the hat along the festival route asking spectators to donate a dollar. With a crowd estimated at several hundreds of thousands, the day's collection would more than pay for the event. The idea was stymied when Metro Toronto Police suggested that passing the hat would make the parade a *paid event*. This would mean hiring more off-duty police for crowd control because it was no longer a free event. This would mean paying Metro Police at least $500,000 to supervise the parade. In essence, the day's collection would go straight into the pockets of the police. So typical of the wider community looking for ways to sponge off Caribana, several people argued.

And why shouldn't they, some members of the community asked, when mainstream businesses can rely every year on a festival that fills their coffers while costing them nothing? Indeed, why feed the cash cow when it can be milked for free?

The election is about how to change this arrangement, how to empower black people to gain full control of the festival by grabbing hold of the levers of power. These include, supposedly, the levers to shut down the festival if they want to and enlarge it if they choose. Choices to be made with or without government funding or approval. This might be no more than a pipe dream. But many hold onto it with fervour—this dream of maintaining control of a festival that captivates so much of a community's energy and spirituality. It is a thing to be passed on with pride to the next generation.

In reality, the election is a channel for the anger of those who cry exploitation. This is another chance to ask why we go to the expense and trouble of organizing an elaborate festival every year only to end up further in debt. With few exceptions, this has been the cycle. Every year the Caribbean Cultural Committee plans a bigger festival; every year more people come out to play *mas* (as Carnival is called in the Caribbean); every year the organizers' debts become more crippling. So from year to year, nobody knows for sure if there will really be a Caribana or if one or more suppliers will petition the Caribbean Cultural Committee into bankruptcy.

Not everyone believes Farrell's goal is attainable, or more specifically, that the wider society will allow it to happen. The sarcasm and the jokes about how Blacks—whether residents of the Toronto area or visitors from around the world—are exploited during the festival are biting and pointed. They crop up in the most unexpected places, any time of the year. "Caribana is a fine example of: (a) diasporic black unity; (b) the celebration of cultural diversity; (c) the Canadian tourism industry at its best; (c) a bunch of Black folks dancin' in de street while corporate 'massa' pockets de cash." So opines columnist McLean Greaves in a humorous spoof in *Word*, Toronto's black cultural magazine.

Along with the roll-call, the words of encouragement and pledges by the politicians of financial support resonate around the hall. There is an undercurrent of optimism at the meeting. Despite the concerns over the voting and tidy way in which the official slate seems unbeatable, there is a feeling that the Caribbean Cultural Committee could be poised for greatness *if* the organization can get its act together, *if* it becomes more accountable and gets better management. For the first time, the committee could become the recipient of meaningful government funding, making the organization even more important in the life of the black and Caribbean community. With more money to spend, the committee can commission more black artists and can support other agencies in the forefront of the political and social struggle for Blacks. Eventually, it would be self-sufficient economically, not requiring government largesse, thereby breaking the image of being a chronic welfare case.

But for these dreams to become real, the undercurrent must come to the surface at this meeting; it must become the dominant wave pushing Caribana on to greater things. And of course, in the short term, these dreams still depend on the goodwill of politicians inside and outside the community. Unfortunately, the community would soon find out the hard way, once again, that political favours and dreams can disappear virtually overnight.

* * *

Among those who arrived early for the meeting is one man who is anxiously signing forms. These are the all-important proxies that will allow him to vote on behalf of members not at the meeting. The man busying himself is Courtney Doldron, an outspoken member of the black and Caribbean community in Toronto, a politician at the community, municipal, provincial and federal levels, but also one of Caribana's most successful costume-band leaders. The band leaders produce the beautiful masquerade costumes that are the source of so much admiration at the Caribana parade. There is always a dispute of some sort involving the band leaders; whether they are paid enough—if at all—for their efforts, whether the Caribbean Cultural Committee offers enough money as prizes and other incentives; whether the band leaders should be running Caribana and not the politicians on the board. Once again this year, the band leaders are threatening to boycott the festival. They are demanding that the Caribbean Cultural Committee recognize their importance by providing $400,000 in prize money and incentives. With an annual budget of about $1.6 million, and a debt that is strangling the committee, the directors argue this price tag is too steep. So there is a stalemate to be inherited by the new board. Doldron is a leader of one of the two associations representing the *mas* bands. He says he wants to get on the board to become the voice of the band leaders in the boardroom.

If elected, this would be a new role for Doldron. Until now, he has been making the board and Caribana look good, contributing to the festival's reputation for high-class entertainment in Canada and abroad. The highlight of Doldron's association with the Caribbean Cultural Committee came in 1994 when he represented Canada in an international costume-band competition in Trinidad. Doldron placed fourth, quite an achievement considering that he was battling top band leaders from around the world. "We jam them down there" is how Doldron explains his success. Doldron's accomplishment, duly noted and complimented in the report for the annual meeting, is another indication of how far Caribana has come, how it has matured since the first festival in 1967. But without money to support the band leaders, it is questionable how much further Caribana can go.

As he shuffles papers, Doldron does not have much time to talk before the annual meeting starts. He wants to make sure that his papers are in order and that he can vote his 35 proxies for himself. For Doldron is not happy with the running of the Caribbean Cultural Committee—it's too disorganized and unfocused, he says—and he plans to shake up the organization when he becomes a director. But first, he has to make sure he has the votes to elect himself because he has no doubt he is up against a very powerful machine spearheaded by Farrell. But with 35 proxies, all in good order, how can he lose? Doldron says smugly. After all, the group's active membership is about 300 and rarely do 100 bother turning out for annual meetings.

Several issues are at stake, most notably the direction in which the current board will take the committee. Will Caribana be transformed into a political tool for the advancement of Blacks and Caribbean people, a means for bringing them economic empowerment by setting the stage for the community to share in the economic spin-offs generated by the festival?

The majority of the current board, including several seeking re-election, want the Caribbean Cultural Committee to be more activist. This means that the radical elements in the community are in the ascendance. They want to use Caribana mainly for the benefit of the black and Caribbean community. They want a North American showcase for black and Caribbean culture and arts. Whether it provides economic benefits for the wider community or becomes a harmless diversion from the trials of everyday life is secondary for this group. In their designs, the economics of Caribana must ultimately translate into political power for the community. They want the Caribbean Cultural Committee, and by extension the community, to share tangibly in the benefits of its creation.

Many are not so sure, however, about how the board plans to achieve its goals, because some members are critical of the current board, feeling it is taking the festival on the wrong path. They believe the board's political goals are blinding directors to the economic reality of the situation. They do not think the board should attempt to drastically transform Caribana into a political tool—and certainly not overnight. Indeed, some doubt if they will ever succeed in making Caribana part of a political agenda, and wonder if even to attempt such would not lead to Caribana's ruin. This is why the election is so crucial. It will show, even by electing one new member to the board, that members are having second thoughts about the current board and the options it has chosen.

But the election is also pivotal for other reasons. One of them is whether the tug of war between the radicals and moderates within the Caribbean Cultural Committee is harming Caribana by paralyzing its planning with infighting. Hanging over the meeting is the news that the executive director of the Caribbean Cultural Committee resigned abruptly only a week before the annual meeting. Rodney Davis, a young accountant credited with bringing a business approach to the organization, left in a huff, claiming that he could no longer accept the meddling of a board that was too interventionist. Specifically, Davis was protesting against Farrell. His departure had all the signs of a power struggle that the executive director lost. Farrell says the disagreement is just another case of battling for accountability, of making sure that the existing board puts procedures in place to make the organization run properly. As Farrell explains, the difference with Davis really boils down to the question of whether an executive director should make commitments for the association without first getting the board's all-clear, without keeping the board informed. Davis claims that he did both, but to many the quarrel smacks of deeper problems of personal conflicts rather than just a board and its executive director disagreeing on a few business procedures. Of late, Davis is seen as a moderate holdout and an irritant to some directors.

For many observers, there was an echo in these arguments. About the same time, they were hearing similar claims from the United States where the venerable National Association for the Advancement of Colored People was tearing itself apart over a question supposedly related to accountability. Maybe this is a sign of how the black community in Canada also moves in step with its U.S. counterpart. But for many, the meeting offers an opportunity for an accounting of what is happening to Caribana, for many members have heard of the split only through snippets in the local community newspapers. And the newspapers make it clear that Davis' departure reflects the infighting between the committee cells over where Caribana is headed.

This meeting is also the first accounting to members, and by extension to the wider community, of what has happened since Farrell pulled off what is considered a political coup and took leadership of the committee a year earlier. Farrell had outmanoeuvred members of the old board, a group mainly composed of businesspeople who had volunteered to rescue Caribana from financial disaster. For three years, the business group produced business plans and a rarity of three consecutive years of profits. When they left, they were promising that a fourth year of profits would wipe out Caribana's debts, allowing an independent and financially secure festival to make a debt-free start a few years on. Profits that would quietly put Caribana on the road to achieving the business goals to which Farrell is re-dedicating his board.

With the removal of the old board, this is the first year for a financial accounting under a new administration. And for the first time in three years, rumour has it, the Caribbean Cultural Committee has reverted to running up losses, adding to a burdensome debt that almost sank the festival four years earlier. The treasurer's report to the meeting will confirm an operating loss for 1994 of $618,000, compared with an operating loss of $443,000 the previous year. This is before the grants from the various governments are factored in, leaving Caribana with a loss of just over $200,000.

There is another factor added to the importance of this meeting and election. Since Caribana's inception, many of the professional and business leaders from the community have served on the Caribbean Cultural Committee. Many of them have gone on to become pioneers for Blacks in law, business and politics. But outside the black and Caribbean community there is always the perception that people who speak on behalf of the community have no legitimacy. Often, columnists and talk show hosts fly into a rage talking about "the self-appointed" leaders and spokesmen in the black community. The clear inference is that people speaking out on issues involving the police, government, immigration, schooling—issues of primary importance to the black community—have no legitimacy or constituency. Sometimes, even members of the black community have cast aspersions at these spokespeople.

* * *

The black community has mostly approached leadership in two ways. There was always the informal method that involved members of the community recognizing some wrong and speaking out against it. If that voice hit a chord and people agreed with the speaker, a leader on a specific issue was born. This leadership shifted from person to person depending on the issue and on the willingness of people to step forward and to speak out. This was the role served traditionally by the clergy in the black community. But of late more secular voices have come forward, sometimes even in opposition to the black clergy.

The other way black leadership evolves is through the organizations that serve the interest of the community. There is leadership from women's groups, from the national associations of the various Caribbean and African countries, from the many social groups and from organizations like the Toronto-based Black Action Defence Committee, which has as its main task being the eyes and ears of the community on policing and legal matters. Among the latter group is the Caribbean Cultural

Committee, which was set up primarily to promote cultural matters.

The Caribbean Cultural Committee has an elected board—not just self-appointed leaders, as the wider society likes to claim. It is a board that is provided for in the organization's bylaws and by the requirements of the Ontario Securities Commission. This makes the elected spokespeople for the Caribbean Cultural Committee as relevant in public debate as heads of business groups, whose ability to speak out on issues of interest to them is never questioned.

The biggest crisis in the history of Caribana and the Caribbean Cultural Committee occurred in 1991. The economics of running a festival and getting no financial return had finally caught up with the organizers. In the previous two years, unseasonably bad weather had ruined many Caribana activities, leaving the Caribbean Cultural Committee heavily in debt. The debts that had accumulated over the years had the festival, and the organizing committee, flat on their backs, apparently ready to expire. Some argued that the Caribbean Cultural Committee made matters worse by trying too hard to retire, in one swipe, the debt that was mounting every year.

The crisis was brought on by a gamble the previous year, when organizers decided to lease the brand-new SkyDome stadium in Toronto for a musical concert. The plan was to put on a heart-stopping show featuring just about every style of Caribbean and black music: calypso, reggae, hip-hop, dance hall, gospel. That the SkyDome, home of the Blue Jays baseball team, was new and shiny, was an added attraction. Around that time, some major international entertainment acts—from Frank Sinatra and Liza Minnelli to tractor pulls—had sold out the stadium. The organizers felt they could do the same, in essence offering a stew of black and Caribbean music under one tent.

It was a gamble that held the potential for big pay-offs. Until then, it was argued that around Caribana time, just about everyone cashed in by putting on a concert of some sort and pocketing the profits. So, why shouldn't the Caribbean Cultural Committee do the same? There was another reason that made the venture even more attractive, if not urgent. A successful concert held the potential of wiping out this debt.

But it was a project fraught with risk. For one thing, the committee was on the hook for the rental of the stadium. When ticket sales did not reach the levels anticipated, the concert was cancelled in the midst of extensive publicity in the community and mainstream media over the marketing debacle. The committee was left with a debt of $600,000, in essence bringing the survival of the festival into question.

Immediately, there were recriminations. Critics argued that it was about time Caribana become profitable, about time people who knew what they were doing ran the board. Some of the loudest voices were in the black and Caribbean community, from people demanding greater accountability from those who held the future of Caribana in trust. The provincial government, one of the largest sponsors, heard the criticisms and threatened to withdraw funding. The municipal government followed. The Caribbean Cultural Committee, at the strong behest of the governments, organized a number of forums or town-hall meetings in the black community to discuss the future of the festival. At the same time, Caribana was put in a form of receivership by its major financial supporters—the governments. A group of high-profile businesspeople from the black community was drafted to run the show while the community was ordered to come up with some consensus on a plan of action.

The consensus of these hearings was, first, that Caribana was poorly planned and the Caribbean Cultural Committee badly mismanaged. For example, it was pointed out that in all its years of running the festival, the committee never took out weather or disaster insurance. This was quite an oversight for a festival that is held almost entirely outdoors and that can be washed out with a good weekend downpour. Fortunately for Caribana, in just about every year the weather co-operated. But when the rains did come, as they did for two consecutive years in 1988 and 1989, they did real damage to the festival's finances.

Second, it had become apparent at the meetings that Caribana did not have a business plan. Events were held on an ad hoc basis. Typically, someone came up with a suggestion for a concert at a stadium and sold the idea to the board. Usually, there was no feasibility or marketing study—just a hunch the event would be profitable. If this proved successful, the event would be tried the next year. If it was a dud, something else would replace it. The committee would pocket the losses. This was what happened with the idea for the SkyDome concert. On the surface the concert sounded like a good idea, but research might have shown the idea was a no-go from the start. For example, the organizers were trying to achieve the impossible by catering to just about every segment of the community: grandmothers interested in gospel music; mothers and fathers who wanted reggae, calypso or soca; youths looking for hip-hop and dance hall.

"If you know anything about young people," says Felix Gulliston, a long-time band leader in the Caribana parade, "you would know they won't go anywhere near concerts where there will be older people. And [youths] are in fact the outgoing people who would spend a frivolous dollar on a concert." Each of these groups, despite having a common black or Caribbean heritage, has different musical tastes, further reinforcing the hard lesson that the black community was never homogeneous and will never be. It is a lesson, as the SkyDome fiasco shows, that occasionally escapes even the most well intentioned in the community.

The town-hall meetings identified two main reasons for the disorganization and poor planning. The first was that Caribana's board was made up of volunteers, but that in deciding to go on the board, members were accepting a full-time, non-paying job. And apart from working very long hours, board members often have to spend their own money when Caribana's cash flow dries up. If the situation improves, the board members are reimbursed. If it doesn't, the money becomes a forgivable loan.

Another problem has been the election of the board. For years, Caribana's board was either dominated by one of two factions in the community. On one side were the radicals who saw the festival as primarily an empowering tool for Blacks. On the other were the moderates, those who felt that Caribana is about culture, about having a good time and that politics shouldn't be the primary concern. From year to year, nobody could determine which faction would hold sway at the annual meeting, and domination depended on which group recruited more members. In the weeks before the annual meeting, the factions would be signing up hundreds of new members, people with no intention of attending the annual meeting or having a say in the running of the festival. They simply paid the membership fee and gave whichever faction they supported the proxy to vote for them. This system did not help the situation; it provided for little continuity in planning and for wild changes in direction from year to year.

The solution, the community suggested, was to have a professional board run the festival. No longer should the board be a resting place for only the popular and the best recruiters in the community. It was decided that the community should look within its ranks and invite businesspeople, accountants, bankers and the like—people who know how to run a business and to make a profit—to view service on the board as part of their community-mindedness.

This is the point at which the "buttoned-down boys," as the business professionals were called, took over the running of Caribana. This turned out to be an unexpected concession to the moderates. From this point on, the Caribbean Cultural Committee became internally torn apart by community politics, by personality clashes and by strong disagreement about what Caribana means for its own people in North America.

CHAPTER 11

CARIBANA CRISIS

The man who was to set about bailing out Caribana from its financial woes was Sam Lewis, a former community liaison consultant in the ministry of the Attorney General in Ontario. A career civil servant, Lewis is considered an authority on carnivals the world over. He recalls playing *mas* in his native Trinidad as a little boy, and has never lost his love for this cultural expression. When the governments pressured the Caribbean Cultural Committee to hand over the running of the festival to a competent individual, Lewis became the natural choice. Lewis and his lieutenants accepted the invitation to manage Caribana in 1991 and to at least stabilize the financial operations. With Lewis in charge, the government came up with temporary funding, enough to shore up the festival. In a short time, Lewis would become known simply as "Mr. Caribana."

Perhaps it is reflective of his civil service experience that Lewis' approach was to quietly go about fixing the problem by making sure he had the best people to do the job. So he canvassed the community for new recruits for the board and put emphasis on bringing in youth representatives. But for continuity, he also looked to the existing board members, even if they did not share his moderate views. One of the people Lewis tapped to help him was a former executive member, the outspoken teacher and politician, Lennox Farrell. Farrell had long been a community activist, remembered by the University of Toronto for creating somewhat of a diplomatic kerfuffle. The ambassador to Canada from apartheid South Africa, Glen Babb, was to speak at the university. Farrell disrupted the proceedings by grabbing the speaker's mace and throwing it at the ambassador. Later, Farrell would run unsuccessfully in provincial and municipal elections.

As a result of the consultations and the heavy presence of the governments demanding changes, the 1992 annual meeting saw a break from the past. Nobody went out and recruited new members to stack the vote. As a result, Lewis got several of his hand-picked people elected. But he ended up with a badly divided board. Lewis, now officially elected as chair, concentrated on putting together a business plan for the organization and on having the people in place to implement it. His emphasis was on retiring the committee's debts. Lewis also set about devising a management structure to look after the day-to-day running of the organization, freeing board members from this onerous task and allowing them to concentrate mainly on policy. Lewis also sought to change the image of Caribana, to focus more on the business of the festival and its contribution to the Canadian economy. And for the first time, he got major sponsors to put money into the festival. Unless Caribana became financially sound, it had no future, he argued.

"In that first year, we worked hard," he recalls. "Thanks to a marketing company that had come on the year before, we were able to get some sponsorship. This was the first time that Caribana was seen in the light that it should have been seen all along—as a contributor to the economy of Ontario. It was difficult. We worked hard and eventually we ended that year with a profit for the first time. We had made a commitment to pay the debt down in three to four years. We felt we could have done it. All of us were committed to doing this." The next year, the members rewarded the board with re-election.

However, at this election Lewis had to vacate the chair because of a bylaw that no one could be chair for two consecutive years. When none of the business types he had brought onto the board volunteered to take on the additional role of chair, Lewis nominated Farrell for the job. But in essence, the board was still primarily under Lewis' control. Another profitable year for Caribana followed, with the business plan becoming more fleshed out and a bit more of the debt retired.

When Lewis nominated Farrell, he thought of it as an interim move and that he would be back as soon as the rules changed. Lewis would later acknowledge that his nomination of Farrell was one of the worst decisions he made and one, he says, that laid the seeds for the destruction of the festival.

However, not every board member was happy with Lewis' style or the way he ran business. The opposition primarily came from the remaining radical board members who felt Lewis was seeking appeasement, that he was putting the onus solely on the Caribbean and black community to save Caribana. More so, they felt the board was selling out Caribana's political ideals to the business sector. And personality conflicts erupted. In the first year, the board had to make a major decision. Because of the poor finances of the corporation, some members on the board wanted the festival cancelled for a year. This would teach the city, country and businesses a lesson. Shutting down the festival would prove that everyone, except the organizers, stood to lose financially. In the meantime, Caribana could spend the year restructuring, instead of rushing to put on another festival.

"There was a very radical faction which felt that there should not have been a parade because of the loss and because of the need for the restructuring," recalls Gulliston, a business manager with Imperial Oil of Canada in Toronto. He was in charge of marketing under Lewis. "They felt that the priority should be on the restructuring. Those of us who worked in the market economy knew if there was not a product for one year that the setback would have been disastrous, that trying to get one million people who were told, because of whatever reason, there wasn't a festival, that getting those people to apportion their vacation times and funds to come into Toronto again would have been extremely difficult. It would set back the festival by 10 years. So looking at it from a marketing perspective, we felt the festival should go on, it should make the change that was necessary right away."

Although the threat of closing down this money-maker wasn't a real one, the possible impact obviously was not lost on the beneficiaries of the parade and the municipal governments. Later, they would act to make sure this threat would never be carried out.

Another divisive point was changing the parade route. For years, the Caribana parade was held on University Avenue in the Toronto downtown core. Nobody seemed happy with this route. The organizers felt it robbed them of the chance to make money because they had no control over the lands along the parade route. This meant they could not claim ownership to Caribana by, for example, charging spectators admission to watch the parade. They could not make vendors buy permits to sell their goods along the parade route. And until they were able to do these things, the businesspeople on the board argued, they would never be able to raise money to defray the cost of mounting the festival.

But others felt differently. There was a symbol of liberation by marching down an avenue of financial towers and seats of power, to rally around the Parliament Buildings, to make fun in front of the courts and to mock the business tycoons. That was the essence of a good carnival, they said—to turn the world on its head so that the powerless can poke fun at the powerful, if only for one day. For one day, symbolically, Blacks controlled the seats of power and the avenue of influence.

The businesspeople on the board wanted the parade to start on the grounds of the Canadian National Exhibition, where spectators could pay to watch the judging of the costumed bands. The parade would move out of the CNE grounds onto Lakeshore Boulevard, at the southern edge of the city. With this arrangement, the Caribbean Cultural Committee could set up a marketplace and sell vendors the necessary permits to operate stalls along the parade route. Opponents argued that the Caribbean Cultural Committee had simply given in to age-old pressure to put the festival out of sight, and that the only humiliation left for the community would be to confine the parade to an enclosed area near the lake, or simply to drown it in the polluted waters of Lake Ontario.

The radicals felt that a parade with as much economic clout as Caribana belonged, by rights, on Yonge Street, the main thoroughfare in Toronto. This was the only way to give the black and Caribbean community respect. On Yonge Street, the parade would bring regular business to a standstill. It would be a political statement by those not counted as part of the mainstream or power elites. Blacks and Caribbean people would flex their political muscles by taking control of this main thoroughfare for at least one day.

The radicals also felt that by moving the parade to the Lakeshore, the committee was giving in to pressure from the police and some people in government. These, they argued, were the people who did not like seeing so many black people on the streets at any one time. The radicals argued that these were the same types who felt that wherever Blacks congregate, there was a penchant for violence. These people wanted the city and region to continue to share the economic benefits of Caribana, but they wanted the parade hidden, moved off to a side street instead of taking centre stage in the downtown core. The radicals would not have this appeasement. There could be no accommodation between the two groups.

"One of the key issues for us in terms of strategic marketing for Caribana was the question of ownership; the product wasn't owned," says Gulliston. "The product is the name Caribana and all of the copyrighting and trademarking was not done. Even if it were done, the practice of people ripping it off was so severe that you couldn't protect it. The question of ownership was key. You must have a venue where it appears that the co-ordinating committee owns the festival, in an area where you have a permit to be there, you have a right to do things commercial in that area. So looking around for an alternative site was key."

In the end, the moderates won the day, and this was partly because of the defection of one radical. This was Rodney Davis, who would later surprise everyone by becoming Caribana's executive director when the radicals came to power. This was the same executive director who would resign weeks before the annual general meeting in February 1995 that I am attending.

Gulliston thinks moving the parade was the right idea. "The way I saw it was that with a festival of one million people you move it to where it is comfortable and where it is commercially viable. When you have a festival that is attracting one million, six hundred thousand people to come into the city, then you have a product so big nobody can ignore you. It doesn't really matter whether you are symbolically on Yonge Street or you are on the Lakeshore. The fact of the matter is that you are what is happening that weekend, that month; you are the biggest festival happening for the year. So you can't be ignored. That was how I felt about that. So the battle was won eventually, after a lot of acrimony, in the [community] newspapers."

But the radicals were not vanquished. They simply bided their time. And at the first opportunity, they pulled off a coup against the moderates. The issue came to a head just before the 1994 annual meeting.

"There became an obvious disenchantment between some members of the board and ourselves," Lewis recalls. "At the time we came into the organization, they started referring to us as the 'buttoned-down boys,' because presumably all of us worked with the private sector or in government in senior managerial positions. What we had brought to the organization was a completely different look. I suspect that some people in the community didn't particularly care for it, because we were not rabble rousers. We were people who came in with a mission, and that mission was to change the fortunes of the organization. So in 1994, there came the big split in the organization when, to our big surprise, all of us who attempted between 1991 and 1994 to rebuild the organization found ourselves on the outside."

Farrell says he broke with Lewis because he wanted a board that was truly democratic and that put the needs and aspirations of the community first. At the 1994 annual meeting, Farrell caught the moderates unawares by resorting to the proven method of signing up more members than anyone else. The coup happened with a Machiavellian touch of planning, timing and execution. Lewis was in Trinidad attending the carnival and showing around the then-Ontario minister of tourism and culture when he received word that he was no longer on the board. The members had ousted Lewis and all his supporters while he was away. The buttoned-down boys and their supporters might have been good at business, but they were hopelessly inept as politicians. Needless to say, the governments that originally had confidence in Lewis—including the city of Toronto, which wrote off $234,000 of debts in 1992—weren't too pleased with this power play. They would bide their time.

Once in power, Farrell showed his opponents how politics can be a weapon by moving quickly. He continued the restructuring by changing the constitution to allow unlimited successive terms as chair. The new board removed the likelihood of a coup against it by getting approval for the bylaw stipulating that membership alone did not qualify for a run at the board. Prospective directors must first work on various committees for two years before they can seek election. And the new board re-dedicated itself to a five-year plan, the cornerstone of which was for Caribana to branch out into other areas of business, including setting up a travel agency and a Caribana museum.

Lewis was not only surprised by the swiftness of his removal but by how quickly he and his supporters were sidelined. "We felt the actions were legitimate but not fair. It wasn't illegal but it certainly left a bad taste in the mouth of a lot of people, in that [stacking the deck at election time] was not the kind of thing that should have been done. We decided that we were going to get out of the business completely, because we realized the existing administration really didn't want us to be assisting in anything."

Sam Lewis says he shares the same general views as Farrell that Caribana should be a vehicle for the cultural, social and political development of the community. He disagrees with Farrell on how this should come about and whether the Caribbean Cultural Committee, as currently set up, can achieve this goal.

"Caribana has to travel simultaneously on three tracks," Lewis says. "Culturally, it has to bring our culture to the highest standard. The whole concept of carnival, of our music, our dance—Caribana can, by working diligently, raise the standard, bring it up to a level that will be recognized just as much as European culture is recognized. However, in moving the cultural aspect of Caribana ahead, you cannot forget or disregard that it should be moved along economically. Caribana, as everyone is aware, contributes a large financial return to not only Ontario but Canada as a whole.

"Yes, there is an economic position that should be taken, where some of the financial rewards should be returned to the community that produces the festival. Finally, when you look at Caribana on any Caribana Saturday and see one million plus people on the street, and you see so many people of colour together, but other people from mainstream Canada out there enjoying themselves, too, relating to one another, you can see the political force and the socio-political force that can be generated through the festival. You have three areas but none should be sacrificed for the other."

Lewis believes that whoever is leading the Caribbean Cultural Committee must always recognize that the three areas must be given equal attention because they are interrelated. "You cannot move ahead with the politics of it and deny the business and the culture. Nor can you move ahead on the culture without recognizing that you also have to move ahead with the economics. It's got to be a question of moving it along on three levels. What that means, then, is that there almost has to be a triumvirate running the organization, one who understand the political, one who understands the business, one who understands the cultural aspects. Because, in a general sense, you may not find one individual possessing all three qualities."

Having the triumvirate would also ensure that people are matched according to their talents and given a clear mandate to complete over a specified time. This way the leadership would not have to be constantly looking over its shoulder to see who was creeping up from behind. Finally, Lewis believes that the community has to re-think how board members are elected and to whom they are accountable. And the first step in this direction would be to disallow the mass recruiting of new members just before annual meetings.

But the biggest danger to Caribana, Lewis says, is that it resumed losing money after three years of profits, after seemingly putting bad management decisions behind it. "I felt that was particularly painful," he says, "because we had set a target date to rid ourselves of this yoke that seemed to be pressing down on the organization."

The Caribbean Cultural Committee should also have a bigger and more permanent staff, he says. Lewis says he was working on this when he was thrown out in what he calls "a retrograde step in 1994." The structure the committee needs would allow the administrative staff to run the festival on a daily basis with the directors acting only as a guide on policy matters. This is in keeping with the findings of a 1989 study by the management consulting firm, Price Waterhouse, on the management of the festival. "Within the Caribbean Cultural Committee's board of directors' frequent meetings, we have observed the board becoming too involved in the day-to-day administration of the organization and there may be a lack of overall perspective on what it is the organization is ultimately trying to accomplish," the report states. "With the historical trend of changing the board of directors' positions relatively frequently, the absence of a firm constitutional mandate exacerbates the problem of individuals [who are] not familiar with the overall direction of the organization and therefore are left to interpret their own vision for the future that may or may not be in harmony with previous decisions."

Six years after this report was published, Rodney Davis claims that he resigned as executive director for these very reasons, because there was no clear line to distinguish between the prerogatives of the board and those of the staff. Because Caribana is a plaything for the politicians in the community and the board members.

Lewis says there is a reason for this. It has to do with the power and visibility that come to anyone sitting on the board. "If you are not careful, you can start to feel powerful and forget what you are doing here is working on behalf of the people and not yourself. For some board members, the greatest thing that has ever happened to them in their lives is that they are now directors of Caribana. So they wouldn't want to give up the power of having their fingers in the pie on a daily basis to an administrative group that will take care of the office functions. That is the problem with the organization." They would not give up, even though they were driving the festival into the ground.

* * *

Finally, the roll-call finishes and the voting begins. Courtney Doldron is among the first to cast his ballots, all 36 of them, all for himself. Yes, Caribana has problems, he states, but he is not willing to put all the blame on Farrell and the so-called radicals. Lewis and his moderates must share the blame. After all, they set up the new constitution for the Caribbean Cultural Committee and were in charge of the very annual meeting at which they were ousted. All that happened is that they got out-hustled by Farrell.

Doldron is still confident that he will sit on the board. As the votes are tallied, he moves among the crowd. The one change he is planning to make is to ensure the board focuses solely on the Caribana parade. As he sees it, the organization should not stray from this main purpose. Neither does he like the idea of a penniless Caribbean Cultural Committee spreading itself ever thinner financially by getting involved in the travel business—as Farrell and his supporters on the board are now planning. This is a recipe for disaster. On the board, he would have to save Caribana from its organizers. And he would start to do that just as soon as the men counting the ballots announce the winners.

Doldron is about to be disappointed. He is outvoted and the official slate carries. This sets up the situation in which, for the next year, the board of directors will be following the existing agenda, under the chairmanship of Lennox Farrell. One of the first announcements from the new board is to press ahead with plans to set up a controversial travel agency called "Canada Caribbean Adventure Vacations" or CARAVAC, a decision that would eventually cost the cash-strapped committee a whopping $170,000 in one year. It is a decision that, with some others, will cripple the finances of the organization to such an extent that the festival's auditors, checking Caribana's books, will balk at giving a qualified opinion.

But in Caribana, where masquerade and deception rule, things are not what they often appear. Just a few months after the meeting, Lennox Farrell is at the receiving end of a coup of sorts. He announces unexpectedly that he is giving up the chair, passing the torch to Peter Marcelline, a long-time ally and a founding member of the Caribbean Cultural Committee. Farrell is to become chairman of CARAVAC, helping Caribana to diversify and make money by offering tourism and travel packages to the hundreds of thousands of visitors coming to Canada for Caribana. Immediately, Farrell finds himself under attack from members of his own board concerned about the direction in which the festival is going, and about the money spent on this venture. CARAVAC is soon portrayed as a white elephant sucking precious funds from the festival. Ultimately, Lennox is threatening that "it looks like I have to clean out the damn board again." Dissident board members take to leaking confidential reports, all with the aim of discrediting and ousting Farrell from the board; executive meetings break down in chaos, occasionally with angry members hurling file folders, briefcases and threats of lawsuits at one another.

By the time the festival rolls around, five months after the election, Caribana is in even worse financial shape. It has come to some accommodation with the *mas* band producers, but friction still remains. Disarray is the order of the day and at every turn. The committee even finds itself having to compete with the associations representing the *mas* band producers at various events. Rival groups and the committee would schedule similar events on the same night in a contest to see who had the bigger following. Indeed, it is usual to see some Caribana board members attending rival events.

But there is an even bigger problem. The Caribbean Cultural Committee relies every year on the provincial government to provide an operating grant of $70,000 to cover the usual last-minute expenses. But times have changed. A new government, Harris' Conservatives, has come to office and has frozen all grants. This could not happen at a worse time for Caribana. It is flat broke and, in the final week before the festival, as hundreds of thousands of people pour into Toronto, there is no certainty there will be a street parade. For in this week, Caribana's banker, the Canadian Imperial Bank of Commerce, has called its loans and lines of credit. It now falls on Mayor Barbara Hall and her ally, councillor Bev Salmon, to live up to their commitment. It takes their personal intervention and some last-minute moral suasion to get the bank to extend the line of credit. In return, the Caribbean Cultural Committee quietly agrees to have auditors from the city monitor all events for which money will change hands. Accountability of a more dangerous sort, this time from outside the black and Caribbean community. For although the city auditors would give Caribana a clean bill of health, this would officially mark the point at which the municipal governments decide it is time they take over the festival, but through the back door.

So, there is a Caribana in 1995, but barely. By now the board of directors is in tatters, with some members refusing to speak to one another. Confidential documents are brought to the board and are on the streets within hours. Some directors privately commission legal opinions on matters before the board, but share the opinion with only a few directors. Everyone appears to have a different vision for the festival. For the radicals, it isn't radical enough; for the moderates, the festival has left its moorings. The costume makers and foreign bands claim they were not paid $80,000 owed them by the committee and they are even more vociferous when the board grudgingly admits it spent at least $100,000 setting up CARAVAC. As fate would have it, this is when Courtney Doldron realizes his dream of becoming a director. With the board so fractured, some directors simply think, What's the use? and give up. Doldron, because he was the runner-up in the election, but perhaps because he unsuccessfully ran for the new Conservative government in the provincial election, might be able to curry some favour for Caribana and is trying desperately to be on friendly terms with the ruling Tories. He is drafted onto the board when fellow directors kick off a member for missing too many consecutive board meetings without permission. The farce has come full circle.

Still, everyone recognizes that the festival cannot continue this way. Caribana and the committee are not only broke, but they are imploding under the weight of community politics. The trophy everyone covets, but fumbles ineptly, has had the gold knocked off it to reveal ugly base metal underneath. The chairman of Metro Toronto, Alan Tonks, offers what, on the surface, appears to be a face-saving task force of Caribana and city officials. Its mandate is to rescue the festival and to set up an infrastructure for the future. On the committee are several businesspeople from the black and wider communities. Perhaps frightened by the very real prospects of no Caribana, the business groups—hotels, restaurants, amusement parks, parking lots, shopping malls and banks—that in the past were so reluctant to contribute financially to Caribana, agree to join the task force. A new team of buttoned-down boys has returned to save Caribana.

This time these business types offer advice only, no cash, and answer only to the funders, the governments. As one director notes, the funders, who promised less than $200,000 for one year's funding, "hold a gun to the head of the Caribbean Cultural Committee to make sure they get their way. Their position will be, you run this festival as we tell you or there will be no money. The Caribbean Cultural Committee has no choice and they know it."

But the businesses make one mistake; instead of suggesting ways to help fund Caribana, they simply pass the buck. They manage to put the focus back on Caribana's board, arguing that Caribana needs to put its house in order and run the festival simply as a business. This is an insult; businesses are once again attempting to rip off the profits from Caribana and to give back nothing in return, and this so incenses members of the black and Caribbean community that for perhaps the first time a genuine movement is launched to scrap the festival. And this time, members of this new coalition intend to carry out their threat. Suddenly, Canadians wake up to news that Caribana is in chaos and facing its biggest crisis.

As the provincial and municipal governments make their move on Caribana, Farrell and his supporters quickly realize that control of the festival is at stake. The task-force meetings show the true intentions of governments and also expose Caribana's weaknesses. Caribana is too dependent on government funding. Its financing is precarious. Out of a budget of $1.6 million annually, Caribana raises only $800,000 on its own. For the remainder it goes, cap in hand, to the governments. This gives the governments the right to call the shots or to withhold funding. And government officials on the task force make sure that members of the Caribbean Cultural Committee understand their position.

And it is a position of utter weakness. Caribana not only has no more money, but it does not have any evidence to support its most basic claims for additional funding. For years, the Caribbean Cultural Committee has claimed that at least one million people attend the annual street parade. Where is the proof? the government and business representatives on the task force ask. Police officials produce photographs of the parade from the air, claiming that the size of the crowd is about 300,000. What they cannot estimate is the turnover rate, Caribana's officials note, because by nature few people take in a full day's activities. Some people attend in the morning and then leave to go to work or attend family or community barbecues, or sight-see around Toronto. Youths tend to come in the evening and stay late into the night for other events. But the police numbers have them worried. So the board members go to Decima Research, the marketing and research people who provided the original estimate, to ask them to explain their numbers. Decima says it will, but only for a fee. Cash-strapped, the committee members beg off and weakly concede the argument over numbers.

Other weaknesses also show up in the Caribbean Cultural Committee's arguments. For example, Caribana officials have always insisted that at least 400,000 Americans arrive annually for the festival. The hoteliers on the task force point out that the Greater Toronto Area has a grand total of 30,000 hotel beds. Where are you placing these 400,000 Americans? the hoteliers ask. Once again, Caribana's representatives are on the defensive. They know that most visitors to Caribana stay with friends and family, which means that the majority of these visitors do not contribute to the hotel coffers.

And on the question of funding, what is Caribana doing to help itself? Once again, the Caribana members bow their heads meekly. The Caribbean Cultural Committee had told the governments following the 1991 crisis that it would rely on corporate sponsorships to reduce dependence on government funding. In 1992, corporate donations hit $400,000 under the buttoned-down boys. In 1995, they came in at about $100,000. Caribana's members have no answers, or at least they can't risk admitting that funding has virtually disappeared because large corporations do not want to be associated with Caribana and its infighting. Only minor sponsorships—$5,000 here or $15,000 there—are available, and they are proving to be more trouble than profit to collect.

And on the question of finance, the Caribana directors know the situation cannot be worse. The festival's auditors are claiming Caribana's debts have ballooned to $700,000, with about $400,000 of this amount owed to the various governments for such things as employee income taxes and the like. And with the auditors' unhappiness with Caribana's cash management, they are not prepared to sign their names to the audited statements—a crippling blow for Caribana's board in its dealing with the task force and with its detractors in the community.

The problem with the auditor is almost farcical: the directors claim the financial situation isn't as bad as the auditors paint it. The problem, they say, is that the committee has hundreds of thousands of dollars in inventory locked away at its former headquarters. Unfortunately, the auditors cannot get to these assets to verify their existence. The assets are in rooms padlocked by the landlord who is angry with the Caribana committee, alleging that the committee is breaking the rental contract by not paying several months rent.

Caribana is now in a worse crisis than when the buttoned-down boys rescued it four years earlier.

The one area that nobody disputes before the task force is that Caribana ploughs hundreds of millions of dollars into the local economy, which means that the main beneficiaries from Caribana are the municipal governments. More than anyone else, they have an overriding reason for ensuring an annual festival. A Caribana, as it would turn out, that will be on the governments' terms if they have to open their cheque books to rescue Caribana from itself one more time.

One month after Caribana 1995, the full implication of the predicament facing the festival comes home to the board of directors. The new provincial government indicates funding will be cut drastically and permanently. The board also starts to get feelers from the task force that the government does not think it is so smart a decision for Caribana to be in the travel business. The task force recommends that the Caribbean Cultural Committee should put all its efforts into providing a successful festival. In other words, the festival should keep churning out money for the local economy, with no real prospect for the Caribbean Cultural Committee and Caribana to benefit. Indeed, the task force would go further. It would suggest that the parade be, for all intents and purposes, run by the people at Ontario Place, a provincial park on the Lakeshore, and that an admission fee be charged. The fee would be collected by Ontario Place, which would run the festival on its grounds. Eventually, Ontario Place would turn over what remained of the admission fees—after paying expenses and the band leaders and musicians—to a much-reduced committee, which would be run by three permanent staff, none of them with any clout.

In essence, Ontario Place would be the vehicle for a reverse takeover of Caribana. The festival would be stripped of its cultural and spiritual importance. Its main purpose would be to produce money for the city. African and Caribbean participants would be reduced to what many critics had always feared—to becoming dancers and performers, but getting nothing in return. For the price of an annual operating grant, the municipal governments would nationalize Caribana, effectively taking it off the streets and moving it into an enclosed area—a location most participants have always rejected. With no money, and a badly divided board, the Caribbean Cultural Committee virtually has no say in what is happening. The gun at the head of the directors is fully loaded and cocked.

With no money to keep CARAVAC operating, the directors and the community are looking at the real possibility of further embarrassment if the tour operator goes under in less than a year. About this time the board starts marketing CARAVAC, quietly seeking potential buyers in the black communities in Canada and the United States. No takers come forward. Then one day, CARAVAC's general manager is talking to Toronto businessman Stan Litchman about the problems of the travel agency. Litchman opines that he might want to buy the agency. Papers are quickly drawn up for the sale of 60 percent of CARAVAC. Caribana would get about $300,000 in cash and an annual licensing fee for the use of its name—money it badly needs to replace funding cuts from the provincial and municipal governments, money it needs to assert itself.

Farrell is among the first to champion the deal, eventually putting his position of director on the line if the deal is rejected. But other board members have their doubts. Four of the 12 members vote against the sale and are adamant that more has been sold than just a travel agency. Caribana and its trademark have been sold, and without even consulting the real owners, the black and Caribbean community. Worse, they argue, it is a sell-out to outside interest. For the buyer is a white Jew, who cannot understand the black community because of his colour and his culture.

* * *

Charles Roach, the man who dreamed up Caribana as a street festival, concedes that the festival is perhaps too big, too successful, to be run on an *ad hoc* basis. Roach, a black nationalist and activist, sounds almost resigned to the fact that Caribana will never become an economic force in the black and Caribbean community. "I immediately saw there was great potential there, but it was not possible to harness that potential and change it into something that is commercial. They [Caribbean Cultural Committee] have never been able to do it and I feel it is something that cannot be done. They keep talking about it. I feel it is something that can't be done, that Caribana will always remain a thing where it would be a good thing for the city, great for all the businesses, great for the airline companies, the buses, the trains, hotels; great for the breweries and the bottlers and those people, but I thought we could not harness anything because we did not have any of that infrastructure there."

Roach's words are prophetic. They were spoken a year before the latest financial crisis at the Caribbean Cultural Committee and soon after the 1995 annual meeting. I am at Roach's office to pick his brains about Caribana, to ask him about his initial expectations for the festival.

Eventually, we get around to discussing what would become of the festival. I ask him what he thought about the notion that the festival had become too big for its own good. That, eventually, the three levels of government might have to move in and take over, especially if the Caribbean Cultural Committee continues to flounder and to be scarred by such deep divisions.

To my surprise, Roach suggests that not only is nationalization possible, but that it can be carried off easily. For Caribana is such a money spinner, the levels of government can no longer sit back and allow a volunteer board to jeopardize a festival so important to the tourism and travel industry. Big business and money wouldn't let it happen because of their vested interests—not in the culture or spirituality of Caribana, but in its money-making potential. And with the bickering between *mas* producers and members of the board so open, with directors so badly divided, it won't cost an entrepreneur much to buy and control Caribana. All the government or an entrepreneur has to do to get control is to provide the $400,000 the *mas* producers demand every year. For when anyone has control of the people who put the costumes on the street, he or she effectively has control of Caribana.

"I think that will be easily done because it is very easy for anyone who has money to take Caribana over, because Caribana has always been weak in its administration, but very strong in spirit."

But even as we talk, we recognize that nationalization would be a bitter pill for the black community to swallow. And it would send a bad signal to communities across the continent. Eventually, parents would be telling their black youths about the time a government robbed a black community of a festival the community had developed on its own, with sparse government assistance. That a government only took over the festival to keep businesses happy. And would the spirit of Caribana be dissipated? Would people feel as strongly connected to a festival if they knew that someone outside the community was pulling the strings, that the revelers had to buy their costumes so that a city and its businesses could make money, could reduce them to performing like so many tourist acts in the Caribbean or Las Vegas, where the performers might appear to be native and cultural, but are simply working for a salary and are not really celebrating their culture?

Would Caribana become hollow? And would the dream of what Caribana could become die because the dream makers were no longer in charge? Who would defend the spirituality of the festival from the rapaciousness of the money makers? Charles Roach's estimate for an asking price would be even richer than we thought. For the board is willing to take $300,000 from Litchman and run. Except that the black community has other ideas.

* * *

It is down to the crucial final week in the life of the CARAVAC deal when a pivotal decision concerning the future ownership of Caribana has to be made. Once again I am in Roach's law office, but this time with about 40 other so-called community elders invited to discuss the future of Caribana. Attending are teachers, businesspeople, school administrators, publishers, community activists, representatives of the Nation of Islam, Caribana musicians and band leaders, Caribana's directors and employees and several of the volunteers who keep the festival running. This group, as Roach explains, is made up of community leaders and opinion shapers. We are meeting with Farrell and other directors to discuss the sale of CARAVAC and whether the Caribbean Cultural Committee should licence anyone the right to use its trademark—Caribana. Six days later, as Roach reminds us, a general meeting of the Caribbean Cultural Committee and interested community members is to vote on the deal and, essentially, on Farrell's future in Caribana. Our deliberations would be crucial, he suggests.

Judging from the stories in the community newspaper, the community is bitterly against the deal. Several people are calling for the resignation of the entire Caribana board and the scuttling of the deal. One of the most vocal critics is the community newspaper *Share*, which simply calls the proposed sale a Caribana sell-out: "And here we thought that the day of black people selling out black people had long ago passed into history. When are we going to learn? When are we going to wake up and realize that there are no white knights coming to save us?

"Maybe the meeting called [in six days] to sell us on the virtues of selling out should be turned into a meeting to nominate a caretaker board to run the organization. Enough is enough."

While this group has no clout in terms of getting the board to adopt a given position, Roach explains, Caribana would ignore the views of the assembled group at its own peril. It would then have to deal with the wrath of the community.

Asking the elders to stand, Roach takes up a porcelain cup and starts with an invocation to the African spirits in the room to guide us in our deliberation. He throws some libation in a corner of the room and offers praises to our ancestors, our elders and our children. Then, we settle down for four hours of intense discussion, starting with perusal of several thick legal documents on the proposed sale. It seems the more people learn about the deal, the more questions they ask and the more answers are proposed, and the more the group is swayed against the deal.

Obviously, the meeting is not going as the directors had hoped. They had planned for an information session in which they would set the agenda and explain details of the deal. But opponents are quick off the mark and in no time the directors and their lawyer are on the defensive, explaining how in their wildest dreams they could have agreed to such a deal, and why they did not make, and were not making, plans to sell the agency to the black community. Why are the directors going outside the black community to sell a part of Caribana? And what about this notion that Litchman would protect Caribana's copyright by fighting in court anyone who abuses it—anyone including many of the small black businesses?

And if CARAVAC is essentially bankrupt, the elders ask, why would any sane businessman spend $300,000, as Litchman is offering, for 60 percent of the company? Is there more to this deal than has been disclosed? And the elders are not pleased when Caribana's lawyer explains that Litchman believes that Caribana's name is worth about $15 million if marketed properly and that is why he wants a piece of the action. Does this mean Blacks need Whites to show them how to conduct their own businesses profitably? they ask. Is the proposed sale another sign of an outsider moving in to fleece a precious community asset? They would have none of it.

Ultimately, as the board and its lawyer suggest, the rationale for doing the deal comes down to a question of a cash-strapped Caribbean Cultural

Committee getting its hands on money quickly to put on the next Caribana festival. It is either take the deal or face the uncertainty of not knowing what will happen next, of knowing that the municipal governments will be imposing their will on the festival in return for another financial bail-out. The choice is clear: the elders should recommend acceptance of a deal that isn't perfect or run the risk of a bankrupt Caribana falling on its knees, shot through the head by the municipal governments.

Finally, Roach calls the meeting to an end. He sums up the proceedings by saying that obviously there is little support for the deal. At the very least, the sale should be delayed until the community can come up with another plan. And getting to the crux of the matter, Roach says that he recognizes a primary reason for the anger at the sale. It is a reason nobody wants to raise openly but which hangs over the entire deal, he says. "It is the Jewishness of Mr. Litchman." Nobody disagrees.

* * *

The air in room A-60 at Jorgenson Hall at the Ryerson Polytechnic University is crackling with tension as Caribana's chairman Peter Marcelline calls the crucial meeting on CARAVAC and the Caribbean Cultural Committee to order. From early on, there is no doubt the board is in for a rough ride. Opponents of the deal seem well organized, perhaps in better shape than the lethargic and dejected-looking board members who support the sale. The opponents come to the meeting with printed handouts, outlining details of the deal, savaging it as another sell-out of black people's interests, condemning the board for mismanagement and supposedly running up losses of over $1 million in recent times, and calling for the mass resignation of all board members to clear the air.

Once again, the job of chairing the meeting falls to Charles Roach. And even Roach, as respected as he is in the community, realizes that this day his is not an easy task. So he tries to lighten the mood by telling a story.

There is tremendous value in the Caribana trademark, he says. He recalls that in 1966, when he and other founders of the festival were searching for a festival name, they could find nothing appropriate. Eventually, one man stepped forward with a suggestion. His name was Fred Hope and he would become Caribana's first paid employee, the equivalent of the current chief executive officer. Hope suggested that since they were starting a Caribbean festival in Canada, why not combine the words Caribbean and Canada and come up with ... Caribana.

But few at the meeting are in a mood for light-hearted banter. And, unlike the meeting of the elders, nobody even tries to pretend race is not at the heart of the criticism of the proposed CARAVAC deal. The issue comes to a head when one woman, a community activist, tells Litchman, "With greatest of respect, white people have never worked in the interest of black people." The loud applause that follows this statement would set the tone for the rest of the meeting. When Litchman's turn comes to speak, he is shouted down. It doesn't help the situation when Litchman says that although he is Jewish, "In my 51 years I have never been called 'white' before."

Litchman is allowed to continue speaking only after one of the board's most vitriolic critics gets his chance at the podium to denounce the deal as a sell-out. At this point, Litchman decides he has had enough. "I withdraw my deal," he says. "The deal is dead." And so is Caribana, he suggests, because the festival is broke.

The end is anticlimactic. Farrell sits slumped in his chair at the front of the hall. Litchman then offers a ray of hope, saying that he is willing to entertain a proposal from the black community and that he is willing to give up the $30,000 he has already advanced to keep CARAVAC afloat.

But for all intents and purposes, the meeting is finished. And so is Farrell's future at Caribana. In a speech, Farrell says he is not bitter but that he has to admit defeat. He will resign from the board of CARAVAC and Caribana. Roach tries to weave the strands of the meeting together, but there is no consensus. Several speakers trot to the podium and talk in generalities about the future of Caribana and whether CARAVAC should be put out of business. One of the most eloquent speeches is from Donnie X, the representative for Minister Farrakhan and the Nation of Islam in Toronto. "This should not be seen as an ending, but as a beginning," he says. NOI would shortly be sending to Caribana a plan that would indicate how the black community can make money from the festival. For after all, he says, we do not own the hotels, buses or the hotdog stands that make money off Caribana. We don't need to kill business ideas like CARAVAC, he offers, but just to massage them so that they suit our community interests.

Suddenly, everyone is talking at the same time. The meeting is in disarray. Roach announces that in light of the chaos and the obvious leadership "vacuum," he is appointing himself the head of a committee to re-examine the CARAVAC deal, essentially to save Caribana. Nobody demurs. After almost 30 years, the future of the festival is in the hands of the man who founded it, or so he thinks.

But before ending the meeting, Roach does one more symbolic thing. He says he wants to finish telling the story of Fred Hope, the playwright and artist who named Caribana. "Caribana can drive people crazy," Roach says. And he recalls that Hope became so consumed with planning the first Caribana that he had a nervous breakdown even before the first costume hit the parade route.

"I can tell you that part of the story now because Fred Hope is no longer with us. He is dead. I will now ask that we all stand and have a moment of silence for Fred Hope, some 27 years after his death, for we have not done that before to mark his passing."

Just about everyone stands. Silence for the first time since the noisy meeting began three hours earlier. But at this moment, it is hard to tell if the silence is for the passing of a founder of Caribana, or almost 30 years later for the death of his dream, the Caribana that we know and love. The dissidents who killed the CARAVAC deal are celebrating. They will set their sights next on taking over Caribana itself, ousting the old board and standing up to the businesses and governments in an attempt to take back the festival by scrapping the task force report. And they will be defiant in their stance, even if it means running the risk of scrapping the festival and making everyone—the black community, the Caribana revelers, the tourists, but particularly the governments and the parasitic businesses—losers in order to make a point.

As I walk away from this meeting it is difficult to determine which is the stronger feeling—anger or disappointment. Already people are meeting in small groups, planning how to take back Caribana. They are exchanging names and telephone numbers, scheming how to thwart the plans by the municipal governments, how to clear out the Caribana board and send a message to the business interests around Toronto by cancelling the festival for a year and allowing the community to regroup. Maybe they are right, I think. Why not do something bold and dramatic since, at this rate, everything seems to be lost?

And I wonder how the governments—all of which are intent these days on downsizing and privatization—can appear to be so hypocritical by taking over Caribana? Will they get away with this move? Or is it still acceptable for governments to treat the black community differently, a hypocrisy that so many in the black community are so quick to buy into? And there is the deep frustration from knowing that in almost three decades Canadian Blacks have nothing to show besides Caribana itself. Even now we cannot decide on what to do with so visible a festival.

But I hope that somehow the black community will find a way to stop the infighting and come up with a plan to take back our festival. Caribana is a family heirloom entrusted to all of us for safekeeping for the generations to come, an heirloom over which the black community must exercise control and preserve as one of the most obvious contributions we have made to this country—indeed, to North America.

* * *

The drama for control of Caribana and the Caribbean Cultural Committee played itself out with the dissidents taking control of the board at a raucous annual general meeting that lasted 12 hours. With these changes, all bets for a Caribana in 1996 were now off. The new board had to make an immediate decision whether to declare the committee bankrupt and to start all over again, perhaps suspending the festival for a year, or even moving the parade out of downtown Toronto. Toronto-area businesses were faced with the very real likelihood of having no Caribana, of proving—as they told the task force—that they really didn't need Caribana to top up their hotel occupancy, to attract patrons to their restaurants or stores. The new board, reinforced by support from the black community for a get-tough posture, called their bluff. The people who produce the costumes for the street parade said they would not participate in the festival unless somebody paid the bills for their start-up costs. And, for the first time, after so many idle threats over the years, the band leaders now appeared to be deadly serious.

Suddenly pressed against the wall, the governments relented. They indicated that the task-force report and the controversial recommendation to change the route of the parade were now negotiable. Businesses would be brought on-stream so that saving Caribana would not be a task only for the new board. Businesses would be asked by the tireless Caribana boosters, Toronto mayor Barbara Hall and Metro chairman Alan Tonks, to contribute $350,000 to make sure that masquerade bands were funded this year. The mayor and the chairman offered personal undertakings—putting their reputations on the line—that they would get businesses to contribute. And the new Caribana board—still broke and still relying on volunteers—set about trying to patch up those glaring areas of mismanagement that led to so divided a board. Special attention, board members promised, would be paid to provide proper financial accounting and to address those concerns raised by Caribana auditors. But even as the frantic work began to make sure Caribana would happen, nobody could be sure how many more Caribanas there would be. There were still too many compromises to be made.

Obviously, there are several messages in this crisis for all of us: that Caribana, like the community that spawns it, has come of age in Canada and can no longer be taken for granted. The flip side of this is, obviously, that Caribana and the community that nurtures it must be counted as an integral part of the wider society, not simply as some exotic appendage to be exploited financially for two weeks and ignored for the rest of the year. And, obviously, just as important a statement to the wider community is that if society does not move fast to meet what might appear to them as wild-eyed demands by today's radicals, they might wake to even bigger demands from tomorrow's black leaders who might appear even more radical. For indeed, for a while nobody thought that a radical like Lennox Farrell, with his dreams of making Caribana an engine of economic growth in the black community, would so soon be considered a conservative. But that is the reality of being black in Canada.

CHAPTER 12

ANGRINON PARK

As I write this chapter, the first real signs of spring are breaking out after a particularly long winter. So typically Canadian. With the days getting longer and the sun's rays stronger, our thoughts turn to the future—in this case to small things like a pleasant summer with lots of fun and time for family and friends. My three-year-old son, Mensah, is particularly looking forward to the warmer days. His unbounded enthusiasm is helping to create the spirit of anticipation among those of us who are a bit more jaded about the present and cynical about the future.

Perhaps nothing would make Mensah happier than to hear that his four-year-old cousin, Ngozi, will be coming from Montreal for an extended stay. This was the case last summer, and perhaps the memories of having someone his age around the house lasted through the dark days of winter. They kept his hopes high when he could not play in a back yard with snowdrifts taller than he was, when he could not run free outdoors dressed just in a T-shirt and shorts—when he was restricted in so many ways. Now, he, too, is looking forward to summer and the freedom it brings. Except how do you explain to a three-year-old that the arrangements for his cousin would take some special planning, for distance is such a major factor. Not like when Mensah's parents and the mother of his favourite cousin were growing up in Barbados and distance was not so important; now it seems to be everything. Oh, how North American we have become. No longer small-island people.

Mensah's innocent hopes for a happy summer are so similar to the hopes that have kept black communities in Canada going for so long. It is an outlook that we in our communities must hold onto for as long as possible. For what good will the future be if we cannot dream? Without hopes that the future can and will be better, we will never get through the lingering dark winters. Without those dreams, our collective memories will force us to admit defeat and ask, Why bother?

We should never forget that many times in the past two hundred years large numbers of Blacks did just that. They abandoned Canada to return to the United States when the dream died here. Among them were many whose ancestors had fled slavery in the South for Canada, but who, on arriving, found that this country wasn't quite the heaven they sang about. They found that, on reflection, maybe they had made a mistake. Once slavery ended, America offered a brighter future. Similarly, we cannot forget the black United Empire Loyalists in Ontario and New Brunswick, and especially in Nova Scotia, who were so betrayed by Canada. These loyalists and their descendants must have wondered why they did not choose a future in an American republic rather than fight alongside loyal monarchists. And as we prepare for the turn of the century, we cannot forget those who came to Canada from Africa and the Caribbean with all those child-like hopes of making a good living, of paving the way for a better future for themselves and their children.

Today, many of these immigrants, particularly the unskilled who came as domestic servants or as nursing assistants in Canadian hospitals, face a bleak retirement—often a retirement forced prematurely on many of them as governments slash funding to hospitals, schools and other institutions. These retirements or lay-offs from the once safe jobs in hospitals and government services are coming too early for many of them. They have not acquired the wealth to allow them to abandon Canada for warmer climes back home. They do not have the nest eggs to see their children through school and university and successfully launch their ships on the seas of life. Many who had invested in real estate, choosing to sacrifice to buy a house or condominium rather than rent, find that in their hour of despair the real-estate market has bottomed out, taking their equity—and future—with it. They feel helpless about their future and the prospects of their offspring. And while many of them still talk of going back home or to warm cities like Atlanta and Miami, they know they are now living a pipe dream, but hoping nobody will be rude enough to wake them.

Their anguish about the future of Blacks in this country shows up in conversations everywhere. It is virtually impossible to attend a meeting of any black association without hearing a keynote speaker making reference to how Blacks in Canada have survived and must continue to survive in the face of big challenges. This is the *raison d'être* for gala events like the annual Harry Jerome Awards in Toronto, where the cream of the Canadian black community meets to celebrate and commiserate, but also to award scholarships and recognition to young people successfully making it out of the isolation of the black community into the mainstream. So we recognize future doctors, lawyers, engineers, musicians and athletes, as well as those older community stalwarts who have worked so hard and long in the trenches. On a smaller scale, there are similar awards handed out by business groups in Montreal and other associations like black women's groups and other professional organizations from one side of the country to the other.

During the winter, I attended a reunion of the Canadian Association of Negro Women. The meeting was to mark the publication of a slim volume of the history of the pioneering work begun almost 50 years ago by these civil-rights activists, who advocated for justice and equity for black people in this country. Once again, the conversations turned to what it will take for Blacks to survive in this country. Everyone was talking about what we as a people can do to ensure a better future, what Blacks must do to show that Canada is as much their country as anyone else's, what examples our so-called role models must set for our youth.

The author of the history, Lawrence Hill, was choked up when he noted in his speech that, as we gathered for this celebration, the black community was in an uproar over unexplainable deaths of our young men. One of them was the seemingly senseless killing of a young black man by a Metro Toronto policeman, and the other was the equally senseless stabbing death of a 15-year-old black youth by another only a few years older. *They* are killing us and *we* are murdering ourselves. But we are killing more of ourselves than they are killing us. Woe is us. Obviously, Hill argued and everyone agreed, the work of the CANWA (Canadian Negro Women Association) is far from over. However, others would have to take up the torch handed off by these pioneers.

And over the winter, I attended various meetings and talked to people about how we must bring our people together. All these discussions and efforts are to make sure the future for Blacks in Canada is nothing like the past or even the present. All the participants are hoping to have their associations or group meetings up and running as soon as spring arrives. They must be ready to act as soon as the black youths start taking to the streets and, unemployed and frustrated, need guidance and assurances. There is that pervasive sense of urgency about the future.

It is hard not to be anxious and concerned about the future, not to wring our hands in despair thinking of the young black children in this country. It is difficult not to worry about how we can possibly survive in a society still so hostile to us, a country in which, compared to other ethnic groups, we have a greater chance of not finishing high school,[5] of ending up in prison, of being unemployed as youths and then as adults, and of being kept away from power and influence, whether in the corporate boardroom or in the political back rooms. A country in which we appear more likely to be shot by police and, according to various authoritative studies, to be dragged before the courts more often, to be granted bail less often and to receive the harshest sentences more often than Whites.

Just as important, it is frustrating to think about how we can survive in a community where we continue to poison one another with illegal drugs and to shoot down one another on the streets and in the homes of our community. It is difficult not to question whether living in isolation, forced or by choice, will make the future any better for us. We have to rethink many of the positions we have always taken in all areas of life. Indeed, of late there has even been a hardening of opinion in some quarters of the black community among those who in frustration lash out at wayward youths and argue that they are getting what they deserve when they die running from police or get killed after a drug deal goes bad. They deserve what they get, for the bad weeds in the community are making us all look bad—all of us, including the large majority who are law abiding, do not carry weapons or deal in drugs. The large majority of us who want to break the defiant culture that produces the outlaws and the bad boys.

But even after the angry outburst and self-pity, invariably the message

5 *Representation of Visible/Racial Minorities in the Toronto Board of Education Work Force*. Toronto: Toronto Board of Education, 1987.

Ontario Royal Commission on Education. Toronto: Ontario Royal Commission on Education, 1995.

Dr. George Dei, *Anti-Racism Education: Theory & Practice.* Halifax: Fernwood Publishers, 1996.

is the same from all quarters: we must not only survive, but keep planning for a better future. We must always believe that all of us are on a journey that will eventually lead us, as the spiritual says, "up the King's Highway." Heaven is always around the corner, maybe as soon as the next summer. As soon as we are fully accepted and respected by the mainstream and when we stop destroying one another.

In this country where we have made our home, to stay after centuries of trial, we have to survive on hope. It is a special community we are building in this country. I was thinking of these circumstances that make us who we are when at the end of last summer it was my job to take Ngozi back home to Montreal. By then he had started to miss his mother and wanted to be back with her. So we boarded a Voyageur bus at midnight, and as we travelled through the night, I kept thinking of my intermittent role in this little boy's life. For here is a young black boy having to travel hundreds of kilometres to make a connection with the nearest members of his family in this country—the same way that my own kids have to make the same trip to Montreal for the same reason. Or when their cousins in New York come across the border to spend the summer vacation or attend a special Christmas reunion, or a family wedding in Montreal or Toronto. When the older cousins from New York teach them the latest slang and music from places like Flatbush Avenue in New York or in their school yards and churches; when they, in turn, teach their New York cousins something or other about Canada. This is how they get a sense of connection, the same way that teenage black youths across the country make a connection when they travel for miles practically every weekend to attend basketball tournaments on either side of the border. Basketball tournaments that are always all-black, with the spectators, players and coaches all one community, unmindful of the different flags on the sides of their rented buses, concerned only about making a connection and keeping the youths off the streets.

The alternative is to jump on a plane for about five hours and fly south. But who has the money to go back home these days? In any case, who is to say that our children can really appreciate the significance of *back home* to us and would not feel as alienated in this foreign country—where they might actually see black prime ministers, presidents, doctors, lawyers, garbage collectors and, yes, criminals—as their parents were when they arrived in Canada only to discover that all the important people were white.

So for most of the year, our kids grow up disconnected from their families and the wider society, having to fall back on special community groups to teach them a sense of belonging and history. This is so different from the life that their parents knew when growing up back home. Then, a family reunion was probably no more than a few minutes drive away, or most likely was within walking distance. Now, my children have to travel hundreds of kilometres. How Canadian we have become. And how much of ourselves have we sacrificed for what seem—in the middle of the night when we can't sleep and we end up scratching our heads and asking why—to be hollow victories?

My trip to Montreal with Ngozi reminded me of the many times, when my two brothers and I were growing up in Barbados, when we took "long vacation" as we called it—because we never had such things as *summer* vacations. We spent two weeks of our six to eight weeks with our grandmother, aunts, cousins and an uncle. For us this was a time to be pampered by members of the family who possibly would not have seen us for a few months. This was a time to rediscover our mother's side of the family as well as to give the grandmother, aunts and cousins we were living with—our father's family—a respite from us. These vacations gave us a sense of belonging. And sometimes Uncle John—the sole male in both of my grandmothers' houses—would join us on the bus as we made our way home in darkness at the end of our reunion.

Now here I was, Uncle Cecil, taking Ngozi back home after playing the role of a father figure for him for about three weeks. Ngozi, Canadian to the bone, born in Montreal to a mother from Barbados and a father from Zaire, with aunts, uncles and cousins scattered around the globe in Barbados, Trinidad, New York, London, Zaire and Toronto and God knows where else. Ngozi, who cannot wait to get back to Montreal and his *garderie*, the day nursery where he is immersed in the language not only of his province but of his Zairian father.

It is for the future of the Ngozis and Mensahs that we must continue to believe in Canada. But not only must we believe: we must do more to break the isolation. We have to take our future in our hands. We are not likely to have much of an effect on the future of this country, on how this country treats us in the workplace, in retirement or vicariously through our children, by staying on the outside looking in. We have to be in the middle of the discussion on the future, a discussion taking place on the very nature of Canada itself. A discussion in which Blacks can make a difference, the same way our forefathers and foremothers left us their proud legacy as United Empire Loyalists fighting against the republicans to the south, to help forge a country called Canada.

* * *

It is hard to think of a more fitting example of the alienation and separation of Blacks in Canada than Angrinon Park. Here we are on the outskirts of Montreal on a weekend that symbolically signals the arrival of summer in what would be one of the most crucial years in Canada's history.

This is the time for Montreal-area Blacks, mainly expatriates from the English-speaking Caribbean, to mentally put away the last of the heavy coats and boots of the past winter. They can roll out their bats, pads and balls for another four to five months of playing in parks their beloved cricket and dominoes, attending picnics and Saturday-night dances. They can linger a bit longer in the bright sunshine outside the several churches at which they worship across the region.

Traditionally, the summer of celebration for members of the Montreal-Caribbean Social Organization starts with a big all-day picnic in Angrinon Park in the industrial city of LaSalle. Here a black visitor from Toronto is made to feel at ease and welcome, where friends and family from around town just drop in to catch up on the gossip and plans for the future.

They eat the special barbecued meats cooking in the oil drums, copiously sprinkled with beer and other spirits. They sit and play dominoes in the shade of trees, nip a strong rum and hastily remove the beer bottles from sight when a police car drives by. All the while, they keep a watchful eye on their children playing on the grass, riding their bikes, playing with dogs, eating hamburgers, hot dogs and other Canadian foods.

But as Blacks from miles around drop by for this summer ritual, there is an uneasiness in the air. They know the start of summer 1995 also unofficially marks the beginning of the latest round in the drive by some elements in Quebec society to make their province an independent country. For even as the Blacks meet in Angrinon Park this Saturday, they are aware that plans are in their final preparation for the annual St. Jean Baptiste march in the heart of Montreal the very next day. This parade would be the first public outpouring of Québécois fervour that would grip the province until all Quebecers decide at the upcoming polls whether their future lies with a federation called Canada or in a sovereign country, Quebec.

None of the Blacks in this park has any doubts where his or her future rests. Or of how their future as a community would benefit most. They are Canadians and federalists to the core. But by a weird twist of fate their federalism also makes them isolationist, cut off from the provincial mainstream, cut off in very much the same way as so many Blacks in the English-speaking part of this country are. This is an irony for the Quebec Blacks, many of whom are seeking strength in their isolation because they want to be Canadian or nothing else. Having already transferred their alliance from their homeland to Canada, they are not now willing to make another transfer. And certainly not to a proposed country where they do not feel welcomed or doubt their children would be free to prosper.

Their immediate worry is about their personal future, and that of their community, if a majority of Quebecers vote to secede from Canada. What would become of the members of the Quebec society whose skins are black, whose culture is black, and who can claim long historical ties to this society, ties that go back to those pioneering days when a black female slave burned down the provincial capital, Quebec City, in a bid for her freedom? So they are faced with a painful choice: do they join the forces of those seeking independence for Quebec? In essence, they would be throwing in their lot with those seeking another form of isolation, this time carving a French nation out of an English-speaking continent if they went this route. Or they could continue to be isolated within the provincial mainstream by rejecting independence for Quebec. Either way, whether they choose Canada or Quebec, they appear destined for some form of separation.

So to a group hovering around the dominoes table, I ask if it is likely that any of them or their friends will participate in the St. Jean Baptiste parade the following day.

"No, man," an elderly man says. "Tomorrow, we stay as far away from downtown as possible. Those people in that parade are fanatics, man. You got to be white and French for them to accept you."

This answer brings nods of approval all around. Then, with each man adding his twist to the story, collectively they recount the incident involving an expatriate from Zaire—for all I know someone who is known by Ngozi's dad—who for several years running has tried to join the St. Jean Baptiste parade. The Zairian has insisted that he would participate on his own terms. He wants to parade in his national costume, praising his heritage, because, he argues, the parade is supposedly a celebration of heritage. The organizers of the parade are adamant that this interloper dress in accordance with their dictates. The organizers decide the theme of each year's parade, and the presence of a Zairian costume, even if the wearer appears to sympathize with them, is ruled out of step.

Naturally, this ruling creates a problem and a major controversy in the media and in places where Blacks meet to talk and socialize. One question that keeps turning up in the media is why would this Zairian want to impose himself on their parade? The corollary in the Black community is why would he even try to go where he obviously isn't welcomed for who he really is? Hearing this discussion, I cannot but think about Ngozi's future—could he be a proud Zairian-Canadian, claiming his father's heritage as well as language, in his beloved *garderie*?

For these dominoes players, there are several lessons to learn from this incident. The first is that Blacks can only join the separatists' debate on the separatists' terms. There is no room for compromise among these "fanatics." The second is that the treatment of the Zairian should send a strong message to all those French-speaking Blacks from other parts of Africa and Haiti who for one minute would believe that language is all there is at the heart of the sovereignty push in Quebec. Language might be a major factor, but colour of skin—or, as some Quebec nationalists say, the *pure laine*—is just as much an issue.

For these reasons, the members of the Montreal-Caribbean Social Organization would have nothing to do with the *nationalistes*' parade in downtown Montreal. Angrinon Park is as far away as possible from the parade as they can get and still be close to their homes. For in many respects, LaSalle is home for many of the Caribbean people—both

English and French speaking. The decay of the old factories in this area is so symbolic of what has happened to the dream of many Blacks living in this country. And in a real sense, the sheer beauty of this park, an oasis for tired eyes and minds, also symbolizes the kind of respite for which these picnickers are looking.

Undoubtedly, the park and its surroundings, the people and their fears and expectations, are so typical of the black experience in Canada and of the harsh decisions Blacks have to make about their future. Decisions that include whether to hold onto the dream that is Canada or to shift to the *rêverie* of an independent Quebec. Or, maybe even something else. But there must be change.

Even among the older people in the park on this, the eve of the independence campaign, it is taken for granted that the black community cannot continue to be on the outside much longer. For already the youths are demanding more than just picnics and cricket and dominoes. They want those gifts and legacy from their parents, but also all the other features of living in this province and country. Maybe that is why this is a picnic essentially for the older immigrants and children too young to defy their parents by not attending. The youths and teenagers of the black community are missing this symbolic start to summer for the community. Undoubtedly, they are looking for answers—and connections—elsewhere. But alas, they, too, would not be at the parade of the nationalists—they have no sense of belonging.

On October 30, 1995, Blacks in Montreal watching TV are feeling that their dream has suddenly become a nightmare, just as so many Black youths in Quebec feel so discarded and left out. The nationalists, those "fanatics," have just gone down to a narrow defeat. Blacks and other ethnic groups are now the whipping boys and girls, just as so many people attending the picnic at Agrinon Park had feared. The leader of the separatist forces is addressing his supporters, Canada and the world. Premier Jacques Parizeau cannot hide his anger. The numbers at the bottom of the television screens across Quebec and Canada tell the story of this narrow miss. Just over 50,000 votes is the difference between defeat and success. And nobody can ignore the emerging analysis of the polling numbers. The separatist forces have been defeated because of a solid federalist vote by the so-called allophones, a mishmash of Blacks and other ethnic groups who essentially do not speak French as a first language.

An emotional Parizeau cannot contain himself. The sovereignty drive is derailed, even if only temporarily, by "money and the ethnic vote," he laments. And in a speech that clearly shows he sees the Quebec society in terms of "them"—*les autres*—and "us"—the *pure laine*—he suggests that the next time a sovereignty vote is held, French Canadians will have to increase the percentage of their solid votes. This is the only way to ensure victory because, obviously, those ethnics cannot be relied on to support the cause. This speech would be filed in the collective memory of Blacks and other ethnic groups. It would have to compete for space in the memory banks already overflowing with stories of all the slights and racist remarks sovereigntist spokespeople have made against these groups over the years. Could a minority group like the province's Blacks and Quebec nationalists ever march in the same parade? On the surface it seems an easier task to mix oil and water or to turn straw into gold.

Obviously, the hurt runs deep. Here in the statements of Parizeau and his lieutenants is further confirmation for Blacks that they would not have a special place in an independent Quebec. How disappointing! For the stories of the ties of Blacks to this province are long and illustrious. They include the heart-rending escapades of escape to freedom from slavery, like that of the slave who burns a city, and stories of hope in the thousands of Caribbean immigrants who arrived in Canada in the 1950s and 1960s looking for a new life. Montreal was, for large numbers of them, their first taste and impression of Canada. Thousands of them never moved on, setting down roots in a part of the country to which they felt an attachment and affinity, even if eventually they would be relegated to the Angrinon Parks on the periphery. They would cultivate an attachment that for French-speaking Blacks from Africa and Haiti appeared even more special because of a shared language.

Montreal has had a long association with Blacks: from the jazz musicians to Jackie Robinson, who used the city to effectively launch his bid to break the colour barrier in American professional baseball. In his biography, *I Never Had It Made*, Robinson tells how Montreal and Canadians had become a refuge for him. The city had become the place he could happily return to from Louisville, where he played his first game in a then all-white league. For in that American city he had heard the taunts of "Hey, black boy, go on back to Canada—and stay."

"Yeah," another one screamed, "and take all your nigger-loving friends with you."

But Montreal was different. "When we arrived in that city, we discovered that the Canadians were up in arms over the way I had been treated.... All through that first game, they booed every time a Louisville player came out of the dugout. It was difficult to be sure how I felt. I didn't approve of this kind of retaliation, but I felt a jubilant sense of gratitude for the way the Canadians express their feelings." Because of this acceptance, thousands of black ball players—including those toiling for the systems of the Montreal Expos and the Toronto Blue Jays—can be thankful.

And Montreal was the home to fiery activists, many of them supporters of Marcus Garvey and his militant Universal Negro Improvement Association. A city where supposedly the mother of none other than Malcolm X received some of her earliest indoctrination as a Garveyite soon after immigrating from the Caribbean island of Grenada. Now, to claim Blacks would not have a special place in a new Quebec seems to defy history. It looks like no more than a continuation of the same old charade of the old Canada to deny—even to the extent of ignoring the Blacks in the standard history books—the contributions of Blacks to the building of the nation.

Indeed, this must have been a tough message for the sprinkling of Black faces in the crowd of nationalists who had assembled on the night of the vote anticipating victory. Many of them had gone out on a limb, breaking ranks with fellow Blacks. Now they would have to go back in their communities and to gatherings like the one in Angrinon Park and face the taunts of federalist Blacks saying, I told you so, and Why bother? What price for bucking trends? It would be just as tough for members of the black community in Montreal to explain how they could even consider supporting separation.

In the days following his speech, Parizeau would offer regrets only for his statement. He would try to explain away his anger as an overflow of the frustration from trying and failing for almost 30 years to persuade ethnic voters to join the march to independence. Now, he says, he has to admit abject failure. He has not been able to win over the ethnic voters.

And perhaps this is the crux of the problem: the separatists have failed to get Blacks and other minority groups to completely swallow their vision of an independent Quebec, a calcified Quebec that does not appear to want to make room for new voices and faces. And it is a Quebec in which the views of one group, the *pure laine* French, is dominant. No thought is given to allowing other points of views, to shaping the separatist outlook to include other groups. Apparently separatism is like religion: you accept it on faith with no deviation, no allowances for the individual. Everyone must conform to the dominant view. Everyone must subscribe to the doctrine that independence is a settling of an old score between the colonial English and French, even though many of the voters care neither for the English nor the French. Even though many newer residents in Quebec do not want to be mercenaries in one of the longest psychological wars in the Western Hemisphere. Even though new recruits might be found by simple gestures such as allowing a Zairian—and potentially, some time in the future, Ngozi—to march in their nationalist parade bedecked in all the splendour of his national costume.

Unfortunately, all these negatives that can be blamed on the *nationalistes* in Quebec can also be laid at the feet of mainstream Canada in every province. For despite centuries in this country, the black experience still amounts to existing outside the mainstream. It is a situation that obviously shouldn't continue for much longer. It's a case in which Blacks will have to make some drastic and radical moves to improve their own situation. Self-interest should govern their dealings in Canada or in an independent Quebec.

To base independence on the settling of old scores between two supposedly founding peoples will not work. Its futility can be seen every year when the St. Jean Baptiste parade happens in downtown Montreal, while other ethnic groups like Blacks put as much distance as possible between themselves and the parade. That is why Angrinon Park becomes the rallying ground for Blacks, where they can meet and talk about the hurt and separation they feel in the Canadian and Quebec society, where they feel they are alone and they must teach their children to band together for a future that is going to be little changed from what their parents endured, and are enduring, whether Quebec remains in

Canada or separates. Where Blacks can wallow in their own misery and isolation.

For the Blacks in Angrinon Park on the day before the St. Jean Baptiste parade were also steeling themselves for a backlash for their vote on the separation issue. Nobody anticipated the kind of tongue-lashing they got from Parizeau on the night of the vote. That was too public and vitriolic for them to even imagine. But what they had anticipated was that they would be blamed for not voting the right way and for being disloyal to Quebec. They would continue to be shut out of jobs, the main reason why unemployment is already so rampant among Black youths. And they were worried that in the event of a decisive vote, one way or the other, they would be abandoned. If the separatists were to win, would Canada support Blacks who are federalists? asks Lloyd Miller, president of an organization of Caribbean immigrants. What about our homes and properties? he wonders. What would become of the hundreds of thousands of Blacks who do not want to live in any other part of the country than Quebec?

In Angrinon Park on the day before the St. Jean Baptiste parade are many Blacks who claimed that they, too, had thought of, or actually joined, the rush of frightened Quebecers heading for Toronto and even the United States. Some of them had been offered good-paying jobs. But when they arrived in Toronto, they found something missing. A part of them was left behind in Quebec. They found the Toronto social life too restricting, sterile and impersonal. Black people are too scattered and disunited there. Most people are concerned only about the escalating values of their house or about making money. Life just wasn't fun, not like in Quebec. So many of them headed back *home*. Now, many of them are in mid-life and their children are getting big. What will become of them if the separatists win and they no longer feel even tolerated in the new Quebec?

"I always say that I have two homes," says Miller. "The first is Jamaica. The other is Quebec. If I am to give up my home in Quebec, I would have to return to my first home."

On the other hand, they worry about a strong federalist vote, of which Blacks would make a major contribution. Such a vote might be misconstrued as a sign everyone is happy with the situation in Canada; that

Blacks, by overwhelmingly supporting federalism, were choosing the status quo. This is not the case, the people gathered in Angrinon Park argue. Blacks want major social changes to the Canada they now live in. They want to find jobs and want their children to feel they have pride of place in the country. They want race relations between Blacks and the police to improve, black youths to stop being hassled and negatively stereotyped, to see themselves reflected positively and daily in the mainstream press and workplaces. They want to feel that despite the fact that some of them speak English, their black culture is different from that of the white English-speaking community. And they don't want to share any of the blame by French-speakers for all the ills of society perpetrated by white English-speaking Quebecers, who were just as mean to Blacks as they were to the French.

For just as the Zairian and Haitian Blacks have discovered that language isn't the only factor governing acceptance in the French-speaking milieu, so the English-speaking Blacks have long realized that they have no prominent status in the white English-speaking world just because of a common language. If it is still true that the battle for Quebec is one of two solitudes, then Blacks now find themselves stranded somewhere in the middle. They cannot be sure if either of the solitudes wants them, or even if they want to join either of the two camps as currently made up.

But this need not be the case. Undoubtedly, the time has come for the sovereigntist leaders and the Black community in Quebec to open serious negotiations to arrive at an accommodation. And perhaps, even more important, the time is ripe for Blacks to seriously consider joining the sovereigntist camp, not so much to fight the old battles of past generations, but to ensure that if the sovereigntists carry the day in some future referendum that Blacks would not be considered an enemy-within in what would be their new country.

For as history has shown, the black experience in the rest of Canada and Quebec has always been the same. We lose when we follow the strategy of those Blacks who congregate in Angrignon Park every year to mark the beginning of summer. When we seek isolation, we do little to improve our lot. We can remain outside the mainstream and refuse to integrate. That is a choice and even a defence mechanism. But there is a price for such a move: it makes us irrelevant to the debate.

Similarly, experience has also shown that we make just as big a mistake when we throw our support in perpetuity to any one party or cause. The price, once again, is that we become irrelevant. We do not shape the debate because our votes are taken for granted.

The alternative is for black leaders in Quebec to show more political savvy and to be daring. They should challenge existing norms and cozy perceptions. They should trample this tendency to isolation. Not only should they negotiate an understanding and possible plank for support for the separatists, but they should also renegotiate their arrangement with the federalist forces. In so doing, the black leadership might not only influence the lives of Blacks in Quebec, but in all Canada.

For it is very unlikely that the federal government would be able to make an accommodation to improve the lot of Blacks in Quebec without extending it to all Blacks across the country. And in this way we would be forcing the federalists to deliver on old promises that life could be good for Blacks who soldiered on to create and maintain a united Canada.

Leadership in the black community has always been based on a group of people recognizing the propitiousness of the times and acting, either alone or in concert, with other groups. With Canada caught in the throes of devising a new deal for everyone, why shouldn't the Blacks of Quebec say to both the federalist and sovereigntist camps, Make me your best offer.

Of course, many would say this would be easier said than done. What about the racist remarks associated for generations with the hard-core separatists? And how can Blacks possibly believe their vote and support are worth the price of bargaining? Well, they do. As a starter, Blacks know that, whether in Quebec or the rest of Canada, their daily life is difficult. They also recognize that this would not be the first time white Canadians entered negotiations with Blacks over questions of sovereignty and establishing a new country. We all know the stories of what happened to the black United Empire Loyalists, those black slaves who were encouraged to fight against the Americans during the War of Independence and for Canada and the monarchy. We know that thousands of them fought and died, helped to found provinces like Ontario and Nova Scotia, and that Canada never fulfilled its promise to them. So there is this precedence of negotiating an understanding, if not of having all sides honour it. Mistreatment of Blacks and other minorities is not something exclusively Québécois. It's very Canadian.

Indeed, some people would say, what about the language problem, where English-speaking Blacks would have to survive in a French-speaking country? Well, what would be so different from what is happening now? How many Blacks are in the provincial civil service or the police services across Montreal? And don't forget that Quebec already has a burgeoning black population that is French speaking. Language should not be a problem for them. But there is more to support this gamble of negotiating with the separatists. If we are looking to the future, and not eternally stuck in the past, we must plan for the likes of Ngozi and all those black kids, who we hope will eventually be bilingual enough to feel unrestricted by language either in Quebec or in the rest of Canada. They could be the generation that will make a connection between the older folks meeting in Angrinon Park and those with the briefcases heading into the professions and businesses—into the heart of the mainstream in the next century.

Blacks across Canada have to recognize that this is a new day in political and constitutional matters. Old allegiances are being re-examined, old agreements are being updated and modernized. Blacks should also enter the social negotiations, but with our eyes open, with a clearly stated position that we will be taking into account past performances as well as promises about the future. We have all heard the hypocrisy in the voices of all those English-speaking Canadians who were so quick to publicly castigate Parizeau and the assortment of sovereignty leaders for their racist remarks about ethnic voters. Yes, they deserved to be denounced. But let us not be fooled by this hypocrisy. Let those doing the denouncing look at themselves in the mirror. Blacks would also recognize that some of the same people offering the loudest criticisms are those who practise racism daily, who do not seem to care about the black and ethnic agenda.

These are the same politicians in English Canada who are fighting against employment equity, pay equity, making the police accountable, relegating Blacks to the parliamentary back benches and no man's land and ignoring many more issues that could make a real change in the daily lives of Blacks and minorities. These are the same politicians who are introducing and instituting terribly mean agendas that hurt the poor and the others in this society.

By seriously negotiating with the federalist and sovereigntist camps, Blacks would also be recognizing the pervasive change in Canadian politics. Perhaps Blacks as a group are among the last of the hold-outs of those supporting a strong federalist state. For decades, immigrant Blacks have been federalists because they identify with the notion that they left their homeland for a country called Canada, not to come to a specific province. Therefore many Blacks in Quebec would argue, just as the president of the West Indies Association of Montreal did, that they immigrated to Canada, not Quebec. They like the option of being able to move to Alberta one day and Nova Scotia the next, if that is what they want to do. They like the certainty of having universal minimums for social benefits across the country, not a patchwork quilt of different standards varying by province.

Second, black immigrants tend to be committed federalists because they have always identified with the image of a strong Canada as developed by former prime minister Pierre Trudeau, who was always popular among black voters. Third, Canadian-born Blacks have supported a strong Canada because a government in Ottawa could always be a counterbalance against their provincial and municipal governments.

But these days, nobody in the mainstream seems to have any taste for a strong, centralist Canada. The operative word in this discussion is devolution. The major opposition parties want the federal government to hand greater powers to the provinces. The provincial governments are in agreement and appear ready for a power-grab. Even the federal government of the day, formed by the party that once had Trudeau as its leader, has adopted the mantra of devolution and decentralization. And Quebec separatists are, of course, looking for a total devolution, so that all federal powers will eventually reside in a sovereign Quebec. Nobody, it seems, is a committed Canadian centralist. Devolution and its companion, self-interest, are the order of the day.

Blacks have to make sure that we, too, move with the times, that we are aware of the changing political winds. History has taught us through many painful examples in Canada and the United States the high political price for staying wedded to an idea whose time has passed. Indeed, one can argue that those Blacks in Quebec who still believe in a strong, central government could very well have this wish met in an independent Quebec. There wouldn't be much talk or need for devolution of anything after independence. Why not try to get in on the ground floor in the building of a strong Quebec?

But there is something else that is missing from the main political agenda. This missing link might be enough to encourage Blacks to support separation. Along with the philosophy of decentralization has come the repudiation of the long-held notion that society has an obligation to help its less fortunate and poor. Many Blacks are counted in this group. The new philosophy across this land is based on the notion that special-interest groups have become too powerful and should be cut down to size. The interests and agendas of these groups should be ignored purposely. A mean streak now characterizes the political landscape. With it has come the dismantling of many institutions that supported the idea of a strong, unified Canada or that helped to ease the inequalities among groups. So that for many people, the current political meanness clearly demonstrates that the Canada of old is gone. Not only does a strong, centralist Canada no longer exist, but a caring has also disappeared, a Canada that at least used to pretend that it subscribed to the notions of helping the unfortunate to achieve their full potential.

The loss of hope for many Blacks has become a big problem. This is particularly true of the youth, who feel there is no legitimate reason for even trying to succeed at anything—especially not integrating into the mainstream. And at the other end of the age scale, the disillusionment is just as present among many Blacks about to retire. These are the people who should be instilling hope in the younger generation, encouraging the young to be as aggressive and optimistic now as the older folks were back then. But hopes and dreams have been sapped by the mean-spiritedness and recrimination that are now so much a part of the Canadian political, social and economic reality.

This is not to say that life would be automatically better for Blacks in an independent Quebec or that there wouldn't be major social, political and economic changes after independence. What it suggests is that Blacks actively get involved in the shaping of a new society. For if we don't, we might find that we have no say much later on. We may discover that much of the political capital and international goodwill that could strengthen our hands in negotiations with the separatists would be much devalued.

Of course, this presupposes that the existing sovereigntist forces would want to open such negotiations or that they would work to break down the suspicions of their fellow residents who don't speak French or are of a different skin colour. For as it is well documented, when it comes to minorities, Quebec society has an unenviable record, comparable to that of the rest of Canada.

But there is reason to believe that sovereigntists continue the negotiations that Parizeau and others claim to have been undertaking for the past three decades. They, too, must recognize the changing face of Quebec politics, and more so, the sterility of political thought, by not having all groups and faces under their umbrella. The battle for sovereignty is a fight for the hearts and minds of people, to get them to believe in a dream, a chance to feel they can fashion the world for themselves and their kids. The chance for a new beginning. If Blacks and other minorities were to put their self-interests first, they might come to the conclusion that there might be an incentive to risk what they already know and enjoy about Canada, for the dream of what an independent Quebec might offer. They might indeed argue that with the backlash anti-immigrant and anti-minority winds blowing, they have little to lose.

For many Blacks understand the need for a people to be sovereign. They know from their history that size of land mass or population doesn't matter as much as a people committed to a dream. Otherwise, how would you account for people in Barbados, St. Lucia, St. Kitts, Ghana, the various ethnic groups in Nigeria and elsewhere in Africa fighting and voting for independence? As in the case of some Blacks from the Caribbean, there are more nationals living in places like New York and London than on the islands, so size of land mass or population doesn't matter. And it is hard for Blacks not to remember the recent history of the native country, deciding on independence, against great odds, against many others asserting that to walk this road is to ensure inevitable failure. But often a dream of a people wanting to be a nation flies in the face of seeming reality. So that wealth, amount of land or population do not matter—just a dream of the future.

This places some of the onus on the sovereigntists to reach out and tap this potential wellspring of goodwill. This is a chance for them to show that an independent Quebec will offer Blacks more than Canada does. And of course, to counter this argument, the federalist forces would have to somehow recommit themselves to the ideals and the agendas of Blacks and other underprivileged groups. Canada, too, would have to change. In either case, Blacks would be at the negotiating table. They would have some say in their future, too.

And what is the international goodwill and capital Blacks can inject into these negotiations? Blacks, for example, might offer Quebec sovereigntists and the federalist camp much more than their votes. They might help to make it easier for an independent Quebec to win acceptance in the international community. Their role could be helpful or obstructionist when Ottawa and Quebec begin the battle over international recognition. If the vote to secede results in a slim majority, then there is no doubt that each side would be doing its utmost to ensure that the international community understands its perspective. For example, it is quite possible for Ottawa to argue that separation calls for more than just a simple majority, that Quebec's territory is divisible, and there might even be a huge disagreement over such issues as portions of the national debt and what obligations to foreigners the new country should assume. This is where black Quebecers would help. They could become unofficial ambassadors for the side they support in the dispute.

A significant portion of new Quebec immigrants are likely to be from French-speaking countries in the Caribbean and Africa. Many of these black countries are members of the Francophone club. Many of the older immigrants are from the English-speaking countries in Africa and the Caribbean that are members of the British Commonwealth. These countries are also members of the United Nations, the Organization of American States, the Organization of African Unity and an assortment of international agencies. The many Caribbean and African countries can champion Quebec's right to self-determination or support Ottawa in these international forums. They would share some vitally important things with Quebec. They might also be very sympathetic to Quebec's aspirations, but would need a nudge to get involved in what in Canada might constitute a domestic dispute.

Within this generation, many of these countries have had to assert their sovereignty and independence, usually through a vote on independence or even a referendum to end a federation. In addition, many of the national heroes in these young countries have argued for generations that the sovereignty of a people has nothing to do with land mass or gross national product, or even the ability to survive. Every year, several prime ministers, presidents, foreign ministers and diplomats arrive in Canada to meet with expatriates. Their concerns are to ensure that their countrymen and women are happy in their new home. Imagine their response when these politicians and diplomats return home and report that some expatriates support a new country. Would they go against the wishes of their expatriates and bow to the diplomatic niceties demanded by Canada for the situation? And turn the situation around: suppose after a close vote for separation, the expatriates report fear and loathing about their future in Quebec. Wouldn't it be natural for these foreign countries to put the interests of their expatriates first and put off immediate recognition of a sovereign Quebec? For these leaders and diplomats, an expatriate is an expatriate. It doesn't matter whether he or she lives in England, the United States, Canada or an independent Quebec. With already stretched financial resources, their primary concern is to prevent a flood of people returning home to the old countries. They would rather the expatriates stay abroad, be happy and productive, and continue to send back their vital remittances.

But Quebec's black community offers more. As the closest neighbour to both Canada and Quebec, the United States would have a pivotal role to play in Quebec independence. By getting Blacks on side, either the sovereigntists or the federalists would have an entrée into the African-American community. Undoubtedly, the African-American leadership will watch with interest what is happening north of the border. And they will echo the fears and concerns of Blacks in Canada and Quebec. These concerns will be amplified in the news media and other avenues of power and influence. The side calling on the African-American leadership and their history of civil rights battles might find itself with a strong ally in Washington and elsewhere.

Regardless of which side the Blacks in Quebec eventually come down on, one thing they know for certain. They will be following in the footsteps of all those Blacks—going back to United Empire Loyalists and before—who have had an impact on what kind of country will exist on the northern part of North America. This is a memory that should be etched in the minds of everyone. A legacy that Blacks should not forget.

* * *

Like many of the Blacks who gather in Angrinon Park every year to officially kick off the summer, my first breath of Canadian air was in Montreal. It was during the Olympics of 1976. And to this day, when I think of Canada and Montreal, I fondly remember the sweet aroma of coffee. Of walking across a pasture on a moonlit night, with the strong smell from a nearby coffee plant on the wind. Of going to a West Indian dance in a school hall, a dance probably held by individual members of the Montreal-Caribbean Social Organization, if not by the organization itself. A dance attended in large part by Blacks—my first introduction to Canada and the isolation of people who looked like me. These are strong memories of enjoying the beauty of the moonlit night, the strong breeze blowing across the field in LaSalle, a short distance from Angrinon Park, and of thinking this is a country of great opportunity. The search for these opportunities and potential brought me back to Canada as a landed immigrant three years later.

Many Blacks still feel this way about Canada and Quebec. Many of them do not want to choose one over the other. But in these times, politicians all over Canada are telling us these are times of tough choices. The strong federalist state, the caring state, that many Blacks associated with Canada are relics of the past, perhaps, just like the lingering smell of the coffee in my memory. Many Blacks are thinking of abandoning Canada, whether to go to the United States—as they did in large numbers after slavery ended when the Canadian dream soured and died—or back to the Caribbean and Africa. With everything in flux, it might be just as easy for the immigrants and the native Blacks to transfer their loyalty again—to a Quebec willing to negotiate and strike a new covenant with them. This might just be the right time for everyone to wake up and smell the coffee, to see the opportunities that could be ahead of us and to simply follow our noses.

But this is just one of the major issues facing Blacks in Canada. Within the community is a raging fire that is consuming even those that lit it. The rage of wondering what has gone wrong for so many. In the United States, immigrants from the Caribbean are considered to be industrious, sometimes even to the point of creating distrust with African-Americans of several generations. This has always been the case. Writing near the turn of the century, W.A. Domingo noted:

> It is probably not realized, indeed, to what extent West Indian Negroes have contributed to the wealth, power and prestige of the United States. Major-General Goethals, chief engineer and builder of the Panama Canal, has testified in glowing language to the fact that when all other labour was tried and failed it was the black men of the Caribbean whose intelligence, skill, muscle and endurance made the union of the Pacific and the Atlantic a reality.
>
> Coming to the United States from countries in which they had experienced no legalized social or occupational disabilities, West Indians very naturally have found it difficult to adapt themselves to the tasks that are, by custom, reserved for Negroes of the North. Skilled at various trades and having a contempt for body service and menial work, many of the immigrants apply for positions that the average Negro has been schooled to regard as restricted to white men only, with the result that through their persistence and doggedness in fighting white labor, West Indians have in many cases been pioneers and shock troops to open a new way for Negroes into new fields of employment.[6]

In his 1983 book, *The Economics and Politics of Race*, African-American economist Thomas Sowell picked up on this theme of the industrious immigrants from the Caribbean, who from the 1920s onwards "were more urban, more skilled, more frugal, and more entrepreneurial":

> These early advantages continue to differentiate West Indian blacks from American blacks. By 1969, black West Indians in

[6] W.A. Domingo, "Gift of the Black Tropics." In *Harlem Renaissance Reader*, ed. David Lavering Lewis. New York: Viking, 1994: p. 12.

> the United States earned 94 percent of the average income of Americans in general, while native blacks earned 62 percent. Second-generation West Indians in the United States earned 15 percent more than the average American. More than half of all black-owned businesses in New York state were owned by West Indian blacks. The highest-ranking blacks in the New York City Police Department in 1970 were all West Indians, as were all the black federal judges in the city. There has been an extraordinary predominance of West Indian directors of black-studies programs in American universities.[7]

Similarly, syndicated newspaper columnist Clarence Page in his 1996 book, *Showing My Color,* was very laudatory about the effects of Caribbean immigrants in the United States. "Korean, Arab, and even some black West Indian merchants, riding into town on a wave of post-1965 immigration polices, have restored enterprise to many blighted urban neighborhoods."[8] Page noted how Haitian immigrants have added verve and life to once-abandoned sections of Miami, creating a prosperous Little Haiti. Why couldn't the same thing happen in Montreal? Not only have Caribbean immigrants, both English-speaking and French-speaking, excelled in business, but also produced many civil-rights leaders and artists: from a Louis Farrakhan to a Colin Powell; from a Shirley Chisolm to a Paule Marshall; from a Sydney Poitier to a Harry Belafonte.

I am not making this point to add to the debate of the rift between Caribbean and American Blacks of several generations. Instead, it is important to look at what Caribbean people have been able to achieve, to make of themselves, in fertile land. And to ask, Why has the same thing not happened in Canada? After all, Canada's black population is primarily Caribbean. They come from among the same Caribbean people who have excelled in the United States. Yet, the results in Canada are markedly different. Why? As I have pointed out, there is a long list of Canadian Blacks—many of them from the Caribbean—who have been as pioneering as those in the United States. But seldom do they get to first base in the Canada that groomed a Jackie Robinson. More than likely, they and their children are negatively stereotyped as no good, as

---

[7] Thomas Sowell, *The Economics and Politics of Race.* New York: W. Morrow, 1983: p. 107.
[8] Clarence Page, *Showing My Color.* New York: HarperCollins, 1996: p.173.

criminals, as ripping off the Canadian society. Seldom are they presented as contributing anything meaningful to Canada.

In his book, Sowell noted similar poor results by Caribbean Blacks in England, "... perhaps because they have arrived later, or because they did not have a large native black population to provide customers for their businesses, clienteles for their professions, or voting support for their political leaders."[9] This might very well be a factor, but cannot be the full explanation. Obviously, the economic climate and the levels of racism must be big factors. Perhaps the institutions that Canada shares with England, and the racism that can permeate them so sublty, are also factors.

Racism, perhaps not as open as in the United States, is as pervasive in Canada. Racism with a smile on its face, as Canadian Blacks like to call the brand they live under. A racism that nonetheless still saps dreams and leads to despair about the future. Such is the current reality of being black in this country at the end of this millennium. A reality that goes back to those days when Blacks first started to arrive in large numbers in this part of the North American continent, when by following the North Star they searched for a place called heaven.

Several things must change on our way to paradise: there must be genuine acceptance, and the media must stop portraying us simply as malcontents and no-good ingrates. We must feel that our heroes are important and are recognized for being Canadian; that race will not matter to the point that we will no longer need to celebrate such things as the appointment of the first Black in any profession or calling; that our cultural institutions will be seen more than simply as money-making businesses but an integral part of the Canadian mosaic; that our boys and girls will not walk the streets fearful of the police and of themselves.

Another sign of our arrival will be when we feel accepted in the boardrooms of businesses and the backrooms of politics, when we are on the front benches in Parliament and when our kids can dream the same dreams as any ambitious white Canadian. And we will stop our wandering in search of this great place when individually we in the Black community feel we can let down our guard and just be ourselves—just a normal Joe or Jill Canuck, who just happens to be black.

[9] Sowell, p. 107.

That we are not carrying the burden of a race on our backs. Then, we would really be in heaven.

Until then, we will continue our search for that paradise we sing of in our Negro gospel hymns. A paradise some of us haven't given up yet, even though, when we travel through the dark night and we look into the heavens, the desired destiny appears as distant as the stars themselves.

INDEX

S

T

W